Rebound

# THE LOEB CLASSICAL LIBRARY

EDITED BY

T E. PAGE, LITT.D.

E. CAPPS, PH.D., LL.D.   W. H. D. ROUSE, LITT.D.

# CATULLUS
# TIBULLUS AND
# PERVIGILIUM
# VENERIS

# CATULLUS TIBULLUS AND PERVIGILIUM VENERIS

LONDON : WILLIAM HEINEMANN
NEW YORK : G. P. PUTNAM'S SONS
MCMXXVIII

*First printed* 1913.
*Reprinted* 1914, 1918, 1919, 1921.
*Reprinted and revised* 1924, 1925, 1928.

*Printed in Great Britain.*

# THE POEMS OF GAIUS VALERIUS CATULLUS TRANSLATED BY F. W. CORNISH M.A., VICE-PROVOST OF ETON COLLEGE AND FORMERLY FELLOW OF KING'S COLLEGE, CAMBRIDGE

v

# INTRODUCTION

Gaius Valerius Catullus, whose name stands not lower than third on the roll of Roman poets, was born at Verona B.C. 84; the son of a wealthy Veronese gentleman, a friend of Julius Caesar. He came from Verona to Rome about 62 B.C. Among his friends and contemporaries were C. Licinius Calvus, the poet, and M. Caelius Rufus, the latter of whom became his rival and enemy.

About 61 B.C., when he was twenty-two, he made the acquaintance of Clodia, wife of Q. Metellus Celer, the most beautiful, powerful, and abandoned woman in Rome, and the bulk of his poems is the history of his fatal love. Lesbia, as he calls her, was as unfaithful to him as to her husband, the consul Q. Metellus Celer, and gave herself for a time to Caelius, the friend of her lover. Her infidelity made havoc of Catullus's life, and his unhappiness was completed by the death of his brother in Asia. Little else is known of him. He travelled in the suite of the praetor Memmius, Lucretius's patron; he quarrelled and made friends with Caesar; he lived in and enjoyed the best society, in all senses, of Rome.

The manuscripts of Catullus, with the exception of Cod. Thuaneus of the ninth century, containing only Carm. LXII., are derived directly or indirectly from

vii

# INTRODUCTION

a manuscript designated V (Veronensis), which is
known to have been at Verona early in the fourteenth
century, and which disappeared before the end of the
century. Two transcripts of this exist: Cod. Sanger-
manensis (G), at Paris, dated October 29, 1375, and
Cod. Oxoniensis or Canonicianus (O), at Oxford,
written about 1400. The symbol V represents the
readings of the lost Cod. Veronensis, as established
by G and O. Other MSS. which stand in a near
relation to G and O and throw light on V are Cod.
Datanus (D), at Berlin, written 1463, to which a high
value is given by Professor Ellis; Cod. Venetus (M),
in the Biblioteca Marciana at Venice; Cod. Romanus
(R), discovered in the Ottoboni collection of the
Vatican library in 1896 by Professor W. G. Hale of
Chicago, and collated by him, as well as by Professor
Ellis, but not yet published: it is nearly allied to O
and G. By the kindness of Professors Hale and
Ellis I have been able to consult the collation of R.
O, G, and R are nearly akin, but their exact rela-
tions to each other and of each of them to V are
not completely made out.

The existing editions are based on these and other
(later) MSS., and also on conjectural emendations
made by the scholars of the Renaissance, chiefly
Italian, among whom Avantius, Muretus, J. C.
Scaliger, Calphurnius, Statius, Lambinus, may be
mentioned, and among later critics Heinsius, Bentley,
Lachmann, Doering, Baehrens, Haupt, Schwabe,
Munro, and Ellis. The present text is substantially
that of Professor Postgate; in most cases where I
have departed from the text Professor Postgate's
reading is given in the notes with the symbol P.

As regards this edition, as well as my former text
and translation of Catullus, published in 1904, my

# INTRODUCTION

grateful thanks are due to Professor Postgate, who has most kindly and carefully helped in the revision of the Latin text, though I must not claim his authority or approval of everything that is printed.

The translator is not responsible for the following poems, in whole or in part: xv., xxi., xxxvii., lxix., lxxi., lxxiv., lxxviii., lxxix., lxxx., lxxxix., xciv., xcvii., c., cx., cxi., cxii., cxiii. These have been paraphrased by W. H. D. Rouse.

I wish also again to express my obligations to Professors Ellis and Hale, to my Eton friends, Mr. H. Macnaghten, Mr. A. B. Ramsay, and Mr. Rawlins, and to Mr. Oliffe L. Richmond, Fellow of King's College, Cambridge, for much help freely given.

FRANCIS WARRE CORNISH

The Cloisters, Eton College
*August* 1912

# PRINCIPAL MANUSCRIPTS OF CATULLUS

*V. Codex Veronensis,* from which all others (except T) are derived; no longer extant.

*E. Codex Sangermanensis* or *Parisiensis;* in the National Library, Paris.

*O. Codex Oxoniensis,* in the Bodleian Library, Oxford.

*D. Codex Datanus,* at Berlin.

*M. Codex Venetus,* in the Library of St. Mark at Venice.

*R. Codex Romanus,* in the Vatican Library, Rome.

*T. Codex Thuaneus,* in the National Library, Paris; contains only Carm. LXII.

# EDITIONS, ETC., REFERRED TO IN THE NOTES

M. H. A. J. Munro: *Criticisms and Elucidations of Catullus*, Cambridge, 1870.

E. R. Ellis: Text and Commentary, Oxford, 1867–1889.

P. J. P. Postgate: *Gai Valerii Catulli Carmina*, London, 1889, and in successive editions of *Corpus Poetarum Latinorum*. Also various papers in philological reviews.

B. Æmil. Baehrens: *Catulli Veronensis Liber*, nova editio, a K. P. Schulze curata, Leipzig, 1883.

M.R. Macnaghten and Ramsay: *Poems of Catullus*, London, 1899.

Rd. O. L. Richmond (MS. notes).

*Hpt.*, Haupt. *Lach.*, Lachmann. *Lamb.*, Lambinus. *Avant.*, Avantius. *Mur.*, Muretus. *Scal.*, Scaliger. *Bentl.*, Bentley. *Heins.*, Heinsius. *Schw.*, Schwabe. *Ital.*, early Italian editions.

# EXPLANATION OF SIGNS

† Reading of *codd.* corrupt or doubtful.
 * Conjectural emendations admitted into the text.
[ ] Conjectural additions.
*** Lacunae in *codd.*
. . . (or blanks).  Passages omitted.

A

7/88

# GAI VALERI CATVLLI
# VERONENSIS LIBER

## I

Cvi dono lepidum novum libellum
arido modo pumice expolitum?
Corneli, tibi: namque tu solebas
meas esse aliquid putare nugas,
iam tum cum ausus es unus Italorum
omne aevum tribus explicare chartis
doctis, Iuppiter, et laboriosis.
quare habe tibi quicquid hoc libelli,
qualecumque; [1] quod, o patrona virgo,
plus uno maneat perenne saeclo.      10

## II

Passer, deliciae meae puellae,
quicum ludere, quem in sinu tenere,
cui primum digitum dare appetenti
et acris solet incitare morsus,
cum desiderio meo nitenti [2]
carum nescio quid lubet iocari,
credo ut, cum gravis acquiescet ardor,
sit solaciolum sui doloris,
tecum ludere sicut ipsa possem
et tristis animi levare curas!      10

---

[1] *Or* qualecumque quidem patronei ut ergo *M.:* qualecumque
mei; patronei ut ergo *Rd.*

[2] *For* nitenti *P. proposes* incidente, *and Prof. Phillimore*
movetur.

2

# THE POEMS OF
## GAIUS VALERIUS CATULLUS

### I

To whom am I to present my pretty new book,
freshly smoothed off with dry pumice-stone ?  To
you, Cornelius : for you used to think that my trifles
were worth something, long ago, when you took
courage, you alone of Italians, to set forth the whole
history of the world in three volumes, learned
volumes, by Jupiter, and laboriously wrought.  So
take and keep for your own this little book, such
as it is, and whatever it is worth ; and may it,
O Virgin my patroness, live and last for more than
one century.

### II

SPARROW, my lady's pet, with whom she often plays
whilst she holds you in her lap, or gives you her
finger-tip to peck and provokes you to bite sharply,
whenever she, the bright-shining lady of my love,
has a mind for some sweet pretty play, in hope, as I
think, that when the sharper smart of love abates,[1]
she may find some small relief from her pain—ah,
might I but play with you as she does, and lighten
the gloomy cares of my heart !

[1] Or *et solaciolum sui doloris, credo, et quo gravis acquiescat
ardor* P. : *cum . . . acquiescet* codd.  But *credo "ut"* may be
a scribe's marginal note upon *et*.

## IIₐ

Tᴀᴍ gratumst mihi quam ferunt puellae
pernici aureolum fuisse malum,
quod zonam soluit diu ligatam.

## III

Lᴠɢᴇᴛᴇ, o Veneres Cupidinesque,
et quantumst hominum venustiorum.
passer mortuus est meae puellae,
passer, deliciae meae puellae,
quem plus illa oculis suis amabat :
nam mellitus erat suamque norat
ipsam [1] tam bene quam puella matrem ;
nec sese a gremio illius movebat,
sed circumsiliens modo huc modo illuc
ad solam dominam usque pipiabat.                    10
qui nunc it per iter tenebricosum
illuc, unde negant redire quemquam.
at vobis male sit, malae tenebrae
Orci, quae omnia bella devoratis :
tam bellum mihi passerem abstulistis.
vae factum male ! vae miselle passer !
tua nunc opera meae puellae
flendo turgiduli rubent ocelli.

## IV

Pʜᴀsᴇʟʟᴠs ille quem videtis, hospites,
ait fuisse navium celerrimus,
neque ullius natantis impetum trabis
nequisse praeter ire, sive palmulis

[1] P. *suggests* ipse.

## IIA (*a fragment*)

.    .    .    .    .

THIS is as welcome to me as to the swift maiden was (they say) the golden apple, which loosed her girdle too long tied.

## III

MOURN, ye Graces and Loves, and all you whom the Graces love. My lady's sparrow is dead, the sparrow my lady's pet, whom she loved more than her very eyes; for honey-sweet he was, and knew his mistress as well as a girl knows her own mother. Nor would he stir from her lap, but hopping now here, now there, would still chirp to his mistress alone. Now he goes along the dark road, thither whence they say no one returns. But curse upon you, cursed shades of Orcus, which devour all pretty things! My pretty sparrow, you have taken him away. Ah, cruel! Ah, poor little bird! All because of you my lady's darling eyes are heavy and red with weeping.

## IV

THE pinnace you see, my friends, says that she was once the fleetest of ships, and that there was never any timber afloat whose speed she was not able to pass, whether she would fly with oar-blades or

opus foret volare sive linteo.
et hoc negat minacis Hadriatici
negare litus insulasve Cycladas
Rhodumque nobilem horridamque Thraciam
Propontida, trucemve Ponticum sinum,
ubi iste post phasellus antea fuit                    10
comata silva : nam Cytorio in iugo
loquente saepe sibilum edidit coma.
Amastri Pontica et Cytore buxifer,
tibi haec fuisse et esse cognitissima
ait phasellus ; ultima ex origine
tuo stetisse dicit in cacumine,
tuo imbuisse palmulas in aequore,
et inde tot per impotentia freta
erum tulisse, laeva sive dextera
vocaret aura, sive utrumque Iuppiter                  20
simul secundus incidisset in pedem ;
neque ulla vota litoralibus deis
sibi esse facta, cum veniret a mari
novissimo [1] hunc ad usque limpidum lacum.
sed haec prius fuere : nunc recondita
senet quiete seque dedicat tibi,
gemelle Castor et gemelle Castoris.


### V

Vivamvs, mea Lesbia, atque amemus,
rumoresque senum severiorum
omnes unius aestimemus assis.
soles occidere et redire possunt :
nobis cum semel occidit brevis lux,
nox est perpetua una dormienda.
da mi basia mille, deinde centum,

---

[1] *Or* novissime *M. and codd.*

with canvas. And this (says she) the shore of the blustering Adriatic does not deny, nor the Cyclad isles and famous Rhodes and the wild Thracian Propontis, nor the gloomy gulf of Pontus, where she who was afterwards a pinnace was formerly a leafy forest: for on the height of Cytorus she often rustled with talking leaves. Pontic Amastris and Cytorus green with box, my galley says that all this was and is well known to thee; she says that from her earliest birthtime she stood on thy summit, in thy waters first dipped her blades, and thence [1] over so many riotous seas brought her owner, whether the breeze from left or right invited, or Jove came down astern on both sheets at once; and that no vows to the gods of the shore were made by her [2] all the time she was sailing from the furthest sea even to this limpid lake.

But these things are past and gone; now she rests in old age and retired leisure, and dedicates herself to thee, twin Castor, and to thee, Castor's twin.

# V

LET us live, my Lesbia, and love, and value at one farthing all the talk of crabbed old men.

Suns may set and rise again. For us, when the short light has once set, remains to be slept the sleep of one unbroken night.

Give me a thousand kisses, then a hundred, then

---

[1] Or "thereafter."
[2] Or "for her."

dein mille altera, dein secunda centum,
deinde usque altera mille, deinde centum.
dein, cum milia multa fecerimus,      **10**
conturbabimus illa, ne sciamus,
aut nequis malus invidere possit,
cum tantum sciat esse basiorum.


## VI

FLAVI, delicias tuas Catullo,
ni sint illepidae atque inelegantes,
velles dicere, nec tacere posses.
verum nescio quid febriculosi
scorti diligis : hoc pudet fateri.
nam te non viduas iacere noctes
nequiquam tacitum,[1] cubile clamat
sertis ac Syrio fragrans olivo,
pulvinusque peraeque et hic et illic
attritus, tremulique quassa lecti      **10**
argutatio inambulatioque.
iam tu ista ipse nihil vales tacere.
cur ? non tam latera ecfututa pandas,
ni tu quid facias ineptiarum.
quare quicquid habes boni malique,
dic nobis.   volo te ac tuos amores
ad caelum lepido vocare versu.


## VII

QVAERIS, quot mihi basiationes
tuae, Lesbia, sint satis superque.
quam magnus numerus Libyssae harenae

---

[1] *P. inserts comma after* tacitum.

another thousand, then a second hundred, then yet another thousand, then a hundred. Then, when we have made up many thousands, we will confuse our counting, that we may not know the reckoning, nor any malicious person blight them with evil eye, when he knows that our kisses are so many.

## VI

FLAVIUS, if it were not that your mistress is rustic and unrefined, you would want to speak of her to your Catullus; you would not be able to help it. But (I am sure) you are in love with some unhealthy-looking wench; and you are ashamed to confess it. But though you are silent, the garlands and perfumes about the bed, and the bed itself, show that you do not sleep alone. Well then, whatever you have to tell, good or bad, let me know it. I wish to call you and your love to the skies by the power of my merry verse.

## VII

You ask how many kissings of you, Lesbia, are enough for me and more than enough. As great as is the number of the Libyan sand that lies on

lasarpiciferis iacet Cyrenis,
oraclum Iovis inter aestuosi
et Batti veteris sacrum sepulcrum,
aut quam sidera multa, cum tacet nox,
furtivos hominum vident amores,
tam te basia multa basiare
vesano satis et super Catullost,                    10
quae nec pernumerare curiosi
possint nec mala fascinare lingua.


# VIII

Miser Catulle, desinas ineptire,
et quod vides perisse perditum ducas.
fulsere quondam candidi tibi soles,
cum ventitabas quo puella ducebat
amata nobis quantum amabitur nulla.
ibi illa multa tum iocosa fiebant,
quae tu volebas nec puella nolebat.
fulsere vere candidi tibi soles.
nunc iam illa non vult : tu quoque,
        impotens, noli,
nec quae fugit sectare, nec miser vive,     10
sed obstinata mente perfer, obdura.
vale, puella.   iam Catullus obdurat,
nec te requiret nec rogabit invitam :
at tu dolebis, cum rogaberis nulla [1]
scelesta, nocte.   quae tibi manet vita ?
quis nunc te adibit ?   cui videberis bella ?
quem nunc amabis ?   cuius esse diceris ?
quem basiabis ?   cui labella mordebis ?
at tu, Catulle, destinatus obdura.

---

[1] nulla. scelesta, vae te, "*Corp. Poet.*" *P. would now read
with Bury* nulla. scelesta, anenti (*cf.* senet, IV. *26*).

silphium-bearing Cyrene, between the oracle of sultry Jove and the sacred tomb of old Battus ; or as many as are the stars, when night is silent, that see the stolen loves of men,—to kiss you with so many kisses, Lesbia, is enough and more than enough for your mad Catullus ; kisses, which neither curious eyes shall count up nor an evil tongue bewitch.

## VIII

Poor Catullus, 'tis time you should cease your folly, and account as lost what you see is lost.  Once the days shone bright on you, when you used to go so often where my mistress led, she who was loved by me as none will ever be loved.  There and then were given us those joys, so many, so merry, which you desired nor did my lady not desire.  Bright to you, truly, shone the days.  Now she desires no more— no more should you desire, poor madman, nor follow her who flies, nor live in misery, but with resolved mind endure, be firm.  Farewell, my mistress ; now Catullus is firm ; he will not seek you nor ask you against your will.  But you will be sorry, when your nightly favours are no more desired.  Ah, poor wretch ! what life is left for you ?  Who now will visit you ? to whom will you seem fair ? whom now will you love ? by whose name will you be called ? whom will you kiss ? whose lips will you bite ?  But you, Catullus, be resolved and firm.

## IX

Verani, omnibus e meis amicis
antistans mihi milibus trecentis,
venistine domum ad tuos Penates
fratresque unanimos anumque matrem ?
venisti.  o mihi nuntii beati !
visam te incolumem audiamque Iliberum
narrantem loca, facta, nationes,
ut mos est tuus, applicansque collum
iucundum os oculosque saviabor.
o quantumst hominum beatiorum,                         10
quid me laetius est beatiusve ?


## X

Varvs me meus ad suos amores
visum duxerat e foro otiosum,
scortillum, ut mihi tum repente visumst,
non sane illepidum neque invenustum.
huc ut venimus, incidere nobis
sermones varii ; in quibus, quid esset
iam Bithynia, quo modo se haberet,
ecquonam mihi profuisset aere.
respondi id quod erat, nihil neque ipsis
* nunc praetoribus esse nec cohorti                    10
cur quisquam caput unctius referret,
praesertim quibus esset irrumator
praetor, nec faceret pili cohortem.

## IX

VERANIUS, preferred by me to three hundred thousand out of all the number of my friends,[1] have you then come home to your own hearth and your affectionate brothers and your aged mother? You have indeed; O joyful news to me! I shall look upon you safe returned, and hear you telling of the country, the history, the various tribes of the Hiberians, as is your way, and drawing your neck nearer to me I shall kiss your beloved mouth and eyes. Oh, of all men more blest than others,[2] who is more glad, more blest than I?

## X

My dear Varus had taken me from the Forum, where I was idling, to pay a visit to his mistress, a little thing, as I thought at a first glance, not at all amiss in manner or looks. When we got there, we fell talking of this and that, and amongst other things, what sort of place Bithynia was now, how its affairs were going on, whether I had made any money there. I answered (what was true) that as things now are, neither praetors themselves nor their staff[3] can find any means of coming back fatter than they went, especially as they had such a beast for a praetor, a fellow who did not care a straw for his subalterns.

---

[1] Or (*o meis a.*) "preferred by me to all my friends, the whole three hundred thousand of them"; or perhaps, "by three hundred miles."

[2] Or *quantumst . . . beatiorum* may = vocative, as III. 2.

[3] Or (*nec*) "neither the people themselves nor the praetors nor their staff." *hoc praetore fuisse* is a possible emendation.

"at certe tamen," inquiunt, "quod illic
natum dicitur esse, comparasti
ad lecticam homines."   ego, ut puellae
unum me facerem beatiorem,
"non" inquam "mihi tam fuit maligne,
ut, provincia quod mala incidisset,
non possem octo homines parare rectos."          20
at mi nullus erat nec hic neque illic,
fractum qui veteris pedem grabati
in collo sibi collocare posset.
hic illa, ut decuit cinaediorem,
"quaeso" inquit "mihi, mi Catulle, paulum
istos : commodum enim volo ¹ ad Sarapim
deferri."   "mane" ² inquio puellae ;
"istud quod modo dixeram me habere,
fugit me ratio : meus sodalis
—Cinnast Gaius—is sibi paravit.                     30
verum, utrum illius an mei, quid ad me ?
utor tam bene quam mihi * paratis.³
sed tu insulsa male ac molesta vivis,
per quam non licet esse neglegentem."


## XI

Fvri et Aureli, comites Catulli,
sive in extremos penetrabit Indos,
litus ut longe resonante Eoa
      tunditur unda,
sive in Hyrcanos Arabasve molles,
seu Sagas sagittiferosque Parthos,

---

¹ commoda nam *codd.*: commodum enim *P.*: da modo *Rd.*
² mane me *codd.*: mane† me *P.*: minime, male me *Rd.*:
memini, mi anime: *al. al.*
³ pararim *codd. is ungrammatical;* paratis *Stat.* (= si
parassem) *harsh.*

14

" Well, but at any rate," say they, "you must have got some bearers for your chair. I am told that is the country where they are bred." I, to make myself out to the girl as specially fortunate above the rest, say, " Things did not go so unkindly with me—bad as the province was which fell to my chance —as to prevent my getting eight straight-backed fellows." Now I had not a single one, here or there, strong enough to hoist on his shoulder the broken leg of an old sofa. Says she (just like her shamelessness), " I beg you, my dear Catullus, do lend me those slaves you speak of for a moment; I want just now to be taken to the temple of Serapis." " Stop," say I to the girl, " what I said just now about those slaves, that they were mine, it was a slip; there is a friend of mine—Gaius Cinna it is—; it was he who bought them for his own use; but it is all one to me whether they are his or mine, I use them just as if I had bought them for myself: but you are a stupid, tiresome thing, who will never let one be off one's guard."

## XI

FURIUS and Aurelius, who will be Catullus's fellow-travellers, whether he makes his way even to distant India, where the shore is beaten by the far-resounding eastern wave, or to Hyrcania and soft Arabia, or to the Sacae and archer Parthians, or those plains [1] which

1 Or "seas," but see Ellis's note.

sive quae septemgeminus colorat
    aequora Nilus,
sive trans altas gradietur Alpes,
Caesaris visens monimenta magni,          10
Gallicum Rhenum, † horribilesque † ulti-
    mosque Britannos,[1]
omnia haec, quaecumque feret voluntas
caelitum, temptare simul parati,
pauca nuntiate meae puellae
    non bona dicta.
cum suis vivat valeatque moechis,
quos simul complexa tenet trecentos,
nullum amans vere, sed identidem omnium
    ilia rumpens:                  20
nec meum respectet, ut ante, amorem,
qui illius culpa cecidit velut prati
ultimi flos, praeter eunte postquam
    tactus aratrost.

## XII

Marrvcine Asini, manu sinistra
non belle uteris in ioco atque vino:
tollis lintea neglegentiorum.
hoc salsum esse putas? fugit te, inepte:
quamvis sordida res et invenustast.
non credis mihi? crede Pollioni
fratri, qui tua furta vel talento
mutari velit: est enim leporum
disertus [2] puer ac facetiarum.
quare aut hendecasyllabos trecentos    10

[1] *Or* horribilem salum ultimosque *M. This is supported by
R., which has* horribiles ult.; *for* horribilē salū ult. *would easily
become* horribiles ult. *Haupt reads* horribile aequor ult.

[2] disertus, dissertus *codd.:* differtus *Passeratius:* diversus
*H.V.M.:* dis ortus *Rd.*

16

sevenfold Nile dyes with his flood, or whether he
will tramp across the high Alps, to visit the memorials
of great Caesar, the Gaulish Rhine, the formidable
Britons, remotest of men—O my friends, ready as
you are to encounter all these risks with me, what-
ever the will of the gods above shall bring, take a
little message, not a kind message, to my mistress.
Bid her live and be happy with her paramours, three
hundred of whom she holds at once in her embrace,
not loving one of them really, but again and again
draining the strength of all. And let her not look to
find my love, as before; my love, which by her fault
has dropped, like a flower on the meadow's edge, when
it has been touched by the plough passing by.

## XII

ASINIUS MARRUCINUS, you do not make a pretty use of
your left hand when we are laughing and drinking;
you take away the napkins of people who are off
their guard. Do you think this a good joke? You
are mistaken, you silly fellow; it is ever so ill-bred,
and in the worst taste. You don't believe me?
believe your brother Pollio, who would be glad to
have your thefts redeemed at the cost of a whole
talent; for he is a boy who is a master of all that is
witty and amusing. So now either look out for three

expecta aut mihi linteum remitte;
quod me non movet aestimatione,
verumst mnemosynum mei sodalis.
nam sudaria Saetaba ex Hiberis[1]
miserunt mihi muneri Fabullus
et Veranius: haec amem necessest
ut Veraniolum meum et Fabullum.

### XIII

CENABIS bene, mi Fabulle, apud me
paucis, si tibi di favent, diebus,
si tecum attuleris bonam atque magnam
cenam, non sine candida puella
et vino et sale et omnibus cachinnis.
haec si, inquam, attuleris, venuste noster,
cenabis bene: nam tui Catulli
plenus sacculus est aranearum.
sed contra accipies meros amores
seu quid suavius elegantiusvest:                    10
nam unguentum dabo, quod meae puellae
donarunt Veneres Cupidinesque,
quod tu cum olfacies, deos rogabis,
totum ut te faciant, Fabulle, nasum.

### XIV

NI te plus oculis meis amarem,
iucundissime Calve, munere isto
odissem te odio Vatiniano:
nam quid feci ego quidve sum locutus,
cur me tot male perderes poetis?
isti di mala multa dent clienti,
qui tantum tibi misit impiorum.

[1] *Or* ex Hibere; exhibere *codd.*

hundred hendecasyllables, or send me back my napkin—which does not concern me for what it is worth, but because it is a keepsake from my old friend; for Fabullus and Veranius sent me some Saetaban napkins as a present from Hiberia. How can I help being fond of these, as I am of my dear Veranius and Fabullus?

## XIII

You shall have a good dinner at my house, Fabullus, in a few days, please the gods, if you bring with you a good dinner and plenty of it, not forgetting a pretty girl and wine and wit and all kinds of laughter. If, I say, you bring all this, my charming friend, you shall have a good dinner; for the purse of your Catullus is full of cobwebs. But on the other hand you shall have from me love's very essence, or what is sweeter or more delicious than love, if sweeter there be; for I will give you some perfume which the Venuses and Loves gave to my lady; and when you snuff its fragrance, you will pray the gods to make you, Fabullus, nothing but nose.

## XIV

If I did not love you more than my own eyes, my dearest Calvus, I should hate you, as we all hate Vatinius, because of this gift of yours; for what have I done, or what have I said, that you should bring destruction upon me with all these poets? May the gods send down all their plagues upon that client of yours who sent you such a set of sinners. But if, as

quod si, ut suspicor, hoc novum ac repertum
munus dat tibi Sulla litterator,
non est mi male, sed bene ac beate,      10
quod non dispereunt tui labores.
di magni, horribilem et sacrum libellum,
quem tu scilicet ad tuum Catullum
misti, continuo ut die periret
Saturnalibus, optimo dierum!
non non hoc tibi, salse, sic abibit:
nam, si luxerit, ad librariorum
curram scrinia, Caesios, Aquinos,
Suffenum, omnia colligam venena,
ac te his suppliciis remunerabor.      20
vos hinc interea valete abite
illuc, unde malum pedem attulistis,
saecli incommoda, pessimi poetae.

## XIVa

Siqvi forte mearum ineptiarum
lectores eritis manusque vestras
non horrebitis admovere nobis

·    ·    ·    ·

## XV

Commendo tibi me ac meos amores,
Aureli. veniam peto pudenter,
ut, si quicquam animo tuo cupisti,
quod castum expeteres et integellum,
conserves puerum mihi pudice,
non dico a populo: nihil veremur
istos, qui in platea modo huc modo illuc
in re praetereunt sua occupati:

I suspect, this new and choice present is given you by
Sulla the schoolmaster, then I am not vexed, but well
and happy, because your labours are not lost. Great
gods! what a portentous and accursed book! And
this was the book which you sent your Catullus, to
kill him off at once on the very day [1] of the Saturnalia,
best of days. No, no, you rogue, this shall not end
so for you. For let the morning only come—I will
be off to the shelves of the booksellers, sweep to-
gether Caesii, Aquini, Suffenus, and all such poisonous
stuff, and with these penalties will I pay you back
for your gift. You poets, meantime, farewell, away
with you, back to that ill place whence you brought
your cursed feet, you burdens of our age, you worst
of poets.

## XIVa (*a fragment*)

O MY readers—if there be any who will read my
nonsense, and not shrink from touching me with
your hands . . .

## XV

To you, Aurelius, I entrust my all, even my loved
one, and I ask a favour of you, a modest favour. If
you have ever with all your soul desired to keep
anything pure and free from stain, then guard my
darling now in safety—I don't mean from the vulgar
throng; I have no fear of such as pass to and fro our
streets absorbed in their own business. 'Tis you I

[1] Or (*continuo* adj.) "the very next day": *cf.* Ov. *Fast.* v. 734,
VI. 720. Or "that very day, the Saturnalia," &c.

verum a te metuo tuoque pene
infesto pueris bonis malisque.                    10
quem tu qua lubet, ut lubet, moveto,
quantum vis, ubi erit foris, paratum:
hunc unum excipio, ut puto, pudenter.
quod si te mala mens furorque vecors
in tantam inpulerit, sceleste, culpam,
ut nostrum insidiis caput lacessas,
a tum te miserum malique fati,
quem attractis pedibus patente porta
percurrent raphanique mugilesque!

## XVI

PEDICABO ego vos et irrumabo,
Aureli pathice et cinaede Furi,
qui me ex versiculis meis putastis,
quod sunt molliculi, parum pudicum.
nam castum esse decet pium poetam
ipsum, versiculos nihil necessest.

## XVII

O COLONIA, quae cupis ponte ludere longo,
et salire paratum habes, sed vereris inepta
crura ponticuli axulis [1] stantis in redivivis,
ne supinus eat cavaque in palude recumbat;
sic tibi bonus ex tua pons libidine fiat,
in quo vel Salisubsili sacra suscipiantur:
munus hoc mihi maximi da, Colonia, risus.
quendam municipem meum de tuo volo ponte

---

[1] *Or* aesculis *A. Palmer.*

22

fear, you and your passions, so fatal to the young, both good and bad alike. Give those passions play where and how you please, ever ready for indulgence when you walk abroad. This one boy I would have you spare : methinks 'tis a modest request. And if infatuate frenzy drive you to the heinous crime of treason against *me*, ah ! then I pity you for your sad fate. For before the city's gaze with fettered feet you shall be tortured as cruelly as an adulterer.


## XVI (*a fragment*)

. . . who have supposed me to be immodest, on account of my verses, because these are rather voluptuous. For the sacred poet ought to be chaste himself, his verses need not be so.


## XVII

O COLONIA, you who wish to have a long bridge on which to celebrate your games, and are quite ready to dance, but fear the ill-jointed legs of your little bridge, standing as it does on old posts done up again, lest it should fall sprawling and sink down in the depths of the mire ;—may you have a good bridge made for you according to your desire, one in which the rites of Salisubsilus himself may be undertaken, on condition that you grant me this gift, Colonia, to make me laugh my loudest. There is a townsman of mine whom I wish to go headlong from your bridge

Ire praecipitem in lutum per caputque pedesque,
verum totius ut lacus putidaeque paludis          10
lividissima maximeque est profunda vorago.
insulsissimus est homo, nec sapit pueri instar
bimuli tremula patris dormientis in ulna.
cui cum sit viridissimo nupta flore puella—
et puella tenellulo delicatior haedo,
asservanda nigerrimis diligentius uvis,—
ludere hanc sinit ut lubet, nec pili facit uni,
nec se sublevat ex sua parte, sed velut alnus
in fossa Liguri iacet suppernata securi,
tantundem omnia sentiens quam si nulla sit
    usquam,                          20
talis iste meus stupor nil videt, nihil audit,
ipse qui sit, utrum sit an non sit, id quoque
    nescit.
nunc eum volo de tuo ponte mittere pronum,
si pote stolidum repente excitare veternum
et supinum animum in gravi derelinquere caeno,
ferream ut soleam tenaci in voragine mula.

## XXI

AVRELI, pater esuritionum,
non harum modo, sed quot aut fuerunt
aut sunt aut aliis erunt in annis,
pedicare cupis meos amores.
nec clam : nam simul es, iocaris una,
haerens ad latus omnia experiris.
frustra : nam insidias mihi instruentem
tangam te prior irrumatione.
atque id si faceres satur, tacerem :

over head and heels into the mud;—only let it be where is the blackest and deepest pit of the whole bog with its stinking morass. The fellow is a perfect blockhead, and has not as much sense as a little baby two years old sleeping in the rocking arms of his father.     He has for wife a girl in the freshest flower of youth,—a girl too, more exquisite than a tender kidling, one who ought to be guarded more diligently than ripest grapes,[1]—and he lets her play as she will, and does not care one straw, and for his part does not stir himself, but lies like an alder in a ditch hamstrung by a Ligurian axe, with just as much perception of everything as if it[2] did not exist anywhere at all. Like this, my booby sees nothing, hears nothing; what he himself is, whether he is or is not, he does not know so much as this. He it is whom I want now to send head foremost from your bridge, to try whether he can all in a moment wake up his stupid lethargy, and leave his sluggish[3] mind there in the nasty sludge, as a mule leaves her iron shoe in the sticky mire.

## XXI

Aurelius, father of all starvations, not these only but all that have been or are or shall be in future years, you wish to sport with my favourite. And not on the quiet: you keep with him, jest in his company, you stick close to his side and leave nothing untried. All in vain: as you plot against me, I'll have at you first. If you had your belly full I should say nothing;

[1] Or (et = sed) "now a maiden . . . ought to be guarded," &c.
[2] Or (nulla) "she."     [3] Or (supinum) "sprawling."

nunc ipsum id doleo, quod esurire      10
†me me puer et sitire discet.
quare desine, dum licet pudico,
ne finem facias, sed irrumatus.


# XXII

SVFFENVS iste, Vare, quem probe nosti,
homost venustus et dicax et urbanus,
idemque longe plurimos facit versus.
puto esse ego illi milia aut decem aut plura
perscripta, nec sic ut fit in palimpsestos [1]
relata : chartae regiae, novi libri,
novi umbilici, lora rubra, membranae,
derecta plumbo, et pumice omnia aequata.
haec cum legas tu, bellus ille et urbanus
Suffenus unus caprimulgus aut fossor      10
rursus videtur : tantum abhorret ac mutat.
hoc quid putemus esse ? qui modo scurra
aut siquid hac re tritius [2] videbatur,
idem infacetost infacetior rure,
simul poemata attigit ; neque idem umquam
aequest beatus ac poema cum scribit :
tam gaudet in se tamque se ipse miratur.
nimirum idem omnes fallimur, nequest quisquam
quem non in aliqua re videre Suffenum
possis. suus cuique attributus est error :      20
sed non videmus manticae quod in tergost.

[1] palimpsesto *codd.* "*can hardly be Latin,*" *M.* ; *but* referre
in palimpseston, *the usual term, does not necessarily exclude* in
palimpsesto relata, *the finished act.* Cf. XXVI. 6.
[2] tristius *of codd. is corrupt. Other emendations are* tersius,
scitius.

as it is, what annoys me is that my lad will learn how
to be hungry and thirsty. Stop, then, while you can
do so unharmed, or you will have to make an end in
very different plight.

## XXII

That Suffenus, Varus, whom you know very well, is
a charming fellow, and has wit and good manners.
He also makes many more verses than any one else.
I suppose he has got some ten thousand or even
more written out in full, and not, as is often done,
put down on old scraps ; imperial paper, new rolls,
new bosses, red ties, parchment wrappers ; [1] all ruled
with lead and smoothed with pumice. When you
come to read these, the fashionable well-bred Suffenus
I spoke of seems to be nothing but any goatherd
or ditcher, to look at him again ; so absurd [2] and
changed he is. How are we to account for this ?
The same man who was just now a dinner-table wit
or something (if such there be) even more practised,
is more clumsy than the clumsy country, whenever
he touches poetry ; and at the same time he is never
so happy as when he is writing a poem, he delights in
himself and admires himself so much. True enough,
we all are under the same delusion, and there is no
one whom you may not see to be a Suffenus in one
thing or another. Everybody has his own delusion
assigned to him : but we do not see that part of the
bag which hangs on our back.

[1] Or (*lora rubra membranae*) "red ties for the wrapper" ;
or (*novi umbilici et lora, rubra membrana* P.) "new bosses and
ties, red parchment wrapper."

[2] *abhorret* = *absurdus est* M. (doubtfully), so *abhorrens*, "un-
couth,"-"out of date." Liv. XXVII. 37, &c.

## XXIII

Fvri, cui neque servus est neque arca
nec cimex neque araneus neque ignis,
verumst et pater et noverca, quorum
dentes vel silicem comesse possunt,
est pulcre tibi cum tuo parente
et cum coniuge lignea parentis.
nec mirum : bene nam valetis omnes,
pulcre concoquitis, nihil timetis,
non incendia, non graves ruinas,
non furta impia, non dolos veneni,        10
non casus alios periculorum.
atqui corpora sicciora cornu
aut siquid magis aridumst habetis
sole et frigore et esuritione.
quare non tibi sit bene ac beate ?
a te sudor abest, abest saliva,
mucusque et mala pituita nasi.
hanc ad munditiem adde mundiorem,
quod culus tibi purior salillost,
nec toto decies cacas in anno,        20
atque id durius est faba et lapillis ;
quod tu si manibus teras fricesque,
non unquam digitum inquinare possis.
haec tu commoda tam beata, Furi,
noli spernere nec putare parvi,
et sestertia quae soles precari
centum desine ; nam sat es beatus.


## XXIV

O qvi flosculus es Iuventiorum,
non horum modo, sed quot aut fuerunt

## XXIII

FURIUS, you who have neither a slave, nor a money-box, nor a bug, nor a spider, nor a fire, but who have a father and a stepmother too, whose teeth can chew even a flintstone, you lead a merry life with your father and that dry stick, your father's wife. No wonder: you all enjoy the best health, your digestions are excellent, you have nothing to be afraid of; fires, dilapidations, cruel pilferings, plots to poison you, other chances of danger. And besides this, your bodies are as dry as horn, or drier still if drier thing there be, what with sun and cold and fasting. How can you, Furius, be otherwise than well and prosperous? You are free from sweat, free from spittle and rheum and troublesome running of the nose.

.    .    .    .    .

Since you have such blessings as these, Furius, do not despise them nor think lightly of them; and cease to pray, as you do, for the hundred sestertia; for you are quite well off enough as it is.

## XXIV

You who are the flower of the Juventii, not only of those we know, but of all who either have been or

aut posthac aliis erunt in annis,
mallem divitias Midae dedisses
isti, cui neque servus est neque arca,
quam sic te sineres ab illo amari.
" quid ? non est homo bellus ? " inquies.  est :
sed bello huic neque servus est neque arca.
hoc tu quamlubet abice elevaque :
nec servum tamen ille habet neque arcam.          10

## XXV

CINAEDE Thalle, mollior cuniculi capillo
vel anseris medullula vel imula oricilla
vel pene languido senis situque araneoso,
idemque Thalle, turbida rapacior procella,
cum † diva mulier aries ostendet † [1] oscitantes,
remitte pallium mihi meum, quod involasti,
sudariumque Saetabum catagraphosque Thynos,
inepte, quae palam soles habere tamquam avita.
quae nunc tuis ab unguibus reglutina et remitte,
ne laneum latusculum manusque mollicellas      10
inusta turpiter tibi flagella conscribillent,
et insolenter aestues velut minuta magno
deprensa navis in mari vesaniente vento.

## XXVI

FVRI, villula nostra non ad Austri
flatus oppositast neque ad Favoni
nec saevi Boreae aut Apheliotae,

---

[1] *Locus desperatus.   The emendations proposed* (atriarios,
munerarios, balnearios, vicarios, &c.) *are no more than ingenious
guesses.   Other emendations carry out the idea of a storm at sea,
as* cum diva mater [Tethys] horias ostendit aestuantes (*Mowat
in* "*Journ. of Philol.*" XIV. *252*).   *Possibly* trabes (cf. IV. 3) *may
be hidden under* aries, *and* oscitantes *may mean* "*gaping.*"

shall be hereafter in other years,—I had rather you had given the riches of Midas to that fellow who has neither servant nor money-box, than so allow yourself to be courted by him. "What? is he not a fine gentleman?" you will say. Oh, yes; but this fine gentleman has neither a servant nor a money-box. You may put this aside and make as little of it as you like: for all that, he has neither a servant nor a money-box.

## XXV

EFFEMINATE Thallus, softer than rabbit's fur or down of goose or lap of ear, or dusty cobweb; and also, Thallus, more ravenous than a sweeping storm when †         † send me back my cloak which you have pounced upon, and my Saetaban napkin and Bithynian tablets, you silly fellow, which you keep by you and make a show of them, as if they were heirlooms. Unglue and let drop these at once from your claws, lest your soft downy flanks and pretty tender hands should have ugly figures branded and scrawled on them by the whip, and lest you should toss about as you are little used to do, like a tiny boat caught in the vast sea, when the wind is madly raging.

## XXVI

FURIUS, my little farm stands exposed not to the blasts of Auster nor Favonius nor fierce Boreas or Apheliotes, but to a call of fifteen thousand two

verum ad milia quindecim et ducentos.
o ventum horribilem atque pestilentem!

## XXVII

Minister vetuli puer Falerni
inger mi calices amariores,
ut lex Postumiae iubet magistrae,
ebrioso acino ebriosioris.[1]
at vos quolubet hinc abite, lymphae,
vini pernicies, et ad severos
migrate: hic merus est Thyonianus.

## XXVIII

Pisonis comites, cohors inanis
aptis sarcinulis et expeditis,
Verani optime tuque mi Fabulle,
quid rerum geritis? satisne cum isto
vappa frigoraque et famem tulistis?
ecquidnam in tabulis patet lucelli
expensum, ut mihi, qui meum secutus
praetorem refero datum lucello
"o Memmi, bene me ac diu supinum
tota ista trabe lentus irrumasti."          10
sed, quantum video, pari fuistis
casu: nam nihilo minore verpa
farti estis.  pete nobiles amicos!
at vobis mala multa di deaeque
dent, opprobria Romuli Remique.

## XXIX

Qvis hoc potest videre, quis potest pati,
nisi impudicus et vorax et aleo,

---

[1] See M.  ebriose *of codd. may be for* ebriosae," *tipsy Postumia,
more tipsy," &c.*  ebria acina *Hpt. P. from Gellius.* VI. 20, 6.

hundred sesterces.   A wind that brings horror and pestilence !

### XXVII

COME, boy, you who serve out the old Falernian, fill up stronger cups for me, as the law of Postumia, mistress of the revels, ordains, Postumia more tipsy than the tipsy grape.   But water, begone, away with you, water, destruction of wine, and take up your abode with scrupulous folk.   This is the pure Thyonian god.

### XXVIII

You subalterns of Piso, a needy train, with baggage handy and easily carried, my excellent Veranius and you, my Fabullus, how are you ?  have you borne cold and hunger with that wind-bag long enough ?  do your account books show any gain, however small, entered on the wrong side, as mine do ?  Why, after following in my praetor's train I put down on the credit side . . . So much for running after powerful friends ! But may the gods and goddesses bring many curses upon you, you blots on the names of Romulus and Remus.

### XXIX

WHO can look upon this, who can suffer this, except he be lost to all shame and voracious and a gambler,

Mamurram habere quod Comata Gallia
habebat ante et ultima Britannia?
cinaede Romule, haec videbis et feres?
[es impudicus et vorax et aleo.]
et ille nunc superbus et superfluens
perambulabit omnium cubilia
ut albulus columbus aut Adoneus?[1]
cinaede Romule, haec videbis et feres?                    10
es impudicus et vorax et aleo.
eone nomine, imperator unice,
fuisti in ultima occidentis insula,
ut ista vostra diffututa Mentula
ducentiens comesset aut trecentiens?
quid est alid[2] sinistra liberalitas?
parum expatravit an parum helluatus est?
paterna prima lancinata sunt bona:
secunda praeda Pontica: inde tertia
Hibera, quam scit amnis aurifer Tagus.                    20
† hunc Galliae timet et Britanniae †[3]
quid hunc malum fovetis?   aut quid hic potest,
nisi uncta devorare patrimonia?
eone nomine urbis † opulentissime[4]
socer generque, perdidistis omnia?


## XXX

ALFENE immemor atque unanimis false sodalibus,
iam te nil miseret, dure, tui dulcis amiculi?

---

[1] idoneus *codd.*          [2] quid istam (*P.*) alit *Pohl.*
[3] *Of the many emendations of this verse these may be mentioned:*
(1) timentque [*or* ne] Galliae hunc. timent Britanniae *vett. edd.*
(*which I translate*); (2) huicne [*or* eine, *or* eatne] Galliae ultima
et Britanniae *P.*
[4] orbis opulentissime *codd.* *Another* locus desperatus, *not
much mended by* urbis o pudet meae *E.*, urbis [orbis] o piissimi
*Hpt. P. al.*, urbis o potissimi *Müller*, ut bis opliti sient *Rd.*

34

that Mamurra should have what Gallia Comata and
furthest Britain had once? Debauched Romulus,
will you see and endure this? [You are shameless
and voracious and a gambler.] And shall he now,
proud and full to overflowing, make a progress
through the beds of all, like a white cock-pigeon or
an Adonis?

Debauched Romulus, will you see and endure this?
You are shameless and voracious and a gambler.
Was it this then, you one and only general, that took
you to the furthest island of the West? was it that
that worn-out profligate of yours, Mentula, should
devour twenty or thirty millions? What else, then,
is perverted liberality, if this be not? Has he not
spent enough on lust and gluttony? His ancestral
property was first torn to shreds; then came his
prize-money from Pontus, then in the third place
that from the Hiberus, of which the gold-bearing
river Tagus can tell. And him do the Gauls and
Britains fear? Why do you both support this
scoundrel? or what can he do but devour rich
patrimonies? Was it for this † that you, father-in-
law and son-in-law, have ruined everything?

## XXX

ALFENUS, ungrateful and false to your faithful com-
rades, do you now cease (ah, cruel!) to pity your
beloved friend? What? do you not shrink from

iam me prodere, iam non dubitas fallere, perfide?
num facta impia fallacum hominum caelicolis placent?
quae [1] tu neglegis, ac me miserum deseris in malis;
eheu quid faciant, dic, homines, cuive habeant fidem?
certe tute iubebas animam tradere, inique, me
inducens in amorem, quasi tuta omnia mi forent.
idem nunc retrahis te ac tua dicta omnia factaque
ventos irrita ferre ac nebulas aerias sinis.                    10
si tu oblitus es, at di meminerunt, meminit Fides,
quae te ut paeniteat postmodo facti faciet tui.


## XXXI

Paene insularum, Sirmio, insularumque
ocelle, quascumque in liquentibus stagnis
marique vasto fert uterque Neptunus,
quam te libenter quamque laetus inviso,
vix mi ipse credens Thyniam atque Bithynos
liquisse campos et videre te in tuto.
o quid solutis est beatius curis,
cum mens onus reponit, ac peregrino
labore fessi venimus larem ad nostrum
desideratoque acquiescimus lecto?                    10
hoc est, quod unumst pro laboribus tantis.
salve, o venusta Sirmio, atque ero gaude:
gaudete vosque, o Lydiae [2] lacus undae:
ridete, quicquid est domi cachinnorum.

1 que codd.  vv. ll. quom, quos, quem.
2 Lydiae Etruscan.  lidie codd.: ludiae (and Lydii) Scaliger
("tumbling"): limpidae Avantius: liquidae P.: al. al.

betraying me, deceiving me, faithless one? Do the deeds of deceivers please the gods above?—All this [1] you disregard, and desert me in my sorrow and trouble; ah, tell me, what are men to do, whom are they to trust? For truly you used to bid me trust my soul to you (ah, unjust!), leading me into love as if all were safe for me; you, who now draw back from me, and let the winds and vapours of the air bear away all your words and deeds unratified. If you have forgotten this, yet the gods remember it, remembers Faith, who will soon make you repent of your deed.

## XXXI

Sirmio, bright eye of peninsulas and islands, all that in liquid lakes or vast ocean either Neptune bears: how willingly and with what joy I revisit you, scarcely trusting myself that I have left Thynia and the Bithynian plains, and that I see you in safety. Ah, what is more blessed than to put cares away, when the mind lays by its burden, and tired with labour of far travel we have come to our own home and rest on the couch we longed for? This it is which alone is worth all these toils. Welcome, lovely Sirmio, and rejoice in your master,[2] and rejoice ye too, waters of the Lydian lake, and laugh out aloud all the laughter you have in your home.[3]

---

[1] M., reading *quom*, puts a comma after *malis;* "since you neglect me, &c., what are men to do?"

[2] Or "for [we should say "with"] your master." "Make cheer for your master."

[3] Or "laugh out, all the laughter there is in my home"; *quicquid est cachinnorum = omnes cachinni* (voc.). *Cf.* III. 2, IX. 10, *quantumst.*

## XXXII

AMABO, mea dulcis Ipsithilla,
meae deliciae, mei lepores,
iube ad te veniam meridiatum.
et si iusseris, illud adiuvato,
nequis liminis obseret tabellam,
neu tibi lubeat foras abire.
sed domi maneas paresque nobis
novem continuas fututiones.
verum, siquid ages, statim iubeto :
nam pransus iaceo, et satur supinus          10
pertundo tunicamque palliumque.

## XXXIII

O FVRVM optime balneariorum
Vibenni pater et cinaede fili,
nam dextra pater inquinatiore,
culo filius est voraciore :
cur non exilium malasque in oras
itis, quandoquidem patris rapinae
notae sunt populo, et nates pilosas,
fili, non potes asse venditare.

## XXXIV

DIANAE sumus in fide
puellae et pueri integri :
[Dianam pueri integri]
    puellaeque canamus.
o Latonia, maximi
magna progenies Iovis,

## XXXII

I ENTREAT you, my sweet Ipsithilla, my darling, my charmer, bid me to come and rest at noonday with you. And if you do bid me, grant me this kindness too, that no one may bar the panel of your threshold, nor you yourself have a fancy to go away, but stay at home. . . . But if you will at all, then bid me come at once. . . .

## XXXIII

CLEVEREST of all clothes-stealers at the baths, father Vibennius and you his profligate son, . . . off with you into banishment and the dismal regions, since the father's plunderings are known to all the world. . . .

## XXXIV

WE girls and chaste boys are lieges of Diana. Diana let us sing, chaste boys and girls. O child of Latona, great offspring of greatest Jove, whom thy mother

quam mater prope Deliam
  deposivit olivam,
montium domina ut fores
silvarumque virentium           10
saltuumque reconditorum
  amniumque sonantum.
tu Lucina dolentibus
Iuno dicta puerperis,
tu potens Trivia et notho's
  dicta lumine Luna.
tu cursu, dea, menstruo
metiens iter annuum
rustica agricolae bonis
  tecta frugibus exples.          20
sis quocumque tibi placet
sancta nomine, Romulique,
antique [1] ut solita's, bona
  sospites ope gentem.

## XXXV

Poetae tenero, meo sodali
velim Caecilio, papyre, dicas
Veronam veniat, Novi relinquens
Comi moenia Lariumque litus :
nam quasdam volo cogitationes
amici accipiat sui meique.
quare, si sapiet, viam vorabit,
quamvis candida miliens puella
euntem revocet manusque collo
ambas iniciens roget morari ;        10
quae nunc, si mihi vera nuntiantur,
illum deperit impotente amore :

[1] Ancique *Scal.*

40

bore by the Delian olive-tree, that thou mightest be the lady of mountains and green woods, and seques-tered glens and sounding rivers ; thou art called Juno Lucina by mothers in pains of travail, thou art called mighty Trivia and Moon with counterfeit light. Thou, goddess, measurest out by monthly course the circuit of the year, thou fillest full with goodly fruits the rustic home of the husbandman. Be thou hal-lowed by whatever name thou wilt ; and as of old thou wert wont, with good help keep safe the race of Romulus.

## XXXV

I ASK you, papyrus page, to tell the gentle poet, my friend Caecilius, to come to Verona, leaving the walls of Novum Comum and the shore of Larius : for I wish him to receive certain thoughts of a friend of his and mine. Wherefore if he is wise he will devour the way with haste, though his fair lady should call him back a thousand times, and throwing both her arms round his neck beg him to delay. She now, if a true tale is brought to me, dotes on him with passionate

nam quo tempore legit incohatam
Dindymi dominam, ex eo misellae
ignes interiorem edunt medullam.
ignosco tibi, Sapphica puella
Musa doctior : est enim venuste
Magna Caecilio incohata Mater.


## XXXVI

ANNALES Volusi, cacata charta,
votum solvite pro mea puella :
nam sanctae Veneri Cupidinique
vovit, si sibi restitutus essem
desissemque truces vibrare iambos,
electissima pessimi poetae
scripta tardipedi deo daturam
infelicibus ustulanda lignis.
et haec pessima se puella vidit
iocosis lepide vovere divis.                                           10
nunc, o caeruleo creata ponto,
quae sanctum Idalium Uriosque apertos
quaeque Ancona Gnidumque harundinosam
colis quaeque Amathunta quaeque Golgos
quaeque Durachium Hadriae tabernam,
acceptum face redditumque votum,
si non illepidum neque invenustumst.
at vos interea venite in ignem,
pleni ruris et infacetiarum
annales Volusi, cacata charta.                                         20

love. For since she read the beginning of his " Lady of Dindymus," ever since then, poor girl, the fires have been wasting her inmost marrow. I can feel for you, maiden more scholarly than the Sapphic Muse ; for Caecilius has indeed made a lovely beginning to his " Magna Mater."

## XXXVI

CHRONICLE of Volusius, filthy waste-paper, discharge a vow on behalf of my love ; for she vowed to holy Venus and to Cupid that if I were restored to her love and ceased to dart fierce iambics, she would give to the lame-footed god the choicest writings of the worst of poets, to be burnt with wood from some accursed tree : and my lady perceived that these were the " worst poems " that she was vowing to the merry gods in pleasant sport.[1] Now therefore, O thou whom the blue sea bare, who inhabitest holy Idalium and open Urii, who dwellest in Ancona and reedy Cnidus and in Amathus and in Golgi, and in Dyrrhachium the meeting-place of all Hadria, record the vow as received and duly paid, so surely as it is not out of taste nor inelegant. Meantime come you here into the fire, you bundle of rusticity and clumsiness, chronicle of Volusius, filthy waste-paper.

[1] Or (*et haec pessima sic puella vidit | ioco se lepido v. d.* P.) " and the lady saw that these were the ' worst writings ' that she was thus devoting to the gods in merry jest "—or *pessima* may go with *puella*, as LV. 10. *vidit* is probably corrupt. By *pessimus poeta* Lesbia meant Catullus ; Catullus, Volusius.

## XXXVII

Salax taberna vosque contubernales,
a pilleatis nona fratribus pila,
solis putatis esse mentulas vobis,
solis licere, quidquid est puellarum,
confutuere et putare ceteros hircos?
an, continenter quod sedetis insulsi
centum an ducenti, non putatis ausurum
me una ducentos irrumare sessores?
atqui putate: namque totius vobis
frontem tabernae scorpionibus scribam.      10
puella nam mi, quae meo sinu fugit,
amata tantum quantum amabitur nulla,
pro qua mihi sunt magna bella pugnata,
consedit istic.   hanc boni beatique
omnes amatis, et quidem, quod indignums
omnes pusilli et semitarii moechi;
tu praeter omnes une de capillatis,
cuniculosae Celtiberiae fili
Egnati, opaca quem bonum facit barba
et dens Hibera defricatus urina      20

## XXXVIII

Malest, Cornifici, tuo Catullo,
malest, me hercule, et [ei] laboriose,[1]
et magis magis in dies et horas.
quem tu, quod minimum facillimumquest,
qua solatus es allocutione?
irascor tibi.   sic meos amores?
paulum quid lubet allocutionis,
maestius lacrimis Simonideis.

> [1] male est me hercle, male et laboriose *Rd*.

## XXXVII

GALLANT pot-house, and you brothers in the service, at the ninth pillar from the temple of the Brothers in the hats (Castor and Pollux), are you the only men, think you? the only ones who have leave to buss all the girls, while you think every one else a goat? Or if you sit in a line, five score or ten maybe, witless all, think you that I cannot settle ten score while they sit? Yet you may think so: for I'll scribble scorpions all over the pot-house front. My girl, who has left my arms, though loved as none ever shall be loved, has taken up her abode there. She is dear to all you men of rank and fortune—indeed, to her shame, all the petty lechers that haunt the byways; to you above all, paragon of long-haired dandies, Egnatius, son of rabbity Celtiberia, made a gentleman by a bushy beard and teeth brushed with your unsavoury Spanish wash.

## XXXVIII

YOUR Catullus is ill at ease, Cornificius, ill and in distress, and that more and more daily and hourly. And you, though that is the lightest and easiest task, have you said one word to console him? I am getting angry with you—what, treat my love so?[1] Give me only some little word of comfort, pathetic as the tears of Simonides!

1 Either (1) "is it thus you treat my friend?" (perhaps alluding to some quarrel with Juventius), or (2) "my tale of love" E.

45

# GAI VALERI CATVLLI LIBER

## XXXIX

EGNATIVS, quod candidos habet dentes,
renidet usquequaque.  si ad rei ventumst
subsellium, cum orator excitat fletum,
renidet ille.  si ad pii rogum fili
lugetur, orba cum flet unicum mater,
renidet ille.  quicquid est, ubicumquest,
quodcumque agit, renidet.  hunc habet morbum,
neque elegantem, ut arbitror, neque urbanum.
quare monendum test mihi, bone Egnati.
si urbanus esses aut Sabinus aut Tiburs          10
aut *porcus [1] Umber aut obesus Etruscus
aut Lanuvinus ater atque dentatus
aut Transpadanus, ut meos quoque attingam,
aut quilubet, qui puriter lavit dentes,
tamen renidere usquequaque te nollem :
nam risu inepto res ineptior nullast.
nunc Celtiber es : Celtiberia in terra,
quod quisque minxit, hoc sibi solet mane
dentem atque russam defricare gingivam ;
ut quo iste vester expolitior dens est,          20
hoc te amplius bibisse praedicet loti.


## XL

QVAENAM te mala mens, miselle Ravide,
agit praecipitem in meos iambos ?
quis deus tibi non bene advocatus
vecordem parat excitare rixam ?
an ut pervenias in ora vulgi ?

---

[1] parcus *codd.* (pinguis *Gloss. Vat.*) : *al.* pastus, fartus :
porcus *Scal.:* P. *suggests* uber Umber.

## XXXIX

EGNATIUS, because he has white teeth, is everlastingly smiling. If people come to the prisoner's bench, when the counsel for the defence is making every one cry, he smiles: if they are mourning at the funeral of a dear son, when the bereaved mother is weeping for her only boy, he smiles: whatever it is, wherever he is, whatever he is doing, he smiles: it is a malady he has, neither an elegant one as I think, nor in good taste. So I must give you a bit of advice, my good Egnatius. If you were a Roman or a Sabine or a Tiburtine or a pig of an Umbrian or a plump Etruscan, or a black and tusky Lanuvian, or a Transpadane (to touch on my own people too), or anybody else who washes his teeth with clean water, still I should not like you to be smiling everlastingly; for there is nothing more silly than a silly laugh. As it is, you are a Celtiberian; now in the Celtiberian country the natives rub their teeth and red gums, we know how; so that the cleaner your teeth are, the dirtier you.

## XL

WHAT infatuation, my poor Ravidus, drives you head-long in the way of my iambics? What god invoked by you amiss is going to stir up a senseless quarrel? Is it that you wish to be talked about? What do

quid vis ?  qualubet esse notus optas ?
eris, quandoquidem meos amores
cum longa voluisti amare poena.

### XLI

AMEANA puella defututa
tota milia me decem poposcit,
ista turpiculo puella naso,
decoctoris amica Formiani.
propinqui, quibus est puella curae,
amicos medicosque convocate :
non est sana puella, nec rogare
qualis sit solet aes imaginosum.

### XLII

ADESTE, hendecasyllabi, quot estis
omnes undique, quotquot estis omnes.
iocum me putat esse moecha turpis,
et negat mihi vestra reddituram
pugillaria, si pati potestis.
persequamur eam, et reflagitemus.
quae sit, quaeritis.  illa, quam videtis
turpe incedere, mimice ac moleste
ridentem catuli ore Gallicani.
circumsistite eam, et reflagitate,                    10
"moecha putida, redde codicillos,
redde, putida moecha, codicillos."
non assis facis ?  o lutum, lupanar,
aut si perditius potes quid esse.
sed non est tamen hoc satis putandum.
quod si non aliud † potest, ruborem

you want? would you be known, no matter how? So you shall, since you have chosen to love my lady,—and long shall you rue it.

## XLI

AMEANA, that worn-out jade, asked me for a round ten thousand; that girl with the ugly snub nose, the mistress of the bankrupt of Formiae. You her relations, who have the charge of the girl, call together friends and doctors: she is not right in her mind, and never asks the looking-glass what she is like.

## XLII

HITHER from all sides, hendecasyllables, as many as there are of you, all of you as many as there are. An ugly drab thinks she may make fun of me, and says she will not give me back your tablets, if you can submit to that. Let us follow her, and demand them back again. You ask who she is? That one whom you see strutting with an ugly gait, grinning like a vulgar mountebank with the gape of a Cisalpine hound. Stand round her and call for them back again. "Dirty drab, give back the tablets, give back the tablets, dirty drab!" Don't you care a penny for that?[1] O filth, O beastliness! or anything else that I can call you worse still! But we must not think this enough. Well, if nothing else can do it, let us

[1] Or *facit.* "She does not care a penny. O filth . . ."

ferreo canis exprimamus ore :
conclamate iterum altiore voce
"moecha putida, redde codicillos,
redde, putida moecha, codicillos."          20
sed nil proficimus, nihil movetur.
mutandast ratio modusque vobis,
siquid proficere amplius potestis :
"pudica et proba, redde codicillos."

## XLIII

SALVE, nec minimo puella naso
nec bello pede nec nigris ocellis
nec longis digitis nec ore sicco
nec sane nimis elegante lingua,
decoctoris amica Formiani.
ten Provincia narrat esse bellam ?
tecum Lesbia nostra comparatur ?
o saeclum insapiens et infacetum !

## XLIV

O FVNDE noster, seu Sabine seu Tiburs,
(nam te esse Tiburtem autumant, quibus
    non est
cordi Catullum laedere : at quibus cordist,
quovis Sabinum pignore esse contendunt)
sed seu Sabine sive verius Tiburs,
fui libenter in tua suburbana
villa, malamque pectore expuli tussim,
non immerenti quam mihi meus venter,
dum sumptuosas appeto, dedit, cenas.
nam, Sestianus dum volo esse conviva,          10

force a blush from the brazen face of the beast: call out again with louder voice, " Dirty drab, give back the tablets, give back the tablets, dirty drab !" [1] We get nothing by that: she does not mind. You must change your plan and method, if you can do better so—" Maiden modest and chaste, give back the tablets."

## XLIII

I GREET you, lady, you who neither have a tiny nose, nor a pretty foot, nor black eyes, nor long fingers, nor dry mouth, nor indeed a very refined tongue, you mistress of the bankrupt of Formiae. Is it you who are pretty, as the Province tells us? is it with you that our Lesbia is compared? Oh, this age ! how tasteless and ill-bred it is !

## XLIV

MY farm, whether Sabine or Tiburtine (for those affirm that you are Tiburtine, who do not love to annoy Catullus, but those who do will wager anything that you are Sabine)—but at all events, whether you are Sabine or more rightly Tiburtine, I was glad to be in your retreat, 'twixt country and town, and to clear my chest of the troublesome cough, which my greediness gave me (not undeservedly) whilst I was running after costly feasts. I wanted to go to dinner

---

[1] Or (*pote, ut ruborem . 1 . ore, conclamate*, &c., M.), " if nothing else can do so, in order to extort a blush from her brazen face, bawl out," &c.

orationem in Antium petitorem
plenam veneni et pestilentiae legi.[1]
hic me gravedo frigida et frequens tussis
quassavit usque dum in tuum sinum fugi
et me recuravi otioque et urtica.
quare refectus maximas tibi grates
ago, meum quod non es ulta peccatum.
nec deprecor iam, si nefaria scripta
Sesti recepso, quin gravedinem et tussim
non mi, sed ipsi Sestio ferat frigus,        **20**
qui tunc vocat me, cum malum librum legi.[2]

## XLV

Acmen Septimius suos amores
tenens in gremio " mea " inquit " Acme,
ni te perdite amo atque amare porro
omnes sum assidue paratus annos
quantum qui pote plurimum perire,
solus in Libya Indiaque tosta
caesio veniam obvius leoni."
hoc ut dixit, Amor, sinistra, † ut ante †
dextra, sternuit approbationem.
at Acme leviter caput reflectens        **10**
et dulcis pueri ebrios ocellos
illo purpureo ore saviata

---

[1] Two explanations of this poem are given, according as
*legi* or *legit* is read in 12, 21.   (1) (*legi*) Catullus, invited to
dine with Sestius, read one of his speeches, caught cold from
it, and did not go to dinner ; (2) (*legit*) Catullus was invited
to dine with Sestius ; went there, heard him read, and came
away with a chill.   Or *pegit*, " composed," Tucker, or *fecit* B.
   [2] legit *codd.*

with Sestius, and so I read a speech of his against the
candidate Antius, full of poison and plague. There-
upon a shivering chill and a constant cough shook
me to pieces, till at last I fled to your bosom, and
set myself right again by a diet of laziness and nettle
broth. So now, having recovered, I return you my
best thanks because you did not punish my error.
And henceforth, if I ever again take in hand the
abominable writings of Sestius, I freely consent that
the chill shall bring catarrh and cough, not upon me,
but upon Sestius himself, for inviting me just when
I have read a stupid book.[1]


## XLV

SEPTIMIUS, holding in his arms his darling Acme, says,
"My Acme, if I do not love thee to desperation, and if I
am not ready to go on loving thee continually through
all my years as much and as distractedly as the most
distracted of lovers, may I in Libya or sunburnt India
meet a green-eyed lion alone." As he said this, Love
on the left, as before on the right, sneezed goodwill.[2]
Then Acme, slightly bending back her head, kissed
with that rosy mouth her sweet love's swimming

---

[1] *tunc . . . cum*, "just when I have read," of a single occasion,
or "only when I happen to read"; *cum* almost = *quoties*.

[2] I follow Dr. Postgate's reading and punctuation. This
makes three sneezes: (1) *dextra* 9, (2) *sinistra* 8 and *sinistram*
17, (3) *dextram* 18; the first from the right, the second from
the left, the third from the right again. *Journal of Philology*,
XVII. 237 *sqq.* See also Dr. Verrall's note, *ibid.* 239 *n.* P. also
suggests *sinistra mutans dextris*, or *sinistra vitans, dextram.*
Munro (*Criticisms*, &c., p. 120) suggests *sinister astans.*

"sic" inquit "mea vita Septimille,
huic uni domino usque serviamus,
ut multo mihi maior acriorque
ignis mollibus ardet in medullis."
hoc ut dixit, Amor, sinistram ut ante,
dextram sternuit approbationem.
nunc ab auspicio bono profecti
mutuis animis amant amantur.                          20
unam Septimius misellus Acmen
mavolt quam Syrias Britanniasque :
uno in Septimio fidelis Acme
facit delicias libidinesque.
quis ullos homines beatiores
vidit, quis Venerem auspicatiorem ?


### XLVI

Iam ver egelidos refert tepores,
iam caeli furor aequinoctialis
iucundis Zephyri silescit auris.
linquantur Phrygii, Catulle, campi
Niceaeque ager uber aestuosae :
ad claras Asiae volemus urbes.
iam mens praetrepidans avet vagari,
iam laeti studio pedes vigescunt.
o dulces comitum valete coetus,
longe quos simul a domo profectos                     10
diversae variae [1] viae reportant.

---

[1] *Perhaps* diversae varie *or* diverse variae.

eyes, and said, "So, my life, my darling Septimius, so may we ever serve this one master as (I swear) more strongly and fiercely burns in me [1] the flame deep in my melting marrow." As she said this, Love, as before on the left, now on the right sneezed goodwill. And now, setting out from this good omen, heart in heart they live, loving and loved. Poor Septimius prefers Acme alone to whole Syrias and Britains. In Septimius, him alone, his faithful Acme takes her fill of loves and pleasures. Who ever saw human beings more blest? Who ever saw a more fortunate love?

## XLVI

Now spring brings back balmy warmth, now the sweet gales of Zephyr are hushing the rage of the equinoctial sky. Deserted be the Phrygian plains, Catullus, and the rich land of burning Nicaea: away let us fly to the renowned cities of Asia. Now my soul flutters in anticipation and yearns to stray; now my eager feet rejoice and grow strong. Farewell, dear bands of fellow travellers, who started together from your far-away home, and whom divided ways through changing scenes are bringing back again.

[1] Or "than for you," understanding *quam tibi*.

## XLVII

Porci et Socration, duae sinistrae
Pisonis, scabies famesque munda,[1]
vos Veraniolo meo et Fabullo
verpus praeposuit Priapus ille?
vos convivia lauta sumptuose
de die facitis? mei sodales
quaerunt in trivio vocationes?

## XLVIII

Mellitos oculos tuos, Iuventi,
siquis me sinat usque basiare,
usque ad milia basiem trecenta,
nec mi umquam videar satur futurus,
non si densior aridis aristis
sit nostrae seges osculationis.

## XLIX

Disertissime Romuli nepotum,
quot sunt quotque fuere, Marce Tulli,
quotque post aliis erunt in annis,
gratias tibi maximas Catullus
agit pessimus omnium poeta,
tanto pessimus omnium poeta
quanto tu optimus omnium's [2] patronus

---

[1] fames munda (*for* mundi *codd.*) = fames mera (cf. *Mart.* iii
lviii. 45).

[2] omnium *codd. :* omnium *R.*

## XLVII

PORCIUS and Socration, Piso's two left hands, you plague and mere famine, has that obscene Priapus preferred you to my dear Veranius and Fabullus? Are you spending money and holding splendid rich banquets at vast expense in broad daylight, whilst my old friends must walk about the streets to hunt for an invitation?

## XLVIII

YOUR honeyed eyes, Juventius, if one should let me go on kissing still, I would kiss them three hundred thousand times, nor would I think I should ever have enough, no, not if the harvest of our kissing were thicker than the ripe ears of corn.

## XLIX

MOST skilled in speech of the descendants of Romulus, all who are, and all who have been, and all who shall be hereafter in other years, Marcus Tullius,—to thee his warmest thanks Catullus gives, the worst of all poets; as much the worst poet of all as you are the best advocate of all.

## L

HESTERNO, Licini, die otiosi
multum lusimus in meis tabellis,
ut convenerat esse delicatos.
scribens versiculos uterque nostrum
ludebat numero modo hoc modo illoc,
reddens mutua per iocum atque vinum.
atque illinc abii tuo lepore
incensus, Licini, facetiisque,
ut nec me miserum cibus iuvaret
nec somnus tegeret quiete ocellos,　　　　　10
sed toto indomitus furore lecto
versarer, cupiens videre lucem,
ut tecum loquerer simulque ut essem.
at defessa labore membra postquam
semimortua lectulo iacebant,
hoc, iucunde, tibi poema feci,
ex quo perspiceres meum dolorem.
nunc audax cave sis, precesque nostras
oramus cave despuas, ocelle,
ne poenas Nemesis reposcat a te.　　　　　20
est vemens dea : laedere hanc caveto.

## LI

ILLE mi par esse deo videtur,
Ille, si fas est, superare divos,
qui sedens adversus identidem te
　　　spectat et audit
dulce ridentem, misero quod omnis
eripit sensus mihi ; nam simul te,
Lesbia, aspexi, nihil est super mi
　　　[vocis in ore]

## L

YESTERDAY, Licinius, we made holiday and played many a game [1] with my tablets, as we had agreed to take our pleasure. Each of us pleased his fancy in writing verses, now in one metre, now in another, answering each other, while we laughed and drank our wine. I came away from this so fired by your wit and fun, Licinius, that food did not ease my pain, nor sleep spread rest over my eyes, but restless and fevered [2] I tossed about all over my bed, longing to see the dawn, that I might talk to you and be with you. But when my limbs were worn out with fatigue and lay half dead on my couch, I made this poem for you, my sweet friend, that from it you might learn my suffering. Now be not too proud, and do not, I pray you, apple of my eye, do not reject my prayers, lest Nemesis demand penalties from you in turn. She is an imperious goddess— beware of offending her.

## LI

HE seems to me to be equal to a god, he, if it may be, seems to surpass the very gods, who sitting opposite you again and again gazes at you and hears you sweetly laughing. Such a thing takes away all my senses, alas! for whenever I see you, Lesbia, at once no sound of voice remains within my mouth, but

---

[1] Or (*invicem*) " in turns."

[2] *indomitus*, "raging," as LXIV. 54, CIII. 2.

lingua sed torpet, tenuis sub artus
flamma demanat, sonitu suopte
tintinant aures, gemina teguntur
    lumina nocte.

10

### LIA

Otivm, Catulle, tibi molestumst:
otio exultas nimiumque gestis.
otium et reges prius et beatas
    perdidit urbes.

### LII

Qvid est, Catulle? quid moraris emori?
sella in curuli Struma Nonius sedet,
per consulatum perierat Vatinius:
quid est, Catulle? quid moraris emori?

### LIII

Risi nescio quem modo e corona,
qui, cum mirifice Vatiniana
meus crimina Calvus explicasset,
admirans ait haec manusque tollens,
"di magni, salaputtium disertum!"

### LIV

Otonis caput (oppidost pusillum)
† et Eri rustice † semilauta crura,

my tongue falters, a subtle flame steals down through
my limbs, my ears ring with inward humming, my
eyes are shrouded in twofold night.[1]

## LIa (*a fragment*)

IDLENESS, Catullus, does you harm, you riot in your
idleness and wanton too much. Idleness ere now
has ruined both kings and wealthy cities.

## LII

WHAT is it, Catullus? why do you not make haste to
die? Nonius Struma[2] sits in a curule chair; Vatinius
forswears himself by his consulship. What is it,
Catullus? why do you not make haste to die?

## LIII

A FELLOW in the crowd made me laugh just now:
when my dear Calvus had drawn out in splendid
style his accusations against Vatinius, he lifted up
his hands in wonder, and "Great gods," says he,
"what an eloquent manikin!"

## LIV

OTHO's head (very small it is) and your half-washed
legs, rustic Erius . . . these points at least, if not all

1 Or (*geminae*) "both my ears . . . my eyes are shrouded
in night." *gemina* has MS. authority, *geminae* is more in
Catullus's manner. *Cf.* LXIII. 75.
2 Or (*struma*) "that wen Nonius."

subtile et leve peditum Libonis,
si non omnia, displicere vellem
tibi et Fuficio seni recocto.


## LIVa

.    .    .    .

Irascere iterum meis iambis
immerentibus, unice imperator.


## LV

Oramvs, si forte non molestumst,
demonstres ubi sint tuae tenebrae.
te campo quaesivimus minore,[1]
te in circo, te in omnibus libellis,
te in templo summi Iovis sacrato;
in Magni simul ambulatione
femellas omnes, amice, prendi,
quas vultu vidi tamen sereno.
a, vel te sic ipse flagitabam,[2]
" Camerium mihi, pessimae puellae ! "                    10
quaedam inquit, nudum reduc[ta pectus],
" en hic in roseis latet papillis."
sed te iam ferre Herculi labos est.                       13
non custos si fingar ille Cretum,                         23
non si Pegaseo ferar volatu,
non Ladas [si] ego pinnipesve Perseus,
non Rhesi niveae citaeque bigae :
adde huc plumipedas volatilesque,
ventorumque simul require cursum ;

[1] *Fr. reads* quaesīmus [= quaesiimus] in minore.
[2] *Probably corrupt.* avelli sinite *Avant. :* avellent . . . puellae ? *E.*

about them, I should wish to be disliked by you
and Fuficius, that old fellow renewed to youth
again.

## LIVₐ (*a fragment*)

·    ·    ·    ·    ·

You will again be angered by my iambics, my inno-
cent iambics, you one and only general.

## LV

I BEG you, if I may without offence, show me where
is your dark corner. I have looked for you in the
lesser Campus, in the Circus, in all the booksellers'
shops, in the hallowed temple of great Jove. And
when I was in Pompey's portico, I stopped all the
women there, my friend, who, however, faced me
with untroubled look. You it was that I kept ask-
ing them for : " Give me my Camerius, you wicked
girls!" One of them, baring her naked bosom,
says, " Look here, he is hiding between my rosy
breasts." Well, to bear with you is now a labour of
Hercules. Not though I should be moulded in brass
like the fabled warder of Crete, not though I were
to soar aloft like flying Pegasus, not if I were Ladas
or wing-rooted Perseus, not if I were the swift snow-
white pair of Rhesus could I overtake you : add to
these the feather-footed gods and the winged, and
with them call for the swiftness of the winds ;—

quos iunctos, Cameri, [ut] mihi dicares,
defessus tamen omnibus medullis                    30
et multis langoribus peresus
essem te, * mi[1] amice, quaeritando.               32
tanto ten fastu negas, amice?                       14
dic nobis ubi sis futurus, ede
audacter, committe, crede luci.
num te lacteolae tenent puellae?
si linguam clauso tenes in ore,
fructus proicies amoris omnes:
verbosa gaudet Venus loquella.                      20
vel si vis, licet obseres palatum,
dum vestri sim[2] particeps amoris.


## LVI

O REM ridiculam, Cato, et iocosam
dignamque auribus et tuo cachinno.
ride, quicquid amas, Cato, Catullum:
res est ridicula et nimis iocosa.
deprendi modo pupulum puellae
crusantem: hunc ego, si placet Dionae,
pro telo rigida mea cecidi.


## LVII

PVLCRE convenit improbis cinaedis,
Mamurrae pathicoque Caesarique.
nec mirum: maculae pares utrisque,
urbana altera et illa Formiana,

[1] mihi *codd.* : mi *Scal.*
[2] vostri sis, nostri sis *codd.*   nostri sis *E. (preferred by P.)*
*would mean "so long as I can get to you and tell my secret."*
*If* vestri sis *is read,* vestri = *tui,* and particeps = potens *or*
compos.

64

though you should harness all these, Camerius, and press them into my service, yet I should be tired out to my very marrow, and worn away with frequent faintness, my friend, while searching for you. Do you deny yourself so haughtily, my friend? Tell us where you are likely to be, out with it boldly, trust me with it, give it to the light. Do the milk-white maids detain you? If you keep your tongue shut up within your mouth, you will waste all the gains of love; Venus loves an utterance full of words. However, if you will, you may lock up your lips, so long as you let me be a sharer in your love.

## LVI

O, CATO, what an absurdly funny thing, worthy for you to hear and laugh at! Laugh, as much as you love Catullus, Cato. The thing is too absurd and funny. . . .

## LVII

WELL agreed are the abominable profligates, Mamurra the effeminate, and Caesar; no wonder either. Like stains, one from the city and one from Formiae, are

impressae resident nec eluentur:
morbosi pariter, gemelli utrique,
uno in lecticulo [1] erudituli ambo,
non hic quam ille magis vorax adulter,
rivales socii puellularum.
pulcre convenit improbis cinaedis.

## LVIII

CAELI, Lesbia nostra, Lesbia illa,
illa Lesbia, quam Catullus unam
plus quam se atque suos amavit omnes,
nunc in quadriviis et angiportis
glubit magnanimi Remi nepotes.

## LIX

BONONIENSIS Rufa Rufulum fellat
uxor Meneni, saepe quam in sepulcretis
vidistis ipso rapere de rogo cenam,
cum devolutum ex igne prosequens panem
ab semiraso tunderetur ustore.

## LX

NVM te leaena montibus Libystinis
aut Scylla latrans infima inguinum parte
tam mente dura procreavit ac taetra,
ut supplicis vocem in novissimo casu
contemptam haberes, a nimis fero corde?

[1] lecticulo *O* : lectulo *caett. codd.* *See M., p. 131.*

deeply impressed on each, and will never be washed out. Diseased alike, very twins, both on one sofa, dilettante writers both, one as greedy in adultery as the other, rivals and partners in love. Well agreed are the abominable profligates.

## LVIII

O, CAELIUS, my Lesbia, that Lesbia, Lesbia whom alone Catullus loved more than himself and all his own, now in the cross-roads and alleys serves the filthy lusts of the descendants of lordly-minded [1] Remus.

## LIX

RUFA of Bononia . . . the wife of Menenius, she whom you have often seen in the graveyards grabbing the baked meats from the very pyre, when as she ran after the loaf rolling down out of the fire she was thumped by the half-shaved slave of the undertaker.

## LX

WAS it a lioness from Libyan mountains or a Scylla barking from her womb below that bare you, you that are so hard-hearted and monstrous as to hold in contempt your suppliant's voice in his last need, ah, too cruel-hearted one ?

1 Or (*magnanimos* or *magnanimis* E., P.) "the high-minded descendants."

## LXI

COLLIS o Heliconii
cultor, Uraniae genus,
qui rapis teneram ad virum
virginem, o Hymenaee Hymen,
    o Hymen Hymenaee,

cinge tempora floribus
suave olentis amaraci,
flammeum cape, laetus huc
huc veni niveo gerens
    luteum pede soccum,          10

excitusque hilari die,
nuptialia concinens
voce carmina tinnula,
pelle humum pedibus, manu
    pineam quate taedam.

namque Vinia Manlio,
qualis Idalium colens
venit ad Phrygium Venus
iudicem, bona cum bona
    nubet alite virgo,          20

floridis velut enitens
myrtus Asia ramulis,
quos Hamadryades deae
ludicrum sibi roscido
    nutriunt † umore.[1]

---

[1] *For* umore *P. reads* alimento, *metri gr.*

## LXI

O HAUNTER of the Heliconian mount, Urania's son, thou who bearest away the tender maid to her bridegroom, O Hymenaeus Hymen, O Hymen Hymenaeus!

Bind thy brows with the flowers of fragrant marjoram, put on the marriage veil, hither, hither merrily come, wearing on thy snow-white foot the yellow shoe,

and wakening on this joyful day, singing with resonant voice the nuptial songs, beat the ground with thy feet, shake with thy hand the pine torch.

For now shall Vinia wed with Manlius, Vinia as fair as Venus who dwells in Idalium, when she came to the Phrygian judge; a good maiden with a good omen,

like the Asian myrtle shining with flowering sprays, which the Hamadryad goddesses with dewy moisture nourish as a plaything for themselves.

quare age huc aditum ferens
perge linquere Thespiae
rupis Aonios specus,
nympha quos super irrigat
    frigerans Aganippe,       **30**

ac domum dominam voca
coniugis cupidam novi,
mentem amore revinciens,
ut tenax edera huc et huc
    arborem implicat errans.

vosque item simul, integrae
virgines, quibus advenit
par dies, agite in modum
dicite " o Hymenaee Hymen,
    o Hymen Hymenaee."      **40**

ut lubentius, audiens
se citarier ad suum
munus, huc aditum ferat
dux bonae Veneris, boni
    coniugator amoris.

quis deus magis est †ama-
tis petendus amantibus ?
quem colent homines magis
caelitum ?  o Hymenaee Hymen,
    o Hymen Hymenaee.      **50**

te suis tremulus parens
invocat, tibi virgines
zonula soluunt sinus,
te timens cupida novus
    captat aure maritus.

Hither then, come hither, haste to leave the Aonian caves of the Thespian rock, which the nymph Aganippe besprinkles with cooling shower from above;

call to her home the lady of the house, full of desire for her bridegroom; bind her heart with love, as here and there the clinging ivy straying clasps the tree.

Ye too with me, unwedded virgins, for whom a like day is coming, come, in measure say, "O Hymenaeus Hymen, O Hymen Hymenaeus!"

that hearing himself summoned to his own office, the god may come more readily hither, the herald of genial Venus, the coupler of honest love.

What god is more worthy to be invoked by lovers who are loved? whom of the heavenly ones shall men worship more than thee? O Hymenaeus Hymen, O Hymen Hymenaeus!

Thee for his children the aged father invokes, for thee the maidens loose their garments from the girdle: for thee the bridegroom listens fearfully with eager ear.

71

tu fero iuveni in manus
floridam ipse puellulam
dedis a gremio suae
matris, o Hymenaee Hymen,
    o Hymen Hymenaee.        60

nil potest sine te Venus,
fama quod bona comprobet,
commodi capere : at potest
te volente.   quis huic deo
    compararier ausit ?

nulla quit sine te domus
liberos dare, nec parens
stirpe nitier : at potest
te volente.   quis huic deo
    compararier ausit ?        70

quae tuis careat sacris,
non queat dare praesides
terra finibus : at queat
te volente.   quis huic deo
    compararier ausit ?

claustra pandite ianuae,
† virgo adest.† [1]   viden ut faces
splendidas quatiunt comas ?
.         .         .

tardet ingenuus pudor :
.         .         .

quem tamen magis audiens      80
    flet, quod ire necesse est.     81

[1] adest *codd.* : ades *Schr. P.* : *or* claustra pandite ianuae,
virgines ; *cf.* 227.

Thou thyself givest into the hands of the fiery youth the blooming maiden from her mother's bosom, O Hymenaeus Hymen, O Hymen Hymenaeus!

No pleasure can Venus take without thee, such as honest fame may approve; but can, if thou art willing. What god dare match himself with this god?

No house without thee can give children, no parent rest on his offspring; but all is well if thou art willing. What god dare match himself with this god?

A land that should want thy sanctities would not be able to produce guardians for its borders—but could, if thou wert willing. What god dare match himself with this god?

Throw open the fastenings of the door; the bride is coming.[1] See you how the torches shake their shining tresses? . . . noble shame delays. . . . Yet listening rather to this, she weeps that she must go.

1 Or (*ades*) "bride, come hither."

flere desine.   non tibi, Au-            86
runculeia, periculumst,
nequa femina pulcrior
clarum ab Oceano diem                    85
    viderit venientem.                   96

talis in vario solet
divitis domini hortulo
stare flos hyacinthinus.
sed moraris, abit dies:                  90
    [prodeas, nova nupta.]

prodeas, nova nupta, si
iam videtur, et audias
nostra verba.   vide ut faces
aureas quatiunt comas:
    prodeas, nova nupta.

non tuus levis in mala
deditus vir adultera
probra turpia persequens
a tuis teneris volet                     100
    secubare papillis,

lenta *qui velut adsitas
vitis implicat arbores,
implicabitur in tuum
complexum.   sed abit dies:
    prodeas, nova nupta.

ɔ cubile, quod omnibus
    .       .       .
    .       .       .
    .       .       .                    110
    candido pede lecti,

Weep no more. Not to you, Aurunculeia, is there danger that any fairer woman shall see [1] the bright day coming from ocean.

So in the gay garden of a rich owner stands a hyacinth flower—but you delay, the day is passing; come forth, O bride.

Come forth, O bride, if now you will, and hear our words. See how the torches shake their golden tresses !—come forth, O bride.

Your husband will not, lightly given to some wicked paramour, and following shameful ways of dishonour, wish to lie away from your soft bosom;

but as the pliant vine entwines the trees planted near it, so will he be entwined in your embrace. But the day is passing; come forth, O bride.

O bridal bed, to all . . .

    .     .     .     .     .

   .     .     .     .     .

white foot . . . bed,

[1] *viderit = visura sit*, translating Callimachus's ὄψεται δώς.

quae tuo veniunt ero,
quanta gaudia, quae vaga
nocte, quae medio die
gaudeat! sed abit dies:
    prodeas, nova nupta.

tollite, o pueri, faces:
flammeum video venire.
ite, concinite in modum
"io Hymen Hymenaee io,
    io Hymen Hymenaee."      120

ne diu taceat procax
Fescennina iocatio,
neu nuces pueris neget
desertum domini [1] audiens
    concubinus amorem.

da nuces pueris, iners
concubine: satis diu
lusisti nucibus: lubet [2]
iam servire Talasio.      130
    concubine, nuces da.

sordebant tibi vilicae,
concubine, hodie atque heri:
nunc tuum cinerarius
tondet os.   miser a miser
    concubine, nuces da.

diceris male te a tuis
unguentate glabris, marite,
abstinere: sed abstine.
io Hymen Hymenaee io,      140
    io Hymen Hymenaee.

[1] *Or* domino.        [2] *Or* iuvet (*Busche*).

What joys are coming for your lord, O what joys for him to know in the fleeting night, joys in the full day!—but the day is passing; come forth, O bride.


Raise aloft the torches, boys: I see the wedding veil coming. Go on, sing in measure, Io Hymen Hymenaeus io, io Hymen Hymenaeus!


Let not the merry Fescennine jesting be silent long, let the favourite boy give away nuts to the slaves, when he hears how his lord has left his love.


Give nuts to the slaves, favourite: your time is past: you have played with nuts long enough: you must now be the servant of Talassius. Give nuts, beloved slave.

To-day and yesterday you disdained the country wives: now the barber shaves your cheeks. Wretched, ah! wretched lover, throw the nuts '


They will say that you, perfumed bridegroom, are unwilling to give up your old pleasures; but abstain. Io Hymen Hymenaeus io, io Hymen Hymenaeus!

scimus haec tibi quae licent
sola cognita : sed marito
ista non eadem licent.
io Hymen Hymenaee io,
    io Hymen Hymenaee.

nupta, tu quoque, quae tuus
vir petet, cave ne neges,
ni petitum aliunde eat.
io Hymen Hymenaee io,         150
    io Hymen Hymenaee.

en tibi domus ut potens
et beata viri tui,
quae tibi sine serviat
(io Hymen Hymenaee io,
    io Hymen Hymenaee),

usque dum tremulum movens
cana tempus anilitas
omnia omnibus annuit.
io Hymen Hymenaee io,        160
    io Hymen Hymenaee.

transfer omine cum bono
limen aureolos pedes,
rasilemque subi forem.
io Hymen Hymenaee io,
    io Hymen Hymenaee.

aspice, intus ut accubans
vir tuus Tyrio in toro
totus immineat tibi.
io Hymen Hymenaee io,        170
    io Hymen Hymenaee.

We know that you are acquainted with no unlawful joys; but a husband has not the same liberty. Io Hymen Hymenaeus io, io Hymen Hymenaeus!

You too, O bride, be sure you refuse not what your husband claims, lest he go elsewhere to find it. Io Hymen Hymenaeus io, io Hymen Hymenaeus!

See how mighty and rich for you is the house of your husband; be content to be mistress here, (Io Hymen Hymenaeus io, io Hymen Hymenaeus!)

even till hoary old age, shaking a trembling head, nods assent to all for all. Io Hymen Hymenaeus io, io Hymen Hymenaeus!

Lift across the threshold with a good omen your golden feet, and enter within the polished door. Io Hymen Hymenaeus io, io Hymen Hymenaeus!

See how your husband within,[1] reclining on a purple couch, is all eagerness for you. Io Hymen Hymenaeus io, io Hymen Hymenaeus!

[1] Or (*unus* codd.) "with no second near him" E.; *i.e.*, at the *cena nuptialis*.

79

illi non minus ac tibi
pectore †uritur [1] intimo
flamma, sed penite magis.
io Hymen Hymenaee io,
    io Hymen Hymenaee.

mitte bracchiolum teres,
praetextate, puellulae :
iam cubile adeat viri.
io Hymen Hymenaee io,        180
    io Hymen Hymenaee.

vos bonae senibus viris
cognitae bene feminae,
collocate puellulam.
io Hymen Hymenaee io,
    io Hymen Hymenaee.

iam licet venias, marite :
uxor in thalamo tibist
ore floridulo nitens,
alba parthenice velut        190
    luteumve papaver.

at, marite, (ita me iuvent
caelites) nihilo minus
pulcher es, neque te Venus
neglegit.  sed abit dies :
    perge, ne remorare.

non diu remoratus es,
iam venis.  bona te Venus
iuverit, quoniam palam
quod cupis capis et bonum    200
    non abscondis amorem.

---

[1] uritur *probably corrupt.* *P. suggests* ille non minus
acribus | pectore uritur intime | flammis.  *Other emendations*
*are* ardet in, pectus uritur intime.

In his inmost heart no less than in yours glows
the flame, but deeper within. Io Hymen Hymenaeus
io, io Hymen Hymenaeus!

Let go, young boy, the smooth arm of the damsel,
let her now come to her husband's bed. Io Hymen
Hymenaeus io, io Hymen Hymenaeus!

Ye, honest matrons, well wedded to ancient hus-
bands, set the damsel in her place. Io Hymen
Hymenaeus io, io Hymen Hymenaeus!

Now you may come, bridegroom; your wife is in the
bride-chamber, shining with flowery face, like a white
daisy or yellow poppy.

But, husband, so the gods help me, you are no
less fair, nor does Venus neglect you. But the day
is passing. Go on then, delay not.

Not long have you delayed. Already you come.
May kindly Venus help you, since openly you take
your desire [1] and do not hide your honest love.

[1] Or (cupis cupis) "desire what you desire." capis is either
the original reading or a very early correction.

ille pulveris Africi
siderumque micantium
subducat numerum prius,
qui vostri numerare vult
multa milia ludi.

ludite ut lubet, et brevi
liberos date.   non decet
tam vetus sine liberis
nomen esse, sed indidem                    210
semper ingenerari.

Torquatus volo parvulus
matris e gremio suae
porrigens teneras manus
dulce rideat ad patrem
semihiante labello.

sit suo similis patri
Manlio et facile † insciis
noscitetur ab † omnibus [1]
et pudicitiam suae [2]                     220
matris indicet ore.

talis illius a bona
matre laus genus approbet,
qualis unica ab optima
matre Telemacho manet
fama Penelopeo.

[1] inscieis . . . omnibus *codd.* omnibus . . . insciis, omni-
bus . . . obviis *are proposed by editors to preserve* synaphea
*but cf. Munro, p. 139.*
[2] suo, *B., P.*

Let him first count up the number of the dust of Africa and of the glittering stars, who would number the many thousands of your joys.

Sport as ye will, and soon bring children forth. It is not fit that so old a name should be without children, but that they should be ever born from the same stock.

I would see a little Torquatus, stretching his baby hands from his mother's lap, smile a sweet smile at his father with lips half parted.

May he be like his father Manlius, and easily be recognised by all, even those who do not know, and declare by his face the fair fame of his mother.

May such praise, due to his chaste mother, approve his descent, as for Telemachus son of Penelope remains unparagoned the honour derived from his noble mother.

claudite ostia, virgines :
lusimus satis.   at, boni
coniuges, bene vivite et
munere assiduo valentem                     230
exercete iuventam.


## LXII

*Iuvenes*

VESPER adest, iuvenes, consurgite : Vesper Olympo
expectata diu vix tandem lumina tollit.
surgere iam tempus, iam pinguis linquere mensas ;
iam veniet virgo, iam dicetur Hymenaeus.

   Hymen o Hymenaee, Hymen ades o Hymenaee !


*Puellae*

cernitis, innuptae, iuvenes ?   consurgite contra ;
nimirum Oetaeos ostendit Noctifer ignes.
sic certest ; viden ut perniciter exiluere ?
non temere exiluere, canent quod † visere par est.

   Hymen o Hymenaee, Hymen ades o Hymenaee !


*Iuvenes*

non facilis nobis, aequales, palma paratast :         11
aspicite, innuptae secum ut meditata requirunt.
non frustra meditantur, habent memorabile quod sit.
nec mirum, penitus quae tota mente laborent.
nos alio mentes, alio divisimus aures ·
iure igitur vincemur ; amat victoria curam.

Maidens, shut the doors. We have sported enough.
But ye, happy pair, live happily, and in your wedded
joys employ your vigorous youth.

## LXII

*Youths.* The evening is come, rise up, ye youths.
Vesper from Olympus [1] now at last is just raising his
long-looked-for light. Now is it time to rise, now to
leave the rich tables ; now will come the bride, now
will the Hymen-song be sung. Hymen, O Hymen-
aeus, Hymen, hither, O Hymenaeus !

*Maidens.* See ye, maidens, the youths ? Rise up
to meet them. For sure the night-star shows his
Oetaean fires. So it is indeed ; see you how nimbly
they have sprung up ? it is not for nothing that they
have sprung up : they will sing something which it
is worth while to look at. Hymen, O Hymenaeus,
Hymen, hither, O Hymenaeus !

*Youths.* No easy palm is set out for us, comrades :
look how the maidens are conning what they have
learnt. Not in vain do they learn, they have there
something worthy of memory ; no wonder, since
they labour deeply with their whole mind. We have
diverted elsewhere our thoughts, elsewhere our ears ;
fairly then shall we be beaten ; victory loveth care

[1] Or "in heaven."

quare nunc animos saltem committite vestros;
dicere iam incipient, iam respondere decebit.

Hymen o Hymenaee, Hymen ades o Hymenaee!

#### Puellae

Hespere, qui caelo fertur crudelior ignis?    20
qui natam possis complexu avellere matris,
complexu [1] matris retinentem avellere natam,
et iuveni ardenti castam donare puellam.
quid faciunt hostes capta crudelius urbe?

Hymen o Hymenaee, Hymen ades o Hymenaee!

#### Iuvenes

Hespere, qui caelo lucet iucundior ignis?
qui desponsa tua firmes conubia flamma,
quae pepigere viri, pepigerunt ante parentes,
nec iunxere prius quam se tuus extulit ardor.
quid datur a divis felici optatius hora?    30

Hymen o Hymenaee, Hymen ades o Hymenaee!

.     .     .     .

#### Puellae

Hesperus e nobis, aequales, abstulit unam

.     .     .     .

#### Iuvenes

namque tuo adventu vigilat custodia semper.
nocte latent fures, quos idem saepe revertens,
Hespere, mutato comprendis nomine Eous.

[Hymen o Hymenaee, Hymen ades o Hymenaee! [2]]

.     .     .     .

---

1 complexu *T., V.*: complexum *P.*     2 *Supplied by P.*

Wherefore now at least match your minds with theirs.[1] Anon they will begin to speak, anon it will be fitting for us to answer. Hymen, O Hymenaeus, Hymen, hither, O Hymenaeus!

*Maidens.* Hesperus, what more cruel fire than thine moves in the sky? for thou canst endure to tear the daughter from her mother's embrace, from her mother's embrace to tear the close-clinging daughter, and give the chaste maiden to the burning youth. What more cruel than this do enemies when a city falls? Hymen, O Hymenaeus, Hymen, hither, O Hymenaeus!

*Youths.* Hesperus, what more welcome fire than thine shines in the sky? for thou with thy flame confirmest the contracted espousals, which husbands and parents have promised beforehand, but unite not till thy flame has arisen. What is given by the gods more desirable than the fortunate hour? Hymen, O Hymenaeus, Hymen, hither, O Hymenaeus!

.     .     .     .     .

*Maidens.* Hesperus, friends, has taken away one of us.

.     .     .     .     .

*Youths.* For at thy coming the guard is always awake. By night thieves hide themselves, whom thou, Hesperus, often overtakest as thou returnest, Hesperus the same but with changed name Eous.[2] [Hymen, O Hymenaeus, Hymen, hither, O Hymenaeus!]

.     .     .     .     .

[1] Or (*convertite* T.) "turn your minds hither."
[2] Or (*eosdem* codd.) "you overtake unchanged." These verses are assigned to the maidens by P.

at lubet innuptis ficto te carpere questu.
quid tum, si carpunt, tacita quem [1] mente requirunt?

Hymen o Hymenaee, Hymen ades o Hymenaee!

### Puellae

ut flos in saeptis secretus nascitur hortis,
ignotus pecori, nullo convulsus aratro,                    40
quem mulcent aurae, firmat sol, educat imber,

. . . . .

multi illum pueri, multae optavere puellae:
idem cum tenui carptus defloruit ungui,
nulli illum pueri, nullae optavere puellae:
sic virgo dum intacta manet, dum cara suis est;
cum castum amisit polluto corpore florem,
nec pueris iucunda manet nec cara puellis.

Hymen o Hymenaee, Hymen ades o Hymenaee!

### Iuvenes

ut vidua in nudo vitis quae nascitur arvo
numquam se extollit, numquam mitem educat
      uvam,                                                50
sed tenerum prono deflectens pondere corpus
iam iam contingit summum radice flagellum;
hanc nulli agricolae, nulli coluere [2] iuvenci.
at si forte eademst ulmo coniuncta marita,
multi illam agricolae, multi coluere iuvenci:
sic virgo dum intacta manet, dum inculta senescit;
cum par conubium maturo tempore adeptast,
cara viro magis et minus est invisa parenti.

[Hymen o Hymenaee, Hymen ades o Hymenaee!]

[1] tacita a l quem B., P.
[2] nulli, a, coluere P.

But girls love to chide thee with feigned com-
plaint. What then, if they chide him whom they
desire in their secret heart? Hymen, O Hymenaeus,
Hymen, hither, O Hymenaeus!

*Maidens.* As a flower springs up secretly in a
fenced garden, unknown to the cattle, torn up [1] by no
plough, which the winds caress, the sun strengthens,
the shower draws forth, many boys, many girls, desire
it; when the same flower fades, nipped by a sharp
nail, no boys, no girls desire it: so a maiden, whilst
she remains untouched, so long is she dear to her
own; when she has lost her chaste flower with sullied
body, she remains neither lovely to boys nor dear to
girls. Hymen, O Hymenaeus, Hymen, hither, O
Hymenaeus!

*Youths.* As an unwedded vine which grows up in
a bare field never raises itself aloft, never brings
forth a mellow grape, but bending its tender form
with downward weight, even now touches the root
with topmost shoot; no farmers, no oxen tend it:
but if it chance to be joined in marriage to the elm,
many farmers, many oxen tend it: so a maiden,
whilst she remains untouched, so long is she aging
untended; [2] but when in ripe season she is matched
in equal wedlock, she is more dear to her husband
and less distasteful to her father. [Hymen, O
Hymenaeus, Hymen, hither, O Hymenaeus!]

[1] Or (*contusus, conclusus,* codd.) "bruised." *convolsus* T.;
cf. LXIV. 40.
[2] Or "whilst . . . whilst." The rendering given here is
from Quintilian, IX. 3, 16.

et [1] tu ne pugna cum tali coniuge, virgo.
non aequumst pugnare, pater cui tradidit ipse,    60
ipse pater cum matre, quibus parere necessest.
virginitas non tota tuast, ex parte parentumst;
tertia pars patrist, pars est data tertia matri,
tertia sola tuast : noli pugnare duobus,
qui genero sua iura simul cum dote dederunt.

   Hymen o Hymenaee, Hymen ades o Hymenaee !


## LXIII

Svper alta vectus Attis celeri rate maria
Phrygium ut nemus citato cupide pede tetigit
adiitque opaca silvis redimita loca deae,
stimulatus ibi furenti rabie, vagus animi,
devolvit ili acuto sibi pondera silice.
itaque ut relicta sensit sibi membra sine viro,
etiam recente terrae sola sanguine maculans
niveis citata cepit manibus leve typanum,
typanum, † tubam Cybelles,† tua, Mater, initia,
quatiensque terga tauri teneris cava digitis    10
canere haec suis adortast tremebunda comitibus.
" agite ite ad alta, Gallae, Cybeles nemora simul,
simul ite, Dindymenae dominae vaga pecora,
aliena quae petentes † velut exules loca celeri † [2]
sectam meam executae duce me mihi comites
rapidum salum tulistis truculentaque pelage [3]

---

[1] et *codd. :* at nec tu *P.*

[2] *Corrupt.*   *P. thinks* velut exules *a gloss on some word* (*perhaps* profugae) *which has dropped out of the text, and proposes to read* aliena q. p. profugae loca celeri (*adv. like* brevi).  *aliena* q. petentes velut exules loca *vulg.*

[3] pelagi *codd. pler.*  pelage *is accepted by Bentley and Lambinus.*

And you, maiden, strive not with such a husband; it is not right to strive with him to whom your father himself gave you, your father himself with your mother, whom you must obey.  Your maidenhead is not all your own; partly it belongs to your parents, a third part is given to your father, a third part to your mother, only a third is yours; do not contend with two, who have given their rights to their son-in-law together with the dowry.  Hymen, O Hymenaeus, Hymen, hither, O Hymenaeus!

## LXIII

BORNE in his swift bark over deep seas, Attis, when eagerly with speedy foot he reached the Phrygian woodland, and entered the goddess's abodes, shadowy, forest-crowned; there, goaded by raging madness, bewildered in mind, he cast down from him with sharp flint-stone the burden of his members.[1] So when she felt her limbs to have lost their manhood, still with fresh blood dabbling the face of the ground, swiftly with snowy hands she seized the light timbrel, timbrel, trumpet [2] of Cybele, thy mysteries, Mother, and shaking with soft fingers the hollow ox-hide thus began she to sing to her companions tremulously : " Come away, ye Gallae, go to the mountain forests of Cybele together, together go, wandering herd of the lady of Dindymus, who swiftly seeking alien homes as exiles, followed my rule as I led you in my train, endured the fast-flowing brine and the savage

[1] Or (*devolvit ile acuto sibi pondere silicis*) " cast down from him his members with the weight of the sharp flint-stone," or (*devolsit* Hpt. B.) " tore off."

[2] Or (*typanum ac typum* M.) " timbrel and medallion " (see M.'s note).

et corpus evirastis Veneris nimio odio,
hilarate erae citatis erroribus animum.
mora tarda mente cedat ; simul ite, sequimini
Phrygiam ad domum Cybelles, Phrygia ad nemora
    deae,                               20
ubi cymbalum sonat vox, ubi tympana reboant,
tibicen ubi canit Phryx curvo grave calamo,
ubi capita Maenades vi iaciunt ederigerae,
ubi sacra sancta acutis ululatibus agitant,
ubi suevit illa divae volitare vaga cohors :
quo nos decet citatis celerare tripudiis."
   Simul haec comitibus Attis cecinit notha mulier,
thiasus repente linguis trepidantibus ululat,
leve tympanum remugit, cava cymbala recrepant,
viridem citus adit Idam properante pede chorus.   30
furibunda simul anhelans vaga vadit, animam agens,
comitata [1] tympano Attis per opaca nemora dux,
veluti iuvenca vitans onus indomita iugi :
rapidae ducem sequuntur Gallae properipedem.
itaque ut domum Cybelles tetigere lassulae,
nimio e labore somnum capiunt sine Cerere.
piger his labante langore oculos sopor operit :
abit in quiete molli rabidus furor animi.
sed ubi oris aurei Sol radiantibus oculis
lustravit aethera album, sola dura, mare ferum,   40
pepulitque noctis umbras vegetis sonipedibus,
ibi Somnus excitum Attin fugiens citus abiit :

        [1] *P. conjectures* tonitante.

seas, and unmanned your bodies from utter abhorrence of love, cheer ye your Lady's heart with swift wanderings.[1]  Let dull delay depart from your mind ; go together, follow to the Phrygian house of Cybele, to the Phrygian forests of the goddess, where the noise of cymbals sounds, where timbrels re-echo, where the Phrygian flute-player blows a deep note on his curved reed, where the Maenads ivy-crowned toss their heads violently, where with shrill yells they shake the holy emblems, where that wandering company of the goddess is wont to rove, whither for us 'tis meet to hasten with rapid dances."

So soon as Attis, woman yet no true one, chanted thus to her companions, the revellers suddenly with quivering tongues yell aloud, the light timbrel rings again, clash again the hollow cymbals, swiftly to green Ida goes the rout with hurrying foot.  Then too frenzied, panting, uncertain, wanders, gasping for breath,[2] attended by the timbrel, Attis, through the dark forests their leader, as a heifer unbroken starting aside from the burden of the yoke.  Fast follow the Gallae their swift-footed leader.  So when they gained the house of Cybele, faint and weary, after much toil they take their rest without bread ; heavy sleep covers their eyes with drooping weariness, the delirious madness of their mind departs in soft slumber.  But when the sun with the flashing eyes of his golden face[3] lightened the clear heaven, the firm lands, the wild sea, and chased away the shades of night with eager tramping steeds refreshed, then Sleep fled from wakened Attis and quickly was gone ; him

1 Or (ero) "at your master's bidding."
2 Or (animi [animo] egens) "reft of sense," or (animae egens) " breathless."
3 Or "the golden-faced sun " = χρυσοφαής.

trepidante eum recepit dea Pasithea sinu.
ita de quiete molli rapida sine rabie
simul ipse [1] pectore Attis sua facta recoluit,
liquidaque mente vidit sine quis ubique foret,
animo aestuante rusum reditum ad vada tetulit.
ibi maria vasta visens lacrimantibus oculis,
patriam allocuta maestast ita voce miseriter.

" Patria o mei creatrix, patria o mea genetrix,    50
ego quam miser relinquens, dominos ut erifugae
famuli solent, ad Idae tetuli nemora pedem,
ut apud nivem et ferarum gelida stabula forem
et earum †omnia adirem [2] furibunda latibula,
ubinam aut quibus locis te positam, patria, reor?
cupit ipsa pupula ad te sibi derigere aciem,
rabie fera carens dum breve tempus animus est.
egone a mea remota haec ferar in nemora domo?
patria, bonis, amicis, genitoribus abero?
abero foro, palaestra, stadio et guminasiis?    60
miser a miser, querendumst etiam atque etiam, anime.
quod enim genus figuraest, ego non quod habuerim?
ego †mulier,[3] ego adolescens, ego ephebus, ego puer,
ego guminasi fui flos, ego eram decus olei:
mihi ianuae frequentes, mihi limina tepida,
mihi floridis corollis redimita domus erat,
linquendum ubi esset orto mihi sole cubiculum.
ego nunc deum ministra et Cybeles famula ferar?

---

   [1] ipsa *R.*: ipse *caett. codd.*
   [2] ut earum omnia adirem *codd.* *P. proposes* et ut omne
earum adirem furibunda latibulum; *Prof. Tyrrell* et ut
excetrarum adirem fur. latibula (excetra = hydra).    operta,
opaca *al.*        [3] ego nam vir *P.* (*perhaps* eram).

the goddess Pasithea received in her fluttering bosom.[1] So after soft slumber, freed from violent madness, as soon as Attis himself in his heart reviewed his own deed, and saw with clear mind what he had lost and where he was, with surging mind again he sped back to the waves. There, looking out upon the waste seas with streaming eyes, thus did she piteously address her country with tearful voice:

"O my country that gavest me life! O my country that barest me! leaving whom, ah wretch! as runaway servants leave their masters, I have borne my foot to the forests of Ida, to live among snows and frozen lairs of wild beasts, and visit in my frenzy all their lurking-dens,—where then or in what region do I think thy place to be, O my country? Mine eye-balls unbidden long to turn their gaze to thee, while for a short space my mind is free from wild frenzy. I, shall I from my own home be borne far away into these forests?[2] from my country, my possessions, my friends, my parents, shall I be absent? absent from the market, the wrestling-place, the racecourse, the playground? unhappy, ah unhappy heart, again, again must thou complain. For what form of human figure is there which I had not? I, to be a woman[3]—I who was a stripling, I a youth, I a boy, I was the flower of the playground, I was once the glory of the palaestra: mine were the crowded doorways, mine the warm thresholds, mine the flowery garlands to deck my house when I was to leave my chamber at sunrise. I, shall I now be called—what? a hand-maid of the gods, a ministress of Cybele? I a Maenad,

---

[1] Or (*trepidantem* R.) "hurrying on his way," or "fluttering."
[2] Or (*remota* acc. pl. neut.) "be borne into these distant forests."
[3] Or (*ego nam vir*) "for I was a man, I a stripling," &c.

ego Maenas, ego mei pars, ego vir sterilis ero ?
ego viridis algida Idae nive amicta loca colam ?      70
ego vitam agam sub altis Phrygiae columinibus
ubi cerva silvicultrix, ubi aper nemorivagus ?
iam iam dolet quod egi, iam iamque paenitet."
    Roseis ut hic labellis sonitus *citus abiit,*
geminas deorum ad aures nova nuntia referens,
ibi iuncta iuga resolvens Cybele leonibus
laevumque pecoris hostem stimulans ita loquitur.
" agedum" inquit " age ferox [i], fac ut hunc furor
    [agitet],
fac uti furoris ictu reditum in nemora ferat,
mea libere nimis qui fugere imperia cupit.      80
age caede terga cauda, tua verbera patere,
fac cuncta mugienti fremitu loca retonent,
rutilam ferox torosa cervice quate iubam."
ait haec minax Cybelle religatque iuga manu.
ferus ipse sese adhortans rapidum incitat animo,[1]
vadit, fremit, refringit virgulta pede vago.
at ubi umida albicantis loca litoris adiit,
tenerumque vidit Attin prope marmora pelagi,
facit impetum : ille demens fugit in nemora fera :
ibi semper omne vitae spatium famula fuit.      90
    Dea magna, dea Cybelle, dea domina Dindymi,
procul a mea tuus sit furor omnis, era, domo :
alios age incitatos, alios age rabidos.

       **1** *The Italian editors read* animum.

I part of myself, a barren man shall I be? I, shall I dwell in icy snow-clad regions of verdant Ida, I pass my life under the high summits of Phrygia, with the hind that haunts the woodland, with the boar that ranges the forest? now, now I rue my deed, now, now I would it were undone."

From his rosy lips as these words issued forth, bringing a new message to both ears of the gods, then Cybele, loosening the fastened yoke from her lions, and goading that foe of the herd who drew on the left, thus speaks: "Come now," she says, "come, go fiercely, let madness hunt him hence, bid him hence by stroke of madness hie him to the forests again, him who would be too free, and run away from my sovereignty. Come, lash back with tail, endure thy own scourging, make all around resound with bellowing roar, shake fiercely on brawny neck thy ruddy mane." Thus says wrathful Cybele, and with her hand unbinds [1] the yoke. The monster stirs his courage and rouses him to fury of heart; he speeds away, he roars, with ranging foot he breaks the brushwood. But when he came to the watery stretches of the white-gleaming shore, and saw tender Attis by the smooth spaces of the sea, he rushes at him—madly flies Attis to the wild woodland. There always for all his lifetime was he a handmaid.

Goddess, great goddess, Cybele, goddess, lady of Dindymus, far from my house be all thy fury, O my queen; others drive thou in frenzy, others drive thou to madness.

1 (*religat*) a very rare usage, but required by the sense *Cf*. 76 and LXIV. 174.

# GAI VALERI CATVLLI LIBER

## LXIV

PELIACO quondam prognatae vertice pinus
dicuntur liquidas Neptuni nasse per undas
Phasidos ad fluctus et fines Aeeteos,
cum lecti iuvenes, Argivae robora pubis,
auratam optantes Colchis avertere pellem
ausi sunt vada salsa cita decurrere puppi,
caerula verrentes abiegnis aequora palmis ;
diva quibus retinens in summis urbibus arces
ipsa levi fecit volitantem flamine currum,
pinea coniungens inflexae texta carinae.                    10
illa rudem cursu † prima ¹ imbuit Amphitriten.

   Quae simul ac rostro ventosum proscidit aequor,
tortaque remigio spumis incanduit unda,
emersere * freti candenti e gurgite vultus
aequoreae monstrum Nereides admirantes.
illa †atque alia ² viderunt luce marinas
mortales oculis nudato corpore Nymphas
nutricum tenus extantis e gurgite cano.
tum Thetidis Peleus incensus fertur amore,
tum Thetis humanos non despexit hymenaeos,      20
tum Thetidi pater ipse iugandum Pelea sensit.
o nimis optato saeclorum tempore nati
heroes, salvete, deum *gens, o bona matrum
progenies salvete iterum *salvete bonarum ;*     23a
vos ego saepe meo vos carmine compellabo :
teque adeo eximie taedis felicibus aucte,
Thessaliae columen Peleu, cui Iuppiter ipse,
ipse suos divum genitor concessit amores.

---

¹ prora *P.* : proram *E.* : prima *vulg.*
² illa atque alia *codd.* *Other emendations are* quaque
alia, at ɛt *P.*] quanam alia *P., E. Harrison,* illac quaque
alia *M.*

98

## LXIV

PINE-TREES of old, born on the top of Pelion, are said
to have swum through the clear waters of Neptune
to the waves of Phasis and the realms of Aeetes,
when the chosen youths, the flower of Argive strength,
desiring to bear away from the Colchians the golden
fleece, dared to course over the salt seas with swift
ship, sweeping the blue expanse with fir-wood blades,
for whom the goddess who holds the fortresses of
city-tops made with her own hands the car flitting
with light breeze, and bound the piny structure of
the bowed keel. That ship first hanselled with
voyage Amphitrite untried before.

So when she ploughed with her beak the windy
expanse, and the wave churned by the oars grew
white with foam-flakes, forth looked from the foam-
ing surge of the sea [1] the Nereids of the deep won-
dering at the strange thing. On that day, if on
any other, mortals saw with their eyes the sea-
Nymphs standing forth from the hoary tide, with
bodies naked as far as the paps. Then is Peleus said
to have caught fire with love of Thetis, then did
Thetis not disdain mortal espousals, then did the
Father himself know in his heart that Peleus must
be joined to Thetis. O ye, in happiest time of ages
born, hail, heroes, sprung from gods! hail, kindly
offspring of good mothers, hail again! you often in
my song, you will I address. And specially thee,
greatly blessed by fortunate marriage torches, main-
stay of Thessaly, Peleus, to whom Jupiter himself,
the king of the gods himself granted his own Love.

---

[1] Or (*feri* codd.) " wild visages."

tene Thetis tenuit pulcherrima Nereine?
tene suam Tethys concessit ducere neptem,
Oceanusque, mari totum qui amplectitur orbem?　30

Quis simul optatae finito tempore luces
advenere, domum conventu tota frequentat
Thessalia, oppletur laetanti regia coetu:
dona ferunt prae se, declarant gaudia vultu.
deseritur *Cieros, linquunt Phthiotica Tempe
Crannonisque domos ac moenia Larisaea,
Pharsalum coeunt, Pharsalia tecta frequentant.
rura colit nemo, mollescunt colla iuvencis,
non humilis curvis purgatur vinea rastris,
non falx attenuat frondatorum arboris umbram,　41
non glaebam prono convellit vomere taurus,　40
squalida desertis rubigo infertur aratris.

Ipsius at sedes, quacumque opulenta recessit
regia, fulgenti splendent auro atque argento.
candet ebur soliis, collucent pocula mensae,
tota domus gaudet regali splendida gaza.
pulvinar vero divae geniale locatur
sedibus in mediis, Indo quod dente politum
tincta tegit roseo conchyli purpura fuco.

Haec vestis priscis hominum variata figuris　50
heroum mira virtutes indicat arte.
namque fluentisono prospectans litore Diae
Thesea cedentem celeri cum classe tuetur
indomitos in corde gerens Ariadna furores;
necdum etiam sese quae visit visere credit,
ut pote fallaci quae tum primum excita somno
100

Thee did fairest Thetis clasp, daughter of Nereus? to thee did Tethys grant to wed her granddaughter, and Oceanus, who circles all the world with sea?

Now when that longed-for day in time fulfilled had come for them, all Thessaly in full assembly crowds the house, the palace is thronged with a joyful company. They bring gifts in their hands, they display joy in their looks. Cieros is deserted; they leave Phthiotic Tempe and the houses of Crannon and the walls of Larissa; at Pharsalus they meet, and flock to the houses of Pharsalus. None now tills the lands; the necks of the steers grow soft; no more is the ground of the vineyard [1] cleared with curved rakes; no more does the pruners' hook thin the shade of the tree; no more does the ox tear up the soil with downward share; rough rust creeps over the deserted ploughs.

But Peleus' own abodes, so far as inward stretched the wealthy palace, with glittering gold and silver shine. White gleams the ivory of the thrones, bright are the cups on the table; the whole house is gay and gorgeous with royal treasure. But see, the royal marriage bed is being set for the goddess in the midst of the palace, smoothly fashioned of Indian tusk, covered with purple tinged with the rosy stain of the shell.

This coverlet, broidered with shapes of ancient men, with wondrous art sets forth the worthy deeds of heroes. For there, looking forth from the wave-sounding shore of Dia, Ariadna sees Theseus, as he sails away with swift fleet, Ariadna bearing wild madness in her heart. Not yet can she believe she beholds what yet she does behold; since now, now first wakened from treacherous sleep she sees herself,

---

[1] Or "the trailing vine."

desertam in sola miseram se cernat harena.
immemor at iuvenis fugiens pellit vada remis,
irrita ventosae linquens promissa procellae.
    Quem procul ex alga maestis Minois ocellis     60
saxea ut effigies bacchantis prospicit, eheu,
prospicit et magnis curarum fluctuat undis,
non flavo retinens subtilem vertice mitram,
non contecta levi velatum [1] pectus amictu,
non tereti strophio lactentis vincta papillas,
omnia quae toto delapsa e corpore passim
ipsius ante pedes fluctus salis adludebant.
sed neque tum mitrae neque tum fluitantis
    amictus
illa vicem curans toto ex te pectore, Theseu,
toto animo, tota pendebat perdita mente.     70
a misera, assiduis quam luctibus externavit
spinosas Erycina serens in pectore curas
illa *ex tempestate, ferox quo tempore Theseus
egressus curvis e litoribus Piraei
attigit iniusti regis Cortynia templa.
    Nam perhibent olim crudeli peste coactam
Androgeoneae poenas exolvere caedis
electos iuvenes simul et decus innuptarum
Cecropiam solitam esse dapem dare Minotauro.
quis angusta malis cum moenia vexarentur,     80
ipse suum Theseus pro caris corpus Athenis
proicere optavit potius quam talia Cretam
funera Cecropiae nec funera portarentur ;
atque ita nave levi nitens ac lenibus auris
magnanimum ad Minoa venit sedesque superbas.
hunc simul ac cupido conspexit lumine virgo
regia, quam suavis expirans castus odores

        [1] velatum *codd.* : nudatum *P. from Schw.*

poor wretch, deserted on the lonely sand. Meanwhile the youth flies and strikes the waters with his oars, leaving unfulfilled his empty pledges to the gusty storm; at whom afar from the weedy beach with streaming eyes the daughter of Minos, like a marble figure of a bacchanal, looks forth, alas! looks forth tempest-tost with great tides of passion. Nor does she still keep the delicate headband on her golden head, nor has her breast veiled by the covering of her light raiment, nor her milk-white [1] bosom bound with the smooth girdle; all these, as they slipt off around her whole body, before her very feet the salt waves lapped. She for her headgear then, she for her floating raiment then, cared not, but on thee, Theseus, with all her thoughts, with all her soul, with all her mind (lost, ah lost!) was hanging, unhappy maid! whom with unceasing floods of grief Erycina maddened, sowing thorny cares in her breast, even from that hour, what time bold Theseus setting forth from the winding shores of Piraeus reached the Gortynian palace of the lawless king.

For they tell how of old, driven by a cruel pestilence to pay a penalty for the slaughter of Androgeos, Cecropia was wont to give as a feast to the Minotaur chosen youths, and with them the flower of unwedded maids. Now when his narrow walls were troubled by these evils, Theseus himself for his dear Athens chose to offer his own body, rather than that such deaths, living deaths, of Cecropia should be borne to Crete. Thus then, speeding his course with light bark and gentle gales, he comes to lordly Minos and his haughty halls. Him when the damsel beheld with eager eye, the princess, whom her chaste couch

[1] Or (*luctantis*) "straining," or (*lucentis*) "shining."

lectulus in molli complexu matris alebat,
quales Eurotae progignunt flumina myrtos
aurave distinctos educit verna colores, 90
non prius ex illo flagrantia declinavit
lumina, quam cuncto concepit corpore flammam
funditus atque imis exarsit tota medullis.
heu misere exagitans immiti [1] corde furores
sancte puer, curis hominum qui gaudia misces,
quaeque regis Golgos quaeque Idalium frondosum,
qualibus incensam iactastis mente puellam
fluctibus in flavo saepe hospite suspirantem!
quantos illa tulit languenti corde timores!
*quam tum* [2] saepe magis fulgore [3] expalluit auri; 100
cum saevum cupiens contra contendere monstrum
aut mortem appeteret Theseus aut praemia laudis.
non ingrata tamen frustra munuscula divis
promittens tacito † succendit vota labello.
nam velut in summo quatientem bracchia Tauro
quercum aut conigeram sudanti cortice pinum
indomitus turbo contorquens flamine robur
eruit (illa procul radicitus exturbata
prona cadit, late *casu cuncta* obvia [4] frangens),
sic domito saevum prostravit corpore Theseus 110
nequiquam vanis iactantem cornua ventis.
inde pedem sospes multa cum laude reflexit
errabunda regens tenui vestigia filo,
ne labyrintheis e flexibus egredientem
tecti frustraretur inobservabilis error.

[1] immiti, in miti *codd.*
[2] quanto *codd.* : quantum, quam tum *edd.* quanto s | aepe
(*for* quantum saepe) *may have come in from* quantos *above.*
[3] fulvore *P. from Ritschl.*
[4] *So P. for* lateque cum eius omnia (obvia) *of codd.* casu
*is dat. Other emendations are* lateque et cominus *Avant.;*
lateque comeis obit omnia *M.;* quaeviscumque obvia *Ellis,*
*Vahlen.*

breathing sweet odours still nursed in her mother's soft embrace, like myrtles which spring by the streams of Eurotas, or the flowers of varied hue which the breath of spring draws forth, she turned not her burning eyes away from him, till she had caught fire in all her heart deep within, and glowed all flame in her inmost marrow. Ah! thou that stirrest cruel madness with ruthless heart, divine boy, who minglest joys of men with cares, and thou, who reignest over Golgi and leafy Idalium, on what billows did ye toss the burning heart of the maiden, often sighing for the golden-headed stranger! what fears did she endure with fainting heart! how often did she then grow paler than the gleam of gold, when Theseus, eager to contend with the savage monster, was setting forth to win either death or the meed of valour! Yet not unsweet were the gifts, though vainly promised to the gods, which she offered [1] with silent lip. For as a tree which waves its boughs on Taurus' top, an oak or a cone-bearing pine with sweating bark, when a vehement storm twists the grain with its blast, and tears it up;—afar, wrenched up by the roots it lies prone, breaking away all that meets its fall—so did Theseus overcome and lay low the bulk of the monster, vainly tossing his horns to the empty winds. Thence he retraced his way, unharmed and with much glory, guiding his devious footsteps by the fine clew, lest as he came forth from the mazy windings of the labyrinth the inextricable entanglement of the building should bewilder him.

[1] Or (*succepit*, P. from Statius) "undertook," or (*suspendit*) "faltered" or "dedicated." *Cf.* Verg. *Georg.* II. 389, *Aen.* XII. 760; Hor. *Carm.* I. v. 15.

Sed quid ego a primo digressus carmine plura
commemorem, ut linquens genitoris filia vultum,
ut consanguineae complexum, ut denique matris,
quae misera in gnata deperdita †leta,[1]
omnibus his Thesei dulcem praeoptarit amorem,　120
aut ut vecta ratis spumosa ad litora Diae,
aut ut eam [molli] devinctam lumina somno
liquerit immemori discedens pectore coniunx?
saepe illam perhibent ardenti corde furentem
clarisonas imo fudisse e pectore voces,
ac tum praeruptos tristem conscendere montes,
unde aciem in pelagi vastos protenderet aestus,
tum tremuli salis adversas procurrere in undas
mollia nudatae tollentem tegmina surae,
atque haec extremis maestam dixisse querellis,　130
frigidulos udo singultus ore cientem.

"Sicine me patriis avectam, perfide, ab aris,
perfide, deserto liquisti in litore, Theseu?
sicine discedens neglecto numine divum
immemor a, devota domum periuria portas?
nullane res potuit crudelis flectere mentis
consilium? tibi nulla fuit clementia praesto,
immite ut nostri vellet miserescere pectus?
at non haec quondam blanda promissa dedisti
voce mihi; non haec miseram sperare iubebas,　140
sed conubia laeta, sed optatos hymenaeos:
quae cuncta aerii discerpunt irrita venti.
iam iam nulla viro iuranti femina credat,
nulla viri speret sermones esse fideles;
quis dum aliquid cupiens animus praegestit
　　　apisci,
nil metuunt iurare, nihil promittere parcunt:
sed simul ac cupidae mentis satiata libidost,

---

[1] lamentatast, laetabatur, &c., are proposed. laetabatur is
nearer the reading of codd. pendet deperdita laeta P.

But why should I leave the first subject of my song and tell of more; how the daughter, flying from her father's face, the embrace of her sister, then of her mother last, who lamented, lost in grief for her daughter—how she chose before all these the sweet love of Theseus; or how the ship was borne to the foaming shores of Dia; or how when her eyes were bound with soft sleep her spouse left her, departing with forgetful mind? Often in the madness of her burning heart they say that she uttered piercing cries from her inmost breast; and now would she sadly climb the rugged mountains, thence to strain her eyes over the waste of ocean-tide; now run out to meet the waters of the rippling brine, lifting the soft vesture of her bared knee. And thus said she mournfully in her last laments, uttering chilly sobs with tearful face:

"Thus then, having borne me afar from my father's home, thus hast thou left me, faithless, faithless Theseus, on the lonely shore? thus departing, unmindful of the will of the gods, forgetful, ah! dost thou carry to thy home the curse of perjury? could nothing bend the purpose of thy cruel mind? was no mercy present in thy soul, to bid thy ruthless heart incline to pity for me? Not such were the promises thou gavest me once with winning voice, not this didst thou bid me hope, ah me![1] no, but a joyful wedlock, but a desired espousal; all which the winds of heaven now blow abroad in vain. Henceforth let no woman believe a man's oath, let none believe that a man's speeches can be trustworthy. They, while their mind desires something and longs eagerly to gain it, nothing fear to swear, nothing spare to promise; but as soon as the lust of their

[1] Or (*misera*) "these miseries."

dicta nihil metuere, nihil periuria curant.
certe ego te in medio versantem turbine leti
eripui, et potius germanum amittere crevi, 150
quam tibi fallaci supremo in tempore dessem;
pro quo dilaceranda feris dabor alitibusque
praeda, neque iniacta tumulabor mortua terra.
quaenam te genuit sola sub rupe leaena?
quod mare conceptum spumantibus expuit undis,
quae Syrtis, quae Scylla rapax, quae vasta Charybdis,
talia qui reddis pro dulci praemia vita?
si tibi non cordi fuerant conubia nostra,
saeva quod horrebas prisci praecepta parentis,
at tamen in vostras potuisti ducere sedes, 160
quae tibi iucundo famularer serva labore,
candida permulcens liquidis vestigia lymphis
purpureave tuum consternens veste cubile.

Sed quid ego ignaris nequiquam conquerar auris,
externata malo, quae nullis sensibus auctae
nec missas audire queunt nec reddere voces?
ille autem prope iam mediis versatur in undis,
nec quisquam apparet vacua mortalis in alga.
sic nimis insultans extremo tempore saeva
fors etiam nostris invidit questibus auris. 170

Iuppiter omnipotens, utinam ne tempore primo
Gnosia Cecropiae tetigissent litora puppes,
indomito nec dira ferens stipendia tauro
perfidus in Creta religasset navita funem,
nec malus hic celans dulci crudelia forma
consilia in nostris requiesset sedibus hospes!
nam quo me referam? quali spe perdita nitor?

greedy mind is satisfied, they fear not then their words, they heed not their perjuries. I—thou knowest it—when thou wert tossing in the very whirl of death, saved thee, and set my heart rather to let my brother go than to fail thee, now faithless found, in thy utmost need. And for this I shall be given to beasts and birds to tear as a prey; my corpse shall have no sepulture, shall be sprinkled with no earth. What lioness bore thee under a desert rock? what sea conceived thee and vomited thee forth from its foaming waves? what Syrtis, what ravening Scylla, what waste Charybdis bore thee, who for sweet life returnest such meed as this? If thou hadst no mind to wed with me for dread of the harsh bidding of thy stern father, yet thou couldst have led me into thy dwellings to serve thee as a slave with labour of love, laving thy white feet with liquid water, or with purple coverlet spreading thy bed.

"But why should I, distracted with woe, cry in vain to the senseless airs—the airs that are endowed with no feeling, and can neither hear nor return the messages of my voice? He meanwhile is now tossing almost in mid-sea, and no human being is seen on the waste and weedy shore. Thus fortune too, full of spite, in this my supreme hour has cruelly grudged all ears to my complaints. Almighty Jupiter, I would the Attic ships had never touched Gnosian shores, nor ever the faithless voyager, bearing the dreadful tribute to the savage bull, had fastened [1] his cable in Crete, nor that this evil man, hiding cruel designs under a fair outside, had reposed in our dwellings as a guest! For whither shall I return, lost, ah, lost? on what hope

---

[1] If *in Cretam* is read, *religasset* would mean "cast off." *Cf.* LXIII. 84.

† Idoneosne [1] petam montes ?   a, gurgite lato
discernens ponti truculentum †ubi dividit aequor *
an patris auxilium sperem ?   quemne ipsa reliqui, 180
respersum iuvenem fraterna caede secuta ?
coniugis an fido consoler memet amore,
quine fugit lentos incurvans gurgite remos ?
praeterea nullo litus,[2] sola insula, tecto,
nec patet egressus pelagi cingentibus undis :
nulla fugae ratio, nulla spes : omnia muta,
omnia sunt deserta, ostentant omnia letum.
non tamen ante mihi languescent lumina morte,
nec prius a fesso secedent corpore sensus,
quam iustam a divis exposcam prodita multam,   190
caelestumque fidem postrema comprecer hora.
    Quare facta virum multantes vindice poena,
Eumenides, quibus anguino redimita capillo
frons expirantis praeportat pectoris iras,
huc huc adventate, meas audite querellas,
quas ego, vae, misera extremis proferre medullis
cogor inops, ardens, amenti caeca furore.
quae quoniam verae nascuntur pectore ab imo,
vos nolite pati nostrum vanescere luctum ;
sed quali solam Theseus me mente reliquit,   200
tali mente, deae, funestet seque suosque."
    Has postquam maesto profudit pectore voces,
supplicium saevis exposcens anxia factis,
annuit invicto caelestum numine rector,

---

[1] ydoneos, idoneos, idmoneos *codd.:* Idomeneos *Lach.*
*P. prefers* Sidonios, *which I translate.*
[2] *A. Palmer would read* colitur *for* litus.

do I lean? shall I seek the mountains of Sidon?
how broad the flood, how savage the tract of sea
which divides them from me! Shall I hope for the
aid of my father?—whom I deserted of my own will,
to follow a lover dabbled with my brother's blood!
Or shall I console myself with the faithful love of
my spouse, who is flying from me, bending his tough
oars in the wave? and here too is naught but the
shore, with never a house, a desert island; no way
to depart opens for me; about me are the waters of
the sea; no means of flight, no hope; all is dumb,
all is desolate; all shows me the face of death. Yet
my eyes shall not grow faint in death, nor shall the
sense fail from my wearied body, before I demand
from the gods just vengeance for my betrayal, and
call upon the faith of the heavenly ones in my last
hour.

"Therefore, O ye that visit the deeds of men with
vengeful pains, ye Eumenides, whose foreheads bound
with snaky hair announce the wrath which breathes
from your breast, hither, hither haste, hear my com-
plaints which I (ah, unhappy!) bring forth from my
inmost heart perforce, helpless, burning, blinded
with raging frenzy. For since my woes come truth-
fully from the depths of my heart, suffer not ye my
grief to come to nothing: but even as Theseus had
the heart to leave me desolate, with such a heart, ye
goddesses, may he bring ruin upon himself and his
own ¹"

When she had poured out these words from
her sad breast, earnestly demanding vengeance for
cruel deeds; the Lord of the heavenly ones bowed
assent with sovereign nod, and at that movement ¹

¹ Or (*quo nutu = cuius nutu*) "at his nod."

quo motu tellus atque horrida contremuerunt
aequora concussitque micantia sidera mundus.
ipse autem caeca mentem caligine Theseus
consitus oblito dimisit pectore cuncta,
quae mandata prius constanti mente tenebat,
dulcia nec maesto sustollens signa parenti          210
sospitem Erechtheum se ostendit visere portum.
   Namque ferunt olim, classi cum moenia divae
linquentem gnatum ventis concrederet Aegeus,
talia complexum iuveni mandata dedisse.
   "Gnate mihi longa iucundior unice vita,          215
reddite in extrema nuper mihi fine senectae,          217
gnate, ego quem in dubios cogor dimittere
   casus,                                      216
quandoquidem fortuna mea ac tua fervida
   virtus
eripit invito mihi te, cui languida nondum
lumina sunt gnati cara saturata figura :          220
non ego te gaudens laetanti pectore mittam,
nec te ferre sinam fortunae signa secundae,
sed primum multas expromam mente querellas,
canitiem terra atque infuso pulvere foedans ;
inde infecta vago suspendam lintea malo,
nostros ut luctus nostraeque incendia mentis
carbasus obscurata † dicet ferrugine Hibera.
quod tibi si sancti concesserit incola Itoni,
quae nostrum genus ac sedes defendere Erechthei
annuit, ut tauri respergas sanguine dextram,          230
tum vero facito ut memori tibi condita corde
haec vigeant mandata, nec ulla oblitteret aetas,
ut simul ac nostros invisent lumina collis,
funestam antennae deponant undique vestem,
candidaque intorti sustollant vela rudentes,

the earth and stormy seas trembled, and the heavens shook the quivering stars. But Theseus himself, darkling in his thoughts with blind dimness, let slip from his forgetful mind all the biddings which formerly he had held firm with constant heart, and raised not the welcome sign to his mourning father, nor showed that he was safely sighting the Erechthean harbour. For they say that erewhile, when Aegeus was trusting his son to the winds, as with his fleet he left the walls of the goddess,[1] he embraced the youth and gave him this charge: " My son, my only son, dearer to me than all my length of days, restored to me but now in the last end of old age, my son, whom I perforce let go forth to doubtful hazards,—since my fortune and thy burning valour tear thee from me, unwilling me, whose failing eyes are not yet satisfied with the dear image of my son, I will not let thee go gladly with cheerful heart, nor suffer thee to bear the tokens of prosperous fortune: but first will bring forth many laments from my heart, soiling my gray hairs with earth and showered dust: thereafter will I hang dyed sails on thy roving mast, that so the tale of my grief [2] and the fire that burns in my heart may be marked by the canvas stained with Iberian azure. But if she who dwells in holy Itonus, who vouchsafes to defend our race and the abodes of Erechtheus, shall grant thee to sprinkle thy right hand with the bull's blood, then be sure that these my commands live, laid up in thy mindful heart, and that no length of time blur them: that as soon as thy eyes shall come within sight of our hills, thy yardarms may lay down from them their mourning raiment, and the twisted cordage raise a

[1] Or (*castae*) " the virgin goddess."
[2] Or (*decet*) " even as the canvas . . . befits our grief."

quam primum cernens ut laeta gaudia mente
agnoscam, cum te reducem aetas prospera sistet."
  Haec mandata prius constanti mente tenentem
Thesea ceu pulsae ventorum flamine nubes
aerium nivei montis liquere cacumen.                    240
at pater, ut summa prospectum ex arce petebat,
anxia in assiduos absumens lumina fletus,
cum primum inflati [1] conspexit lintea veli,
praecipitem sese scopulorum e verti ceiecit,
amissum credens immiti Thesea fato.
sic funesta domus ingressus tecta paterna
morte ferox Theseus qualem Minoidi luctum
obtulerat mente immemori talem ipse recepit.
quae tum prospectans cedentem maesta carinam
multiplices animo volvebat saucia curas.                250
  At parte ex alia florens volitabat Iacchus
cum thiaso Satyrorum et Nysigenis Silenis,
te quaerens, Ariadna, tuoque incensus amore.


　　　．　　　　．　　　　．　　　　．　　　　．　　　　．


qui tum [2] alacres passim lymphata mente furebant
euhoe bacchantes, euhoe capita inflectentes.
  Harum pars tecta quatiebant cuspide thyrsos,
pars e divulso iactabant membra iuvenco,
pars sese tortis serpentibus incingebant,
pars obscura cavis celebrabant orgia cistis,
orgia, quae frustra cupiunt audire profani;           260
plangebant aliae proceris tympana palmis
aut tereti tenues tinnitus aere ciebant,

---

[1] infecti *P. with the Italian editors.*
[2] *If* quae tum *is read, we must suppose a lacuna after 253 :*
*1)* qui tum (*of codd.*), *a lacuna after 255, unless we read* horum
256, *with Lachmann : if* quicum (*B.*), bacchantes *must be taken*
*as* βάκχαι. *254, 255 are more appropriate to Bacchanalians*
*than to Satyrs and Sileni.*

white sail: that so I may see at once and gladly welcome the signs of joy, when a happy hour shall set thee here in thy home again."

These charges at first did Theseus preserve with constant mind; but then they left him, as clouds driven by the breath of the winds leave the lofty head of the snowy mountain. But the father, as he gazed out from his tower-top, wasting his longing eyes in constant tear-floods, when first he saw the canvas of the bellying sail, threw himself headlong from the summit of the rocks, believing Theseus destroyed by ruthless fate. Thus bold Theseus, as he entered the chambers of his home, darkened with mourning for his father's death, himself received such grief as by forgetfulness of heart he had caused to the daughter of Minos. And she the while, gazing out tearfully at the receding ship, was revolving manifold cares in her wounded heart.

In another part of the tapestry youthful Bacchus was wandering with the rout of Satyrs and the Nysa-born Sileni, seeking thee, Ariadna, and fired with thy love; . . . who then, busy here and there, were raging with frenzied mind, while "Evoe!" they cried tumultuously, "Evoe!" shaking their heads.

Some of them were waving thyrsi with shrouded points, some tossing about the limbs of a mangled steer, some girding themselves with writhing serpents: some bearing in solemn procession dark mysteries enclosed in caskets, mysteries which the profane desire in vain to hear. Others beat timbrels with uplifted hands, or raised clear clashings with cymbals of rounded bronze: many blew horns with

multis raucisonos efflabant cornua bombos,
barbaraque horribili stridebat tibia cantu.
  Talibus amplifice vestis decorata figuris
pulvinar complexa suo velabat amictu.
quae postquam cupide spectando Thessala pubes
expletast, sanctis coepit decedere divis.
hic, qualis flatu placidum mare matutino
horrificans Zephyrus proclivis incitat undas          270
Aurora exoriente vagi sub limina Solis,
quae tarde primum clementi flamine pulsae
procedunt, leviterque sonant plangore cachinni,
post vento crescente magis magis increbescunt
purpureaque procul nantes ab luce refulgent,
sic ibi vestibuli[1] linquentes regia tecta
ad se quisque vago passim pede discedebant.
  Quorum post abitum princeps e vertice Peli
advenit Chiron portans silvestria dona ;
nam quoscumque ferunt campi, quos Thessala
        magnis                                         280
montibus ora creat, quos propter fluminis undas
aura aperit flores tepidi fecunda Favoni,
hos indistinctis plexos tulit ipse corollis,
quo permulsa domus iucundo risit odore.
confestim Penios adest, viridantia Tempe,
Tempe, quae silvae cingunt super impendentes,
† Minosim[2] linquens † Doris[3] celebranda choreis,
non vacuus : namque ille tulit radicitus altas
fagos ac recto proceras stipite laurus,
non sine nutanti platano lentaque sorore             290
flammati Phaethontis et aeria cupressu.
haec circum sedes late contexta locavit,

---

  [1] vestibuli *codd.*: vestibulo *P. with Schrader.*
  [2] *For* Minosim *of codd. other readings are* Haemonisin *P. from Heins.*, Magnessum *E. al. al.*
  [3] Doris *codd. omn.   Edd. read* doctis, claris, crebris, &c.

harsh-sounding drone, and the barbarian pipe shrilled
with dreadful din.

Such were the figures that richly adorned the
tapestry which embraced and shrouded with its folds
the royal couch.  Now when the Thessalian youth
had gazed their fill, fixing their eager eyes on these
wonders, they began to give place to the holy gods.
Hereupon, as the west wind ruffling the quiet sea
with its breath at morn urges on the sloping waves,
when the Dawn is rising up to the gates of the
travelling Sun, the waters slowly at first, driven by
gentle breeze, step on and lightly sound with plash of
laughter ; then as the breeze grows fresh they crowd
on close and closer, and floating afar reflect a bright-
ness from the crimson light ; so now, leaving the royal
buildings of the portal, hither and thither variously
with devious feet the guests passed away.

After their departure, from the top of Pelion came
Chiron leading the way, and bearing woodland gifts.
For all the flowers that the plains bear, all that the
Thessalian region brings to birth on its mighty moun-
tains, all the flowers that near the river's streams the
fruitful gale of warm Favonius discloses, these he
brought himself, woven in mingled garlands, cheered
with whose grateful odour the house smiled its glad-
ness.  Forthwith Penëus is there, leaving verdant
Tempe, Tempe girt with impendent forests [       ]
to be haunted by Dorian dances ; not empty-handed,
for he bore, torn up by the roots, lofty beeches and
tall bay-trees with upright stem, and with them the
nodding plane and the swaying sister of flame-
devoured Phaethon, and the tall cypress.  All these
he wove far and wide around their home, that the

vestibulum ut molli velatum fronde vireret.
post hunc consequitur sollerti corde Prometheus,
extenuata gerens veteris vestigia poenae,
quam quondam † silici restrictus membra catena
persolvit pendens e verticibus praeruptis.
inde pater divum sancta cum coniuge natisque
advenit, caelo te solum, Phoebe, relinquens
unigenamque simul cultricem montibus † Idri :      300
Pelea nam tecum pariter soror aspernatast
nec Thetidis taedas voluit celebrare iugalis.

Qui postquam niveis flexerunt sedibus artus,
large multiplici constructae sunt dape mensae,
cum interea infirmo quatientes corpora motu
veridicos Parcae coeperunt edere cantus.
his corpus tremulum complectens undique vestis
candida purpurea *talos incinxerat ora,
at roseae niveo residebant vertice vittae,
aeternumque manus carpebant rite laborem.       310
laeva colum molli lana retinebat amictum,
dextera tum leviter deducens fila supinis
formabat digitis, tum prono in pollice torquens
libratum tereti versabat turbine fusum,
atque ita decerpens aequabat semper opus dens,
laneaque aridulis haerebant morsa labellis,
quae prius in levi fuerant extantia filo :
ante pedes autem candentis mollia lanae
vellera virgati custodibant calathisci.
haec tum clarisona pellentes vellera voce          320
talia divino fuderunt carmine fata,
carmine, perfidiae quod post nulla arguet aetas.

118

portal might be greenly embowered with soft foliage.
Him follows Prometheus wise of heart, bearing the
faded scars of the ancient penalty which whilom, his
limbs bound fast to the rock [1] with chains, he paid,
hanging from the craggy summits. Then came the
Father of the gods with his divine wife and his sons,
leaving thee, Phoebus, alone in heaven, and with thee
thine own sister who dwells in the heights of Idrus;
for as thou didst, so did thy sister scorn Peleus, nor
deigned to be present at the nuptial torches of Thetis.

So when they had reclined their limbs on the
white couches, bountifully were the tables piled with
varied dainties: whilst in the meantime, swaying
their bodies with palsied motion, the Parcae began to
utter soothtelling chants. White raiment enfolding
their aged limbs robed their ankles with a crimson
border; on their snowy heads rested rosy bands,[2]
while their hands duly plied the eternal task. The
left hand held the distaff clothed with soft wool;
then the right hand lightly drawing out the threads
with upturned fingers shaped them, then with down-
ward thumb twirled the spindle poised with rounded
whorl; and so with their teeth they still plucked the
threads and made the work even. Bitten ends of
wool clung to their dry lips, which had before stood
out from the smooth yarn: and at their feet soft
fleeces of white-shining wool were kept safe in baskets
of osier. They then, as they struck the wool, sang
with clear voice, and thus poured forth the Fates in
divine chant. That chant no length of time shall
prove untruthful.

---

[1] *silici* may be abl., "on the rock." Or (*Scythica*) "with
Scythian chain." Perhaps (P.) *in silici.*

[2] Or (*annoso niveae*) "snow-white bands rested on their
aged heads." *at roseo niveae* codd,

O decus eximium magnis virtutibus augens,
Emathiae tutamen opis, clarissime nato,
accipe, quod laeta tibi pandunt luce sorores,
veridicum oraclum.    sed vos, quae fata sequuntur,
  currite ducentes subtegmina, currite, fusi.

adveniet tibi iam portans optata maritis
Hesperus, adveniet fausto cum sidere coniunx,
quae tibi * flexanimo mentem perfundat amore * 1   *330*
languidulosque paret tecum coniungere somnos,
levia substernens robusto bracchia collo.
  currite ducentes subtegmina, currite, fusi.

nulla domus tales umquam contexit amores,
nullus amor tali coniunxit foedere amantes,
qualis adest Thetidi, qualis concordia Peleo.
  currite ducentes subtegmina, currite, fusi.

nascetur vobis expers terroris Achilles,
hostibus haud tergo, sed forti pectore notus,
qui persaepe vago victor certamine cursus          *340*
flammea praevertet celeris vestigia cervae.
  currite ducentes subtegmina, currite, fusi.

non illi quisquam bello se conferet heros,
cum Phrygii Teucro manabunt sanguine * rivi,
Troicaque obsidens longinquo moenia bello
periuri Pelopis vastabit tertius heres.
  currite ducentes subtegmina, currite, fusi.

illius egregias virtutes claraque facta
saepe fatebuntur gnatorum in funere matres,

---

1 *The codd. have* quae tibi flexo animo mentis perfundat
amorem.  *I print Muretus's emendation, which is accepted by
almost all editors.*

" O thou who crownest high renown with great deeds of virtue, bulwark of Emathian power, famed for thy son to be, receive the truthful oracle which on this happy day the Sisters reveal to thee; but run ye on, drawing the woof-threads which the fates follow, ye spindles, run.

" Soon will Hesperus come to thee, Hesperus, who brings longed-for gifts to the wedded, soon will come thy wife with happy star, to shed over thy spirit soul-quelling love, and join with thee languorous slumbers, laying her smooth arms under thy strong neck. Run, drawing the woof-threads, ye spindles, run.

" No house ever harboured such loves as these; no love ever joined lovers in such a bond as links Thetis with Peleus, Peleus with Thetis. Run, drawing the woof-threads, ye spindles, run.

" There shall be born to you a son that knows not fear, Achilles, known to his enemies not by his back but by his stout breast; who right often winner in the contest of the wide-ranging race shall outstrip the flame-fleet footsteps of the flying hind. Run, drawing the woof-threads, ye spindles, run.

" Against him not a hero shall match himself in war, when the Phrygian streams shall flow with Teucrian blood, and the third heir of Pelops shall lay waste the Trojan walls, with tedious war beleaguering. Run, drawing the woof-threads, ye spindles, run.

" The hero's surpassing achievements and renowned deeds often shall mothers own at the burial

121

cum * incultum cano * solvent a vertice crinem   350
putridaque infirmis variabunt pectora palmis.
    currite ducentes subtegmina, currite, fusi.

namque velut densas praecerpens [1] cultor [2] aristas
sole sub ardenti flaventia demetit arva,
Troiugenum infesto prosternet corpora ferro.
    currite ducentes subtegmina, currite, fusi.

testis erit magnis virtutibus unda Scamandri,
quae passim rapido diffunditur Hellesponto,
cuius iter caesis angustans corporum acervis
alta tepefaciet permixta flumina caede.     360
    currite ducentes subtegmina, currite, fusi.

    .     .     .     .     .

denique testis erit morti quoque reddita praeda,
cum teres excelso coacervatum aggere bustum
excipiet niveos percussae virginis artus.
    currite ducentes subtegmina, currite, fusi.

nam simul ac fessis dederit fors copiam Achivis
urbis Dardaniae Neptunia solvere vincla,
alta Polyxenia madefient caede sepulcra,
quae, velut ancipiti succumbens victima ferro,
proiciet truncum submisso poplite corpus.     370
    currite ducentes subtegmina, currite, fusi.

quare agite optatos animi coniungite amores.
accipiat coniunx felici foedere divam,
dedatur cupido iamdudum nupta marito.
    currite ducentes subtegmina, currite, fusi.

---

[1] praecernens *codd. pler.* : praecerpens *E.* : praesternens *or*
prosternens *P.*

[2] cultor *codd. pler.* : messor *O.*

122

of their sons, loosing dishevelled hair from hoary head, and marring their withered breasts with weak hands. Run, drawing the woof-threads, ye spindles, run.

" For as the husbandman cropping the thick ears of corn under the burning sun mows down the yellow fields, so shall he lay low with foeman's steel the bodies of the sons of Troy. Run, drawing the woof-threads, ye spindles, run.

" Witness of his great deeds of valour shall be the wave of Scamander which pours itself forth abroad in the current of Hellespont, whose channel he shall choke with heaps of slain corpses, and make the deep streams warm with mingled blood. Run, drawing the woof-threads, ye spindles, run.

. . . . . .

" Lastly, witness too shall be the prize assigned to him in death, when the rounded barrow heaped up with lofty mound shall receive the snowy limbs of the slaughtered maiden. Run, drawing the woof-threads, ye spindles, run.

" For so soon as Fortune shall give to the weary Achaeans power to loose the Neptune-forged circlet of the Dardanian town, the high tomb shall be wetted with Polyxena's blood, who like a victim falling under the two-edged steel, shall bend her knee and bow her headless trunk. Run, drawing the woof-threads, ye spindles, run.

" Come then, unite the loves which your souls desire : let the husband receive in happy bonds the goddess, let the bride be given up—nay now !—to her eager spouse. Run, drawing the woof-threads, ye spindles, run.

123

non illam nutrix orienti luce revisens
hesterno collum poterit circumdare filo,
anxia nec mater discordis maesta puellae
secubitu caros mittet sperare nepotes.                    380
    currite ducentes subtegmina, currite, fusi.

Talia praefantes quondam felicia † Pelei [1]
carmina divino cecinerunt pectore Parcae.
praesentes namque [2] ante domos invisere castas
heroum et sese mortali ostendere coetu
caelicolae nondum spreta pietate solebant.
saepe pater divum templo in fulgente revisens
annua cum festis venissent sacra diebus,
conspexit terra centum procumbere tauros.
saepe vagus Liber Parnasi vertice summo         390
Thyadas effusis euantis crinibus egit,
cum Delphi tota certatim ex urbe ruentes
acciperent laeti divum fumantibus aris.
saepe in letifero belli certamine Mavors
aut rapidi Tritonis era aut Rhamnusia virgo
armatas hominumst praesens hortata catervas.
sed postquam tellus scelerest imbuta nefando,
iustitiamque omnes cupida de mente fugarunt,
perfudere manus fraterno sanguine fratres,
destitit extinctos natus lugere parentes,        400
optavit genitor primaevi funera nati,
liber † ut innuptae poteretur flore novercae,† [3]
ignaro mater substernens se impia nato
impia non veritast divos scelerare parentes : [4]

---

[1] Pelei *codd.*, *which* (cf. *336*) *must be genitive.   The simplest
emendation is* Peleo.

[2] Or (*Earle and P.*) Parcae | praesentes ; namque, &c.

[3] novercae *codd.   P. would read* nuriclae.   *Perhaps* liber uti
nuptae poteretur flore novellae.

[4] parentes *codd. opt. :* penates *Itali.   The expression* dei
parentes *is found in inscriptions.*

124

"When her nurse visits her again with the morning light, she will not be able to circle her neck with yesterday's riband; nor shall her anxious mother, saddened by lone-lying of an unkindly bride, give up the hope of dear descendants. Run, drawing the woof-threads, ye spindles, run."

Such strains of divination, foreboding happiness to Peleus, sang the Fates from prophetic breast in days of yore. For in bodily presence of old, before religion was despised, the heavenly ones were wont to visit pious homes of heroes, and show themselves to mortal company. Often the Father of the gods coming down again, in his bright temple, when yearly feasts had come on his holy days, saw a hundred bulls fall to the ground. Often Liber roving on the topmost height of Parnassus drove the Thyades crying "Evoe!" with flying hair, when the Delphians, racing eagerly from all the town, joyfully received the god with smoking altars. Often in the death-bearing strife of war Mavors or the Lady of swift Triton or the Rhamnusian Virgin by their presence stirred up the courage of armed bands of men. But when the earth was dyed with hideous crime, and all men banished justice from their greedy souls, and brothers sprinkled their hands with brothers' blood, the son left off to mourn his parents' death, the father wished for the death of his young son, that he might without hindrance enjoy the flower of a young bride, the unnatural mother impiously coupling with her unconscious son did not fear to sin against parental gods : [1]—

[1] Or (penates) "the gods of the household." parentes "deified parents."

omnia fanda nefanda malo permixta furore
iustificam nobis mentem avertere deorum.
quare nec tales dignantur visere coetus,
nec se contingi patiuntur lumine claro.


## LXV


Etsi me assiduo confectum cura dolore
    sevocat a doctis, Hortale, virginibus,
nec potis est dulcis Musarum expromere fetus
    mens animi, tantis fluctuat ipsa malis:
namque mei nuper Lethaeo gurgite fratris
    pallidulum manans alluit unda pedem,
Troia Rhoeteo quem subter litore tellus
    ereptum nostris obterit ex oculis.

      .        .        .        .        .

[alloquar, audiero numquam tua facta loquentem,]
    numquam ego te, vita frater amabilior,        10
aspiciam posthac.   at certe semper amabo,
    semper maesta tua carmina morte * canam,
qualia sub densis ramorum concinit umbris
    Daulias absumpti fata gemens Ityli.
sed tamen in tantis maeroribus, Hortale, mitto
    haec expressa tibi carmina Battiadae,
ne tua dicta vagis nequiquam credita ventis
    effluxisse meo forte putes animo,
ut missum sponsi furtivo munere malum
    procurrit casto virginis e gremio,        20

then all right and wrong, confounded in impious madness, turned from us the righteous will of the gods. Wherefore they deign not to visit such companies, nor endure the touch of clear daylight.


## LXV

### To Hortalus

THOUGH I am worn out with constant grief, Hortalus, and sorrow calls me away, apart from the learned Maids, nor can the thoughts of my heart utter the sweet births of the Muses, tossed as it is with such waves of trouble;—so lately the creeping wave of the Lethaean flood has lapped my own brother's death-pale foot, on whom, torn away from our sight, under the shore of Rhoeteum the soil of Troy lies heavy.

.    .    .    .    .

Never shall I speak to thee, never hear thee tell of thy life; never shall I see thee again, brother more beloved than life: but surely I shall always love thee, always sing[1] strains of mourning for thy death, as under the thick shadows of the boughs sings the Daulian bird bewailing the fate of Itylus lost. Yet, in such sorrows, Hortalus, I send to you these verses of Battiades translated, lest haply you should think that your words have slipped from my mind, vainly committed to wandering winds: as an apple sent as a secret gift from her betrothed lover falls out from the chaste bosom of the girl, which—

---

[1] Or (tegam) "keep veiled in silence."

quod miserae oblitae molli sub veste locatum,
  dum adventu **matris** prosilit, excutitur :
atque illud prono praeceps agitur decursu,
  huic manat tristi conscius ore rubor.


# LXVI


Omnia qui magni dispexit lumina mundi,
  qui stellarum ortus comperit atque obitus,
flammeus ut rapidi solis nitor obscuretur,
  ut cedant certis sidera temporibus,
ut Triviam furtim sub Latmia saxa relegans
  dulcis amor gyro devocet aerio,
idem me ille Conon caelesti in lumine vidit
  e Beroniceo vertice caesariem
fulgentem clare, quam †multis illa dearum†
  levia protendens bracchia pollicitast,            10
qua rex tempestate novo auctus hymenaeo
  vastatum finis iverat Assyrios,
dulcia nocturnae portans vestigia rixae,
  quam de virgineis gesserat exuviis.
estne novis nuptis odio Venus †atque parentum† [1]
  frustrantur falsis gaudia lacrimulis,
ubertim thalami quas intra limina fundunt ?
  non, ita me divi, vera gemunt, iuerint.
id mea me multis docuit regina querellis
  invisente novo proelia torva viro.               20
at tu non orbum luxti deserta cubile,
  sed fratris cari flebile discidium !
quam penitus maestas exedit cura medullas !
  ut tibi tum toto pectore sollicitae

---

[1] *Or* maritum (= maritorum) *P. from B. Schmidt.* **anne**
**parumper, patrantum, parantum, parentes, an quod aventum**
*are proposed.*

poor child, she forgot it!—put away in her soft gown, is shaken out as she starts forward when her mother comes; then, see, onward, downward swiftly it rolls and runs; a conscious blush creeps over her downcast face.

## LXVI

### The Lock of Berenice

CONON, he who scanned all the lights of the vast sky, who learnt the risings of the stars and their settings, how the flaming blaze of the swift sun suffers eclipse, how the stars recede at set seasons, how sweet love calls Trivia from her airy circuit, banishing her secretly to the rocky cave of Latmus—that same Conon saw me shining brightly among the lights of heaven, me, the lock from the head of Berenice, me whom she vowed to many of the goddesses, stretching forth her smooth arms, at that season when the king, blest in his new marriage, had gone to waste the Assyrian borders. . . . Is Venus hated by brides? and do they mock the joys of parents with false tears, which they shed plentifully within their virgin bowers? No, so may the gods help me, they lament not truly. This my queen taught me by all her lamentations, when her newly wedded husband went forth to grim war. But your tears, forsooth, were not shed for the desertion of your widowed bed, but for the mournful parting from your dear brother, when sorrow gnawed the inmost marrow of your sad heart. At that time how from your whole breast did your

sensibus ereptis mens excidit! at te ego certe
  cognoram a parva virgine magnanimam.
anne bonum oblita's facinus, quo regium adepta's
  coniugium, * quo non fortius ausit* alis?
sed tum maesta virum mittens quae verba locuta's!
  Iuppiter, ut tristi lumina saepe manu!      30
quis te mutavit tantus deus? an quod amantes
  non longe a caro corpore abesse volunt?
atque ibi me cunctis pro dulci coniuge divis
  non sine taurino sanguine pollicita's,
si reditum tetulisset.   is haud in tempore longo
  captam Asiam Aegypti finibus addiderat.
quis ego pro factis caelesti reddita coetu
  pristina vota novo munere dissoluo.
invita, o regina, tuo de vertice cessi,
  invita: adiuro teque tuumque caput,      40
digna ferat quod siquis inaniter adiurarit:
  sed qui se ferro postulet esse parem?
ille quoque eversus mons est, quem maximum in
      † oris [1]
  progenies Thiae clara supervehitur,
cum Medi peperere [2] novum mare, cumque iuventus
  per medium classi barbara navit Athon.
quid facient crines, cum ferro talia cedant?
  Iuppiter, ut Chalybon omne genus pereat,
et qui principio sub terra quaerere venas
  institit ac ferri stringere duritiem!      50
abiunctae paulo ante comae mea fata sorores
  lugebant, cum se Memnonis Aethiopis

[1] oris *codd.: al.* orbe.
[2] propere *codd.: al.* pepulere, rupere.

anxious spirit fail, bereft of sense! and yet truly I knew you to be stout-hearted from young girlhood. Have you forgotten the brave deed by which you gained a royal marriage, braver deed than which none other could ever dare?[1] But at that time in your grief, when parting from your husband, what words did you utter! How often, O Jupiter, did you brush away the tears with your hand! What mighty god has changed you thus? is it that lovers cannot bear to be far away from the side of him they love? And there to all the gods for your dear husband's welfare you vowed me not without blood of bulls, so he should complete his return. He in no long time had added conquered Asia to the territories of Egypt. This is done; and now I am given as due to the host of heaven, and pay your former vows with a new offering. Unwillingly, O queen, I was parted from your head, unwillingly, I swear both by you and by your head; by which if any swear vainly, let him reap a worthy recompense.—But what man can claim to be as strong as steel? Even that mountain was overthrown, the greatest of all in those shores which the bright son of Thia traverses, when the Medes created a new sea, and when the youth of Persia swam in their fleet through mid Athos. What shall locks of hair do, when such things as this yield to steel? O, Jupiter, may all the race of the Chalybes perish, and he, who first began to seek for veins underground, and to forge hard bars of iron!

⁵¹ My sister locks, sundered from me just before, were mourning for my fate, when the own brother of Ethiopian Memnon appeared, striking the air with

---

[1] Or (*quod non fortior ausit alis* codd.) " which none else could venture and so win the title of braver," E. The reading in the text is that of Muretus.

unigena impellens nutantibus aera pennis
  obtulit Arsinoes Locridos ales equus,
isque per aetherias me tollens avolat umbras
  et Veneris casto collocat in gremio.
ipsa suum Zephyritis eo famulum legarat,
  Graia Canopeis incola litoribus.
*inde Venus* vario [1] ne solum in lumine caeli
  ex Ariadneis aurea temporibus                             60
fixa corona foret, sed nos quoque fulgeremus
  devotae flavi verticis exuviae,
uvidulam a *fletu cedentem ad templa deum me
  sidus in antiquis diva novum posuit :
Virginis et saevi contingens namque Leonis
  lumina, Callisto iuncta Lycaoniae,
vertor in occasum, tardum dux ante Booten,
  qui vix sero alto mergitur Oceano.
sed quamquam me nocte premunt vestigia divum,
  lux autem canae Tethyi restituit,                         70
(pace tua fari hic liceat, Rhamnusia virgo,
  namque ego non ullo vera timore tegam,
nec si me infestis discerpent sidera dictis,
  condita quin veri pectoris evoluam) :
non his tam laetor rebus, quam me afore semper,
  afore me a dominae vertice discrucior,
quicum ego, dum virgo quondam fuit, omnibus
  †expers
  unguentis, una milia multa bibi.
nunc vos, optato cum iunxit lumine taeda,
  non prius unanimis corpora coniugibus               80
tradite nudantes reiecta veste papillas
  quam iucunda mihi munera libet onyx,
vester onyx, casto colitis quae iura cubili.
  sed quae se impuro dedit adulterio,

  [1] hii (hi) dii ven ibi vario *codd.* : hic iuveni Ismario *E.* : hic
dii ("*bright*") *H.V.M.* : invida enim *Vahlen* : inde Venus *P.*
132

waving wings, the winged courser of Locrian Arsinoe.
And he sweeping me away flies through the airs
of heaven and places me in the holy bosom of
Venus. On that service had the Lady of Zephyrium,
the Grecian queen, who sojourns on the shores of
Canopus, herself sent her own minister. Then
Venus—that among the various lights of heaven,
not only should the golden crown taken from the
brows of Ariadne be fixed, but that I also might
shine, the dedicated spoil of Berenice's sunny head—
me too, wet with tears, and transported to the abodes
of the gods, me a new constellation among the ancient
stars did the goddess set; for I, touching the fires of
the Virgin and the raging Lion, and close by Callisto
daughter of Lycaon, move to my setting, while I point
the way before slow Bootes, who scarce late at night
dips in deep ocean. But though at night the footsteps
of the gods press close upon me, whilst by day I am
restored to gray Tethys (under thy sufferance let me
speak this, O Virgin of Rhamnus ; no fear shall make
me hide the truth, no, not even though the stars shall
rend me with angry words will I refrain from uttering
the secrets of a true heart), I do not so much rejoice
in this good fortune, as grieve that parted, ever parted
must I be from the head of my lady ; with whom of
old, while she was still a virgin, delighting herself[1]
with all kinds of perfumes, I drank many thousands.

79 Now, ye maidens, when the torch has united
you with welcome light, yield not your bodies to your
loving spouses, baring your breasts with vesture
opened, before the onyx jar offers pleasant gifts to
me, the jar which is yours, who reverence marriage
in chaste wedlock. But as for her who gives

---

[1] *expers* (codd.) "apart from," *expersa* "sprinkled with." I
translate *explens unguentis se* M.

illius a, mala dona levis bibat irrita pulvis :
   namque ego ab indignis praemia nulla peto.
sed magis, o nuptae, semper concordia vestras
   semper amor sedes incolat assiduus.
tu vero, regina, tuens cum sidera divam
   placabis festis luminibus Venerem,        90
\*unguinis [1] expertem non \*siveris [2] esse tuam me,
   sed potius largis affice muneribus.
sidera cur \*retinent? [3]   iterum\* coma regia fiam :
   proximus Hydrochoi fulgoret Oarion !


# LXVII


O DVLCI iucunda viro, iucunda parenti,
   salve, teque bona Iuppiter auctet ope,
ianua, quam Balbo dicunt servisse benigne
   olim, cum sedes ipse senex tenuit,
quamque ferunt rursus nato servire maligne,
   postquam es porrecto facta marita sene.
dic agedum nobis, quare mutata feraris
   in dominum veterem deseruisse fidem.
" non (ita Caecilio placeam, cui tradita nunc sum)
   culpa meast, quamquam dicitur esse mea,    10
nec peccatum a me quisquam pote dicere quic-
      quam :
   verum †istius populi [4] ianua qui te facit,†

---

[1] sanguinis *codd.* : unguinis *Bentl.*

[2] non vestris (vrīs) *codd.* : *probably* ᵛᵉ *written* si ᵛᵉ ris, ve siris,
vestris = siveris (*Scal.*).

[3] cur iterent *codd.* : corruerint *Lach.* : cur retinent *P.*
*from Markland.*

[4] verum istius (isti) populi *codd.* (1) verum . . . is mos
populi, (2) verum est vox populi, &c., *have been conjectured.*
(1) *seems most probable.*

134

herself up to foul adultery, ah! let the light dust
drink up her worthless gifts unratified: for I ask
no offerings from the unworthy. But rather, O ye
brides, may concord evermore dwell in your homes,
ever abiding Love. And you, my queen, when
gazing up to the stars you propitiate Venus with
festal lamps, let not me your handmaid want per-
fumes, but rather enrich me with bounteous gifts.
Why do the stars keep me here? I would fain be
the queen's lock once more; and let Orion blaze
next to Aquarius.

## LXVII

### *Catullus*

HAIL, house-door, once dear to a well-beloved husband
and dear to his father; hail, and may Jupiter bless
you with kindly help; you door, who once, they say,
did kindly service to Balbus, when the old man him-
self held the house, and who since then, as they tell
us, are doing grudging service to his son,[1] now that
the old man is dead and laid out, and you are become
the door of a wedded house.

7 Come tell us why you are said to be changed,
and to have deserted your old faithfulness to your
master.

### *House-door*

It is not—so may I please Caecilius, whose property
I am now become—it is not my fault, though it is
said to be mine, nor can any one speak of any wrong
done by me. But of course people will have it that

---

1 Or (*voto servisse maligno*) "lent yourself to the service of
an ill-affected vow" (whether "of its new mistress" (E.) or
"the old man's dying wish" (M.) ), or (*voto servisse maligne*)
"to have carried out scurvily his wish and prayer" (M.).

qui, quacumque aliquid reperitur non bene factum,
  ad me omnes clamant: ianua, culpa tuast."
non istuc satis est uno te dicere verbo,
  sed facere ut quivis sentiat et videat.
"qui possum?  nemo quaerit nec scire laborat."
  nos volumus: nobis dicere ne dubita.
"primum igitur, virgo quod fertur tradita nobis,
  falsumst.  non illam vir prior attigerat,                    20
languidior tenera cui pendens sicula beta
  nunquam se mediam sustulit ad tunicam:
sed pater illius gnati violasse cubile
  dicitur et miseram conscelerasse domum;
sive quod impia mens caeco flagrabat amore,
  seu quod iners sterili semine natus erat,
et quaerendus is unde foret nervosius illud,
  quod posset zonam solvere virgineam."
egregium narras mira pietate parentem,
  qui ipse sui gnati minxerit in gremium.                      30
"atqui non solum hoc se dicit cognitum habere
  Brixia † Chinea suppositum specula,†
flavus quam molli percurrit flumine Melo,
  Brixia Veronae mater amata meae;
sed de Postumio et Corneli narrat amore,
  cum quibus illa malum fecit adulterium."
dixerit hic aliquis: "quid?  tu istaec, ianua,
  nosti?
  cui numquam domini limine abesse licet,

the door does it all; all of them, whenever any ill deed is discovered, cry out to me, "House-door, the fault is yours."

### Catullus

It is not enough for you to say that with a single word, but so to do that any one may feel it and see it.

### House-door

How can I? No one asks or cares to know.

### Catullus

I wish to know—do not scruple to tell me.

### House-door

First then, that she came to us a virgin is untrue. She gave her maidenhead, not to her husband, but to his father.

### Catullus

What? A father in love with his own daughter-in-law? An affectionate father indeed!

### House-door

And yet this not only does Brixia say she well knows, Brixia that lies close under the citadel of Chinea, the town through which runs the soft stream of golden Melo, Brixia dear mother of my own Verona; but she tells stories about Postumius, and the amours of Cornelius, with whom she enjoyed unlawful love.

### Catullus

Here some one will say: "What, house-door, do you know all this, you who never may be away from your master's threshold, nor hear the people talk, but

nec populum auscultare, sed hic suffixa tigillo
  tantum operire soles aut aperire domum?"     40
"saepe illam audivi furtiva voce loquentem
  solam cum ancillis haec sua flagitia,
nomine dicentem quos diximus, ut pote quae mi
  speraret nec linguam esse nec auriculam.
praeterea addebat quendam, quem dicere nolo
  nomine, ne tollat rubra supercilia.
longus homost, magnas cui lites intulit olim
  falsum mendaci ventre puerperium."


## LXVIII


Qvod mihi fortuna casuque oppressus acerbo
  conscriptum hoc lacrimis mittis epistolium,
naufragum ut eiectum spumantibus aequoris undis
  sublevem et a mortis limine restituam,
quem neque sancta Venus molli requiescere somno
  desertum in lecto caelibe perpetitur,
nec veterum dulci scriptorum carmine Musae
  oblectant, cum mens anxia pervigilat ;
id gratumst mihi, me quoniam tibi dicis amicum,
  muneraque et Musarum hinc petis et Veneris :     10
sed tibi ne mea sint ignota incommoda, Manli,
  neu me odisse putes hospitis officium,
accipe, quis merser fortunae fluctibus ipse,
  ne amplius a misero dona beata petas.

fixed under this lintel have nothing to do but to shut or open the house ? [1]

### House-door

I have often heard her telling these crimes of hers with hushed voice alone with her maids, speaking of those by name of whom I spoke ; she thought, no doubt, that I had neither tongue nor ear. She added besides one whom I do not choose to mention by name, lest he should arch his red brows. He is a tall man, and was once troubled with a great law-suit, from a falsely imputed child-birth.


# LXVIII

### To Manlius

THAT you, weighed down as you are by fortune and bitter chance, should send me this letter written with tears, to bid me succour a shipwrecked man cast up by the foaming waters of the sea, and restore him from the threshold of death, whom neither does holy Venus suffer to rest, deserted in his widowed bed, nor do the Muses charm him with the sweet poetry of ancient writers, when his mind keeps anxious vigil ;—this is grateful to me, since you call me your friend, and come to me for the gifts both of the Muses and of Love.

11 But, dear Manlius, that my troubles may not be unknown to you, and that you may not think I am tired of the duty of a friend, let me tell you what are the waves of fortune in which I too am whelmed ; so will you not again require gifts of happiness from one who is unblest.

1 37–40 may be given either to Catullus or to the House-door.

tempore quo primum vestis mihi tradita purast,
    iucundum cum aetas florida ver ageret,
multa satis lusi : non est dea nescia nostri,
    quae dulcem curis miscet amaritiem :
sed totum hoc studium luctu fraterna mihi mors
    abstulit.   o misero frater adempte mihi,      20
tu mea tu moriens fregisti commoda, frater,
    tecum una totast nostra sepulta domus,
omnia tecum una perierunt gaudia nostra,
    quae tuus in vita dulcis alebat amor.
cuius ego interitu tota de mente fugavi
    haec studia atque omnes delicias animi.
quare, quod scribis " Veronae turpe, Catulle,
    esse, quod hic quisquis de meliore notast
frigida deserto tepefecit membra cubili,"
    id, Manli, non est turpe, magis miserumst.    30
ignosces igitur, si, quae mihi luctus ademit,
    haec tibi non tribuo munera, cum nequeo.
nam, quod scriptorum non magnast copia apud me,
    hoc fit, quod Romae vivimus : illa domus,
illa mihi sedes, illic mea carpitur aetas :
    huc una ex multis capsula me sequitur.
quod cum ita sit, nolim statuas nos mente maligr.a
    id facere aut animo non satis ingenuo,
quod tibi non utriusque petenti copia praestost :
    ultro ego deferrem, copia siqua foret    40

15 At the time when first a white dress was given to me, when my youth in its flower was keeping jocund spring-time, I wrote merry poems enough ; not unknown am I to the goddess who mingles with her cares a sweet bitterness.

19 But all care for this is gone from me by my brother's death. Ah me unhappy, who have lost you, my brother ! You, brother, you by your death have destroyed my happiness ; with you all my house is buried. With you all my joys have died, which your sweet love cherished, while yet you lived. By reason of your death, I have banished from all my mind these thoughts and all the pleasures of my heart.

27 And so, when you write, "It is no credit to you, Catullus, to be at Verona ; because here, where I am, all the young men of better condition warm their cold limbs in the bed deserted by you" ; that, Manlius, is rather a misfortune than a discredit. You will forgive me then, if I do not render to you those services which grief has taken from me at a time when I cannot do it.

33 For as for my not having plenty of authors at hand, that is because I live at Rome : that is my home, that is my abode, there my life is spent ; when I come here only one small box out of many attends me. And since this is so, I would not have you judge that it is due to niggardly mind or ungenerous temper, that you have not received a full supply of what you ask of each kind : I would have offered it unasked, if I had any such resources.

# GAI VALERI CATVLLI LIBER

## LXVIIIA

Non possum reticere, deae, qua me Allius in re
    iuverit aut quantis iuverit officiis :
ne fugiens saeclis obliviscentibus aetas
    illius hoc caeca nocte tegat studium :
sed dicam vobis, vos porro dicite multis
    milibus et facite haec charta loquatur anus

     .     .     .     .     .

    notescatque magis mortuus atque magis,
nec tenuem texens sublimis aranea telam
50   in deserto Alli nomine opus faciat.          10
nam mihi quam dederit duplex Amathusia
    curam,
    scitis, et in quo me torruerit [1] genere,
cum tantum arderem quantum Trinacria rupes
    lymphaque in Oetaeis Malia Thermopylis,
maesta neque assiduo tabescere lumina fletu
    cessarent tristique imbre madere genae.
qualis in aerii perlucens vertice montis
    rivus muscoso prosilit e lapide,
qui cum de prona praeceps est valle volutus,
60   per medium densi [2] transit iter populi,      20
dulce viatori lasso in sudore levamen,
    cum gravis exustos aestus hiulcat agros :
hic, velut in nigro iactatis turbine nautis
    lenius aspirans aura secunda venit
iam prece Pollucis, iam Castoris implorata,
    tale fuit nobis Allius auxilium.

---

[1] Or (corruerit) *ruined, or* in me quo corruerit genere ; *cf.*
*Hor.* "*Carm.*" I. *xix. 9.*

[2] densi *codd.*  *P. proposes* ridens *or* splendens.

## LXVIIIA

I CANNOT, O ye goddesses, refrain from telling what
the matter was in which Allius helped me, and how
greatly he helped me by his services, lest time flying
with forgetful ages hide in blind night this kindly
zeal of his. But to you I will tell it; do you hand
on the tale to many thousands, and let the paper
speak this in its old age.

· · · · · ·

and let him be famous more and more in death;
and let not the spider who weaves her thin web
aloft spread her work over the neglected name of
Allius. For how much sorrow of heart the wily
goddess of Amathus gave me, ye know, and in
what fashion she scorched me. When I was burn-
ing as hotly as the Trinacrian rock and the Malian
water at Oetean Thermopylae, when my sad eyes
never rested from wasting with perpetual tears,
nor my cheeks from streaming with a flood of
sorrow;—as at the top of a lofty mountain a bright
stream leaps forth from a moss-grown rock, and
gushing headlong down the steep valley crosses the
mid way thronged by the people, a sweet solace in
his labour to the weary wayfarer when sultry heat
makes the parched fields to gape; and as to mariners
tossed by the black storm comes a favouring breeze
with gentler breath, sought by prayer now to Pollux,
now to Castor;—such an aid to me was Allius; he

    is clausum lato patefecit limite campum,
       isque domum nobis isque dedit dominam,
    ad quam communes exerceremus amores.
70   quo mea se molli candida diva pede          30
       intulit et trito fulgentem in limine plantam
       innixa arguta constituit solea;
    coniugis ut quondam flagrans advenit amore
       Protesilaeam Laudamia domum
    inceptam frustra, nondum cum sanguine sacro
       hostia caelestis pacificasset eros.
    nil mihi tam valde placeat, Rhamnusia virgo,
       quod temere invitis suscipiatur eris.
    quam ieiuna pium desideret ara cruorem,
80   doctast amisso Laudamia viro,          40
    coniugis ante coacta novi dimittere collum
       quam veniens una atque altera rursus hiemps
    noctibus in longis avidum saturasset amorem,
       posset ut abrupto vivere coniugio,
    quod scibant Parcae non longo tempore abesse,
       si miles muros isset ad Iliacos:
    nam tum Helenae raptu primores Argivorum
       coeperat ad sese Troia ciere viros.
    Troia (nefas) commune sepulcrum Asiae Europae-
        que,
90   Troia virum et virtutum omnium acerba cinis,  50
    *quaene etiam* [1] nostro letum miserabile fratri
       attulit.  ei misero frater adempte mihi,
    ei misero fratri iucundum lumen ademptum,
       tecum una totast nostra sepulta domus;
    omnia tecum una perierunt gaudia nostra,
       quae tuus in vita dulcis alebat amor.

---

[1] q ue vetet id *oodd.*, quaene etiam *Heins. is commonly read. Other conjectures are* quae taetre id *M.*, qualiter id (et?) *E.*, quae vel idem *M.R.*

opened a broad track across the fenced field, he gave
me access to a house and its mistress, under whose
roof we should together enjoy each his own love.
Thither my fair goddess delicately stepped, and set
the sole of her shining foot on the smooth threshold,
as she pressed on her slender [1] sandal: even as once
Laodamia came burning with love to the house of
Protesilaus, that house begun in vain, since not yet had
a victim's sacred blood appeased the Lords of heaven.
Lady of Rhamnus, never may that please me which
is undertaken amiss without the will of our Lords.

[39] How much the starved altar craves for the blood
of pious sacrifices, Laodamia learnt by the loss of her
husband; forced to loose her arms from the neck of
her new spouse, before the coming of one and then
a second winter with its long nights should content
her passionate love, that she might endure to live,
though her husband was taken from her; [2] and this
the Fates had ordained to come in no long time, if
once he went as a soldier to the walls of Ilium.

[47] For then it was, because of the rape of Helen,
that Troy began to summon against herself the chief-
tains of the Argives, Troy—O horror!—the common
grave of Europe and Asia, Troy the untimely tomb of
all heroes and heroic deeds: Troy brought pitiable
death to my brother also; alas! my brother, taken
from me unhappy, alas! dear light of my eyes, taken
from thy unhappy brother: [3] with thee now is all my
house buried; all my joys have perished together
with thee, which while thou wert alive thy sweet

---

[1] Or "creaking."

[2] *abrupto = abrepto* M.; *cf.* Verg. *Aen.* XII. 451. Or "though
her marriage bond was broken off."

[3] Or "alas for the lovely light of life taken away from my
unhappy brother."

quem nunc tam longe non inter nota sepulcra
    nec prope cognatos compositum cineres,
sed Troia obscena, Troia infelice sepultum
100    detinet extremo terra aliena solo.        60
ad quam tum properans fertur [simul] undique [1]
    pubes
    Graeca penetralis deseruisse focos,
ne Paris abducta gavisus libera moecha
    otia pacato degeret in thalamo.
quo tibi tum casu, pulcherrima Laudamia,
    ereptumst vita dulcius atque anima
coniugium : tanto te absorbens vertice amoris
    aestus in abruptum detulerat barathrum,
quale ferunt Grai Pheneum prope Cylleneum
110    siccare emulsa pingue palude solum,        70
quod quondam caesis montis fodisse medullis
    audit falsiparens Amphitryoniades,
tempore quo certa Stymphalia monstra sagitta
    perculit imperio deterioris eri,
pluribus ut caeli tereretur ianua divis,
    Hebe nec longa virginitate foret.
sed tuus altus amor barathro fuit altior illo,
    qui tamen indomitam [2] ferre iugum docuit :
nam nec tam carum confecto aetate parenti
120    una caput seri nata nepotis alit,        80
qui, cum divitiis vix tandem inventus avitis
    nomen testatas intulit in tabulas,
impia derisi gentilis gaudia tollens
    suscitat a cano vulturium capiti :
nec tantum niveo gavisast ulla columbo
    compar, quae multo dicitur improbius
oscula mordenti semper decerpere rostro,
    quam quae praecipue multivolast mulier.

---

[1] [simul] undique.  vi vindice *A. Palmer.*
[2] taurum domitum (*or* indomitum) *Rd.*

love cherished. Thee now far, far away, not among
familiar graves, nor laid to rest near the ashes of thy
kinsfolk, but buried in hateful Troy, ill-omened Troy,
a foreign land holds in a distant soil.

⁶¹ To Troy at that time all the youth of Greece is
said to have hastened together, deserting their hearths
and homes, that Paris might not enjoy undisturbed
leisure in a peaceful chamber, rejoicing in the rape
of his paramour.

⁶⁵ By that sad chance then, fairest Laodamia, wast
thou bereft of thy husband, sweeter to thee than life
and soul; so strong the tide of love, so whelming
the eddy that bore thee into the sheer abyss, deep
as that gulf which (say the Greeks) near Cyllenian
Pheneus drains away the swamp, and dries up the
rich soil which of old the false-fathered son of
Amphitryon is said to have dug out, cutting away
the heart of the hill, what time with sure shaft
he hit the monsters of Stymphalus at the bidding
of a meaner lord, that the door of heaven might be
frequented by more gods, and that Hebe might not
long be unmated. But deeper than that gulf was
thy deep love, which taught thee though untamed
to bear the yoke.

⁷⁹ Not so dear to her age-stricken parent is the head
of the late-born grandchild which his only daughter
nurses, who, scarce at length appearing as an heir to
ancestral wealth, and having his name brought into
the witnessed tablets, puts an end to the unnatural
joy of the kinsman, now in his turn derided, and
drives away the vulture that waits for the hoary
head; nor did ever dove delight so much in her
snowy mate, though the dove bites and bills and
snatches kisses more wantonly than any woman, be
she amorous beyond others' measure. You alone

147

sed tu horum magnos vicisti sola furores,
130   ut semel es flavo conciliata viro.      90
    aut nihil aut paulo cui tum concedere digna
      lux mea se nostrum contulit in gremium,
    quam circumcursans hinc illinc saepe Cupido
      fulgebat crocina candidus in tunica.
    quae tamenetsi uno non est contenta Catullo,
      rara verecundae furta feremus erae,
    ne nimium simus stultorum more molesti.
    saepe etiam Iuno, maxima caelicolum,
    coniugis in culpa flagrantem *concoquit [1] iram,
140   noscens omnivoli plurima *furta [2] Iovis.   100
† atque nec divis homines componier aequumst,

     •     •     •     •     •

    ingratum tremuli tolle parentis onus. [3]
    nec tamen illa mihi dextra deducta [4] paterna
      fragrantem Assyrio venit odore domum,
    sed furtiva dedit †mira munuscula nocte,
      ipsius ex ipso dempta viri gremio.
    quare illud satis est, si nobis is datur unis,
      quem lapide illa, dies, candidiore notat.

    Hoc tibi, quod potui, confectum carmine munus
150   pro multis, Alli, redditur officiis,      110
    ne vestrum scabra tangat rubigine nomen
      haec atque illa dies atque alia atque alia.
    huc addent divi quam plurima, quae Themis olim
      antiquis solitast munera ferre piis:

---

[1] cotidiana *codd. Other conjectures are* continet, contudit, condidit. *P. proposes* flagrante excanduit ira.

[2] facta *codd.:* furta *Edd.*

[3] onus *codd.:* opus *P.*

[4] *Or* dextra de ducta *P., since the father had nothing to do with the* deductio *of the bride. Cf. P.'s* "Catulliana," *in ' Journal of Class. Philology,"* XVII. *p.* 255.

surpassed the passion of these, when once you were matched with your golden-haired husband.

⁹¹ Even so kind, or but little less, was she, my bright one, who came into my arms; and often around her flitting hither and thither Cupid shone fair in vest of saffron hue. And though she is not content with Catullus alone, I will bear the faults, for few they are, of my modest mistress, lest we become as tiresome as jealous fools. Juno, too, greatest of the heavenly ones, often keeps down her anger for her husband's fault, as she learns the many loves of all-amorous Jove. Yet since it is not fit that men should be compared with gods    .        .        .
away, then, with the hateful severity of an anxious father.¹ And after all she did not come for me led by her father's hand into a house fragrant with Assyrian odours, but gave me in the wondrous ² night sweet stolen gifts, taken from the very bosom of her husband himself. Wherefore it is enough if to me alone is granted the day ³ which she marks with a whiter stone.

This gift—'twas all I could—set forth in verse is returned to you, Allius, for many kind offices; lest this and that day, and another and another should touch your name with corroding rust. To this the gods will add those countless gifts which Themis of old was wont to give to pious men of ancient time.

---

1 Or "take up the weary burden of the decrepit father"; with allusion to a supposed episode of Aeneas and Anchises in the lost verses.

2 Or (muta) "silent," or (multa) "at dead of night."

3 dies (diem), see M.'s note, p. 192.

sitis felices et tu simul et tua vita
    et domus [illa], in qua [1] lusimus, et domina,
et qui principio nobis †terram dedit aufert,† [2]
    a quo sunt primo * mi omnia nata bona.
et longe ante omnes mihi quae me carior ipsost,
160    lux mea, qua viva vivere dulce mihist.    120


## LXIX

Noli admirari, quare tibi femina nulla,
    Rufe, velit tenerum supposuisse femur,
non si illam rarae labefactes munere vestis
    aut perluciduli deliciis lapidis.
laedit te quaedam mala fabula, qua tibi fertur
    valle sub alarum trux habitare caper.
hunc metuunt omnes.  neque mirum : nam
      mala valde est
    bestia, nec quicum bella puella cubet.
quare aut crudelem nasorum interfice pestem
    aut admirari desine cur fugiunt.    10


## LXX

Nvlli se dicit mulier mea nubere malle
    quam mihi, non si se Iuppiter ipse petat.
dicit : sed mulier cupido quod dicit amanti
    in vento et rapida scribere oportet aqua.

---

[1] *Or* in qua una *Rd.*
[2] *M. translates* terram "*firm ground.*"  *Under* aufert *some name, as* Anser, Ufens Afer (Auster *Rd.*), *may be concealed.*

May ye be happy, both you, and with you your dear
Life, and the house in which you and I sported, and its
mistress, and he who first [          ] for us, from whom
first all those good things had their springing for me.
And far before all, she who is dearer to me than
myself, my Light, whose life alone makes it sweet to
me to live.

## LXIX

You need not wonder why no dainty woman cares to
come to your arms, Rufus, not though you may shake
her by the gift of a dress of fine texture, or some
delightful transparent jewel. What hurts you is a
slander that says you have the rank goat under your
armpits: this is what they all fear, and no wonder;
'tis a horrid beast, and no bedfellow for a pretty
girl. Then kill that which so cruelly outrages our
noses, or wonder no more why they run away.

## LXX

The woman I love says that there is no one whom
she would rather marry than me, not if Jupiter
himself were to woo her. Says;—but what a woman
says to her ardent lover should be written in wind
and running water.

## LXXI

Siqvoi iure bono sacer alarum obstitit hircus,
  aut siquem merito tarda podagra secat,
aemulus iste, toro qui vestro exercet amorem,
  mirificest a te nactus utrumque [1] malum.
nam quotiens futuit, totiens ulciscitur ambos:
  illam affligit odore, ipse perit podagra.

## LXXII

Dicebas quondam solum te nosse Catullum,
  Lesbia, nec prae me velle tenere Iovem.
dilexi tum te non tantum ut vulgus amicam,
  sed pater ut gnatos diligit et generos.
nunc te cognovi: quare etsi impensius uror,
  multo mi tamen es vilior et levior.
qui potis est? inquis. quod amantem iniuria talis
  cogit amare magis, sed bene velle minus.

## LXXIII

Desine de quoquam quicquam bene velle mereri
  aut aliquem fieri posse putare pium.
omnia sunt ingrata, nihil fecisse benigne;
  immo etiam taedet, [taedet] obestque magis: [2]
ut mihi, quem nemo gravius nec acerbius urget,
  quam modo qui me unum atque unicum amicum
  habuit.

[1] a se . . ., utrimque *P.*
[2] immo etiam tedet obestque magisque magis *codd. The
emendation in the text is that of Statius, Muretus, and other
early scholars. P. reads* immo taedet obestque et magis atque
magis.

## LXXI

IF there ever was a good fellow afflicted with rankness, or one who was racked for his sins with the gout, your rival who shares your privileges has got both from you to a marvel. Whenever they meet, they both pay dear for it; she is overwhelmed with the gust, he half dead with the gout.

## LXXII

You used once to say that Catullus was your only friend. Lesbia, and that you would not prefer Jupiter himself to me. I loved you then, not only as the common sort love a mistress, but as a father loves his sons and sons-in-law. Now I know you; and therefore, though I burn more ardently, yet you are in my sight much less worthy and lighter. How can that be? you say. Because such an injury as this drives a lover to be more of a lover, but less of a friend.

## LXXIII

LEAVE off wishing to deserve any thanks from any one, or thinking that any one can ever become grateful. All this wins no thanks; to have acted kindly is nothing, rather it is wearisome, wearisome and harmful; so is it now with me, who am vexed and troubled by no one so bitterly as by him who but now held me for his one and only friend.

## LXXIV

Gellivs audierat, patruum obiurgare solere
    siquis delicias diceret aut faceret.
hoc ne ipsi accideret, patrui perdepsuit ipsam
    uxorem et patruum reddidit Harpocratem.
quod voluit fecit : nam, quamvis irrumet ipsum
    nunc patruum, verbum non faciet patruus.

## LXXV

Hvc est mens deducta tua, mea Lesbia, culpa,[1]
    atque ita se officio perdidit ipsa suo,
ut iam nec bene velle queat tibi, si optima fias,
    nec desistere amare, omnia si facias.

## LXXVI

Siqva recordanti benefacta priora voluptas
    est homini, cum se cogitat esse pium,
nec sanctam violasse fidem, nec foedere in ullo
    divum ad fallendos numine abusum homines,
multa parata manent in longa aetate, Catulle,
    ex hoc ingrato gaudia amore tibi.
nam quaecumque homines bene cuiquam aut dicere
      possunt
    aut facere, haec a te dictaque factaque sunt ;
omnia quae ingratae perierunt credita menti.
    quare cur tu te iam [2] amplius excrucies ?    10

---

  [1] *Or* tua mea, Lesbia, culpa *P.*
  [2] *Or* quare iam te cur *E. :* quare cur tu te ipse *P. from E.*

## LXXIV

GELLIUS had heard that his uncle used to reprove any one who talked of indulgence or used it. To avoid this himself, he seduced his uncle's own wife, and so made him dumbness on a monument. He did what he wanted; for even if he should tackle the uncle himself, uncle will not say a word.

## LXXV

To this point is my mind reduced by your fault, my Lesbia, and has so ruined itself by its own devotion, that now it can neither wish you well though you should become the best of women, nor cease to love you though you do the worst that can be done.

## LXXVI

IF a man can take any pleasure in recalling the thought of kindnesses done, when he thinks that he has been a true friend; and that he has not broken sacred faith, nor in any compact has used the majesty of the gods in order to deceive men, then there are many joys in a long life for you, Catullus, earned from this thankless love. For whatever kindness man can show to man by word or deed has been said and done by you. All this was entrusted to an ungrateful heart, and is lost: why then should you torment yourself now any more? Why do you not

quin tu animum offirmas atque istinc teque reducis
  et dis invitis desinis esse miser?
difficilest longum subito deponere amorem.
  difficilest, verum hoc qualubet efficias.
una salus haec est, hoc est tibi pervincendum:
  hoc facias, sive id non pote sive pote.
o di, si vestrumst misereri, aut si quibus umquam
  extremam iam ipsa in morte tulistis opem,
me miserum aspicite et, si vitam puriter egi,
  eripite hanc pestem perniciemque mihi.      20
heu, mihi surrepens imos ut torpor in artus
  expulit ex omni pectore laetitias!
non iam illud quaero, contra me ut diligat illa,
  aut, quod non potis est, esse pudica velit:
ipse valere opto et taetrum hunc deponere morbum.
  o di, reddite mi hoc pro pietate mea.


## LXXVII

Rvfe mihi frustra ac nequiquam credite amico
  (frustra? immo magno cum pretio atque malo),
sicine subrepsti mi, atque intestina perurens
  ei misero eripuisti omnia nostra bona?
eripuisti, heu heu nostrae crudele venenum
  vitae, heu heu nostrae pestis amicitiae.


## LXXVIII

Gallvs habet fratres, quorumst lepidissima coniunx
  alterius, lepidus filius alterius.
Gallus homost bellus: nam dulces iungit amores,
  cum puero ut bello bella puella cubet.

settle your mind firmly, and draw back, and cease to be miserable, in despite of the gods? It is difficult suddenly to lay aside a long-cherished love. It is difficult; but you should accomplish it, one way or another. This is the only safety, this you must carry through, this you are to do, whether it is possible or impossible. Ye gods, if mercy is your attribute, or if ye ever brought aid to any at the very moment of death, look upon me in my trouble, and if I have led a pure life, take away this plague and ruin from me. Ah me! what a lethargy creeps into my inmost joints, and has cast out all joys from my heart! No longer is this my prayer, that she should love me in return, or, for that is impossible, that she should consent to be chaste. I would myself be well again and put away this baleful sickness. O ye gods, grant me this in return for my piety.

## LXXVII

Rufus, whom I, your friend, trusted in vain, and to no purpose—in vain? nay, rather at a great and ruinous price—have you stolen into my heart and burning into my vitals torn away, alas, all my blessings? Torn away, alas, alas! you the cruel poison of my life, alas, alas! you the deadly bane of my friendship.

## LXXVIII

Gallus has two brothers; one has a most charming wife, the other a charming boy. Gallus is a gallant: he helps love's course, and brings the gallant lad to the arms of the gallant lass. Gallus is a fool, and does

157

Gallus homost stultus nec se videt esse maritum,
    qui patruus patrui monstret adulterium.
sed nunc id doleo, quod purae pura puellae
    savia comminxit spurca saliva tua.
verum id non impune feres ; nam te omnia saecla
    noscent, et qui sis fama loquetur anus.     10


## LXXIX

Lesbivs est pulcer : quid ni ?    quem Lesbia malit
    quam te cum tota gente, Catulle, tua.
sed tamen hic pulcer vendat cum gente Catullum,
    si tria notorum savia reppererit.


## LXXX

Qvid dicam, Gelli, quare rosea ista labella
    hiberna fiant candidiora nive,
mane domo cum exis et cum te octava quiete
    e molli longo suscitat hora die ?
nescio quid certest : an vere fama susurrat
    grandia te medii tenta vorare viri ?
sic certest : clamant Victoris rupta miselli
    ilia, et emulso labra notata sero.


## LXXXI

Nemone in tanto potuit populo esse, Iuventi,
    bellus homo, quem tu diligere inciperes,
praeterquam iste tuus moribunda ab sede Pisauri
    hospes inaurata pallidior statua,
qui tibi nunc cordist, quem tu praeponere nobis
    audes, et nescis quod facinus facias ?

not see that he has a wife of his own, when he teaches a nephew how to seduce an uncle's wife. But now what annoys me is that your nasty spittle has touched the pure lips of a pure girl. But you shall not have it gratis; all generations shall know you, and beldame Rumour shall tell what you are.

## LXXIX

Lesbius is a pretty boy; why not? since Lesbia likes him better than you, Catullus, with all your kin. But this pretty boy would sell Catullus and all his kin if he could find three acquaintances to vouch for him.

## LXXX

What reason can I give, Gellius, why those ruddy lips become whiter than snow when you rise in the morning or the eighth hour awakes you from your soft siesta in the long hours of the day? Something there is assuredly: is the gossip true that you are given to vice? So it is assuredly: the signs attest it.

## LXXXI

Could there not, Juventius, be found in all this people a pretty fellow whom you might begin to like, besides that friend of yours from the sickly region of Pisaurum, paler than a gilded statue, who now is dear to you, whom you presume to prefer to me, and know not what a deed you do?

## LXXXII

Qvinti, si tibi vis oculos debere Catullum
    aut aliud siquid carius est oculis,
eripere ei noli, multo quod carius illi
    est oculis seu quid carius est oculis.

## LXXXIII

Lesbia mi praesente viro mala plurima dicit:
    haec illi fatuo maxima laetitiast.
mule, nihil sentis.   si nostri oblita taceret,
    sana esset: nunc quod gannit et obloquitur,
non solum meminit, sed quae multo acrior est res,
    iratast.   hoc est, uritur et loquitur.

## LXXXIV

*Chommoda* dicebat, si quando *commoda* vellet
    dicere, et *insidias* Arrius *hinsidias,*
et tum mirifice sperabat se esse locutum,
    cum quantum poterat dixerat *hinsidias.*
credo, sic mater, sic Liber avunculus eius,
    sic maternus avus dixerat atque avia.
hoc misso in Syriam requierant omnibus aures:
    audibant eadem haec leniter et leviter,

## LXXXII

QUINTIUS, if you wish Catullus to owe his eyes to you, or aught else that is dearer than eyes, if dearer aught there be, do not take from him what is much dearer to him than his eyes, or aught besides that dearer is than eyes.

## LXXXIII

LESBIA says many hard things to me in the presence of her husband, a great joy to the fool. Dull mule, you understand nothing. If she forgot me and were silent, she would be heart-whole. But as it is, her snarling and railing means this: she not only remembers, but—a much more serious thing—she is angry; that is, she burns,[1] and so she talks.

## LXXXIV

ARRIUS if he wanted to say "honours" used to say "*h*onours," and for "intrigue" "*h*intrigue"; and thought he had spoken marvellous well, whenever he said "*h*ambush" with as much emphasis as possible. So, no doubt, his mother had said, so Liber [2] his uncle, so his grandfather and grandmother on the mother's side. When he was sent into Syria, all our ears had a holiday; they heard the same syllables pronounced quietly and lightly, and had no

---

[1] Or (*coquitur*) "she is burning"; but *cf.* Carm. XCII. A. Palmer and P. prefer *queritur*.

[2] Or (*liber* P., *al.*) "the freeman"—*i.e.*, the first of the family who was free-born.

nec sibi postilla metuebant talia verba,
  cum subito affertur nuntius horribilis,    10
Ionios fluctus, postquam illuc Arrius isset,
  iam non *Ionios* esse, sed *Hionios*.


## LXXXV

ODI et amo.   quare id faciam, fortasse requiris.
  nescio, sed fieri sentio et excrucior.


## LXXXVI

QVINTIA formosast multis; mihi candida, longa,
  rectast.   haec ego sic singula confiteor,
totum illud formosa nego : nam nulla venustas,
  nulla in tam magnost corpore mica salis.
Lesbia formosast, quae cum pulcherrima totast,
  tum omnibus una omnis surripuit Veneres.


## LXXXVII

NVLLA potest mulier tantum se dicere amatam
  vere, quantum a me Lesbia amata mea's.
nulla fides ullo fuit umquam foedere tanta,
  quanta in amore tuo ex parte reperta meast.


## LXXXVIII

QVID facit is, Gelli, qui cum matre atque sorore
  prurit et abiectis pervigilat tunicis?
quid facit is, patruum qui non sinit esse maritum?
  ecquid scis quantum suscipiat sceleris?

fear of such words for the future : when on a sudden a dreadful message arrives, that the Ionian waves, ever since Arrius went there, are henceforth not " Ionian," but " *H*ionian."

## LXXXV

I HATE and love. Why I do so, perhaps you ask. I know not, but I feel it, and I am in torment.

## LXXXVI

QUINTIA is thought beautiful by many ; I think her fair, tall, and straight. I so far allow each of these points, but I demur to " beautiful," for she has no grace ; there is not in the whole compass of her tall person one grain of salt. Lesbia is beautiful : for she possesses all the beauties, and has stolen all the graces from all the women alone for herself.

## LXXXVII

No woman can say truly that she has been loved as much as you, Lesbia mine, were loved by me. No faithfulness in any bond was ever such as has been found on my part in my love for you.

## LXXXVIII

WHAT is he doing, Gellius, who keeps vigil with mother and sister, tunics all thrown off ? What is he doing, who will not let his uncle be a husband ? Do you know how much guilt he incurs ? More he

163

suscipit, o Gelli, quantum non ultima Tethys
  nec genitor Nympharum abluit Oceanus :
nam nihil est quicquam sceleris quo prodeat ultra,
  non si demisso se ipse voret capite.

### LXXXIX

Gellivs est tenuis : quid ni ?   quoi tam bona mater
  tamque valens vivat tamque venusta soror
tamque bonus patruus tamque omnia plena puellis
  cognatis, quare is desinat esse macer ?
qui ut nihil attingat, nisi quod fas tangere non est,
  quantumvis quare sit macer invenies.

### XC

Nascatvr magus ex Gelli matrisque nefando
  coniugio et discat Persicum aruspicium :
nam magus ex matre et gnato gignatur oportet,
  si verast Persarum impia religio,
gnatus [1] ut accepto veneretur carmine divos
  omentum in flamma pingue liquefaciens.

### XCI

Non ideo, Gelli, sperabam te mihi fidum
  in misero hoc nostro, hoc perdito amore fore,
quod te cognossem bene constantemve putarem
  aut posse a turpi mentem inhibere probro,

---

[1] gnatus *codd.*   *Other readings are* gratus, gnarus, gnavus.

incurs than furthest Tethys can wash away, or Ocean-
father of the nymphs : for there is no guilt what,
ever beyond for him to attain to.


## LXXXIX

GELLIUS is thin, and well he may be ; with a mother
so kind and so lusty and lively, and a sister so
charming, and so kind an uncle, and so many girls of
his acquaintance all over the place, why should he
cease to be lean?  Even if he touch nothing but
what none may touch, you will find any number of
reasons why he should be lean.


## XC

FROM the unholy commerce of Gellius and his mother
let a Magian be born, and learn the Persian art of
soothsaying ; for a Magian must be the offspring of
mother and son, if the unnatural religion of the Per-
sians is true, so that their child may worship the
gods with acceptable hymns, whilst melting the fat
caul in the altar flame.


## XCI

I HOPED, Gellius, that you would be true to me in
this miserable, this ruinous love of mine, not on the
ground that I knew you,[1] or thought that you were
truly honourable or could restrain your mind from
baseness or villainy, but because I saw that she,

---

[1] Or (*non nossem* Avant.) "it was not that I did not know
you [as I did]."

sed neque quod matrem nec germanam esse
    videbam
hanc tibi, cuius me magnus edebat amor.
et quamvis tecum multo coniungerer usu,
    non satis id causae credideram esse tibi.
tu satis id duxti : tantum tibi gaudium in omni
    culpast, in quacumque est aliquid sceleris.         10


## XCII

Lesbia mi dicit semper male nec tacet umquam
    de me : Lesbia me dispeream nisi amat.
quo signo ? quia sunt totidem mea : deprecor illam
    assidue, verum dispeream nisi amo.


## XCIII

Nil nimium studeo, Caesar, tibi velle placere,
    nec scire utrum sis albus an ater homo.


## XCIV

Mentvla moechatur.  moechatur mentula ?   certe
hoc est quod dicunt, ipsa ollera olla legit.


## XCV

Zmyrna mei Cinnae, nonam post denique messem
    quam coeptast nonamque edita post hiemem,
milia cum interea quingenta †Hortensius uno [1]

.        .        .        .        .       .

[1] *M. supplies the lacuna by* Hatrianus in uno | versiculorum
anno putidus evomuit.

whose mighty love was consuming me, was neither mother nor sister of yours. And although I was connected with you by much familiar friendship, I had not thought that that was reason enough for you. You thought it enough : so much delight do you take in any vice in which there is something of dishonour.

## XCII

LESBIA always speaks ill of me, and is always talking about me. May I perish if Lesbia does not love me. By what token? because it is just the same with me. I am perpetually crying out upon her, but may I perish if I do not love her.

## XCIII

I HAVE no very great desire to make myself agreeable to you, Caesar, nor to know whether your complexion is light or dark.

## XCIV

ROGER plays the gallant : say you so in truth? Sure enough this is the proverb, the pot finds its own herbs.

## XCV

MY friend Cinna's *Smyrna*, published at last nine harvest-tides and nine winters after it was begun, whilst Hortensius [has brought out] five hundred thousand [verses] in one [year].

Zmyrna cavas Satrachi penitus mittetur ad undas,
    Zmyrnam cana diu saecula pervoluent.
at Volusi annales Paduam morientur ad ipsam
    et laxas scombris saepe dabunt tunicas.
parva mei mihi sint cordi monumenta [sodalis],
    at populus tumido gaudeat Antimacho.      10


## XCVI

Si quicquam mutis gratum acceptumve sepulcris
    accidere a nostro, Calve, dolore potest,
quo desiderio veteres renovamus amores
    atque olim amissas flemus amicitias,
certe non tanto mors immatura dolorist
    Quintiliae, quantum gaudet amore tuo.


## XCVII

Non (ita me di ament) quicquam referre putavi,
    utrumne os an culum olfacerem Aemilio.
nilo mundius hoc, niloque immundius, illud,
    verum etiam culus mundior et melior :
nam sine dentibus est : os dentis sesquipedalis,
    gingivas vero ploxeni habet veteris,
praeterea rictum qualem diffissus in aestu
    meientis mulae cunnus habere solet.
hic futuit multas et se facit esse venustum,
    et non pistrino traditur atque asino ?      10
quem siqua attingit, non illam posse putemus
    aegroti culum lingere carnificis ?

*Smyrna* will travel as far away as the deep-channelled streams of Satrachus. But the Annals of Volusius will die by the river Padua where they were born, and will often furnish a loose wrapper for mackerels. Let the modest memorials of my friend [1] be dear to me, and let the vulgar rejoice in their windy Antimachus.

## XCVI

IF the silent grave can receive any pleasure, or sweetness at all from our grief, Calvus, the grief and regret with which we make our old loves live again,[2] and weep for long-lost friendships, surely Quintilia feels less sorrow for her too early death, than pleasure from your love.

## XCVII

I SWEAR I didn't think it mattered one straw whether I sniffed Aemilius's head or his tail: neither was better or worse than t'other; or rather his tail was the better and smarter of the two, for it has no teeth. His mouth has teeth half a yard long, gums, moreover, like an old cart-frame, gaping like a mule in summer. He courts many a woman and makes himself out a charmer, and yet he is not passed over to the grinding-mill and its ass. If any woman touches him, don't we think that she is capable of fondling a sick hangman?

[1] Or (*Phalaeci*) "of my own Phalaecus" M.
[2] Or (*quom* M. and P.) "when in sorrow," &c.

## XCVIII

In te, si in quemquam, dici pote, putide Victi,
  id quod verbosis dicitur et fatuis.
ista cum lingua, si usus veniat tibi, possis
  culos et crepidas lingere carpatinas.
si nos omnino vis omnes perdere, Victi,
  hiscas: omnino quod cupis efficies.

## XCIX

Svrripvi tibi dum ludis, mellite Iuventi,
  saviolum dulci dulcius ambrosia.
verum id non impune tuli: namque amplius horam
  suffixum in summa me memini esse cruce,
dum tibi me purgo nec possum fletibus ullis
  tantillum vestrae demere saevitiae.
nam simul id factumst, multis diluta labella
  guttis abstersisti omnibus articulis,
ne quicquam nostro contractum exore maneret,
  tanquam commictae spurca saliva lupae.          10

.      .      .      .      .      .

praeterea infesto miserum me tradere Amori
  non cessasti omnique excruciare modo,
ut mi ex ambrosia mutatum iam foret illud
  saviolum tristi tristius helleboro.
quam quoniam poenam misero proponis amori [1]
  numquam iam posthac basia surripiam.

---

[1] amori *codd.:* amoris *P.*

## XCVIII

You if any man, disgusting Victius, deserve what is said about chatterboxes and idiots. With a tongue like that, given the chance you might lick a rustic's clogs. If you wish to destroy us all utterly, Victius, just utter a syllable: you'll utterly do what you wish.

## XCIX

I STOLE a kiss from you, honey-sweet Juventius, while you were playing, a kiss sweeter than sweet ambrosia. But not unpunished; for I remember how for more than an hour I hung impaled on the top of the gallows tree, while I was excusing myself to you, yet could not with all my tears take away ever so little from your anger; for no sooner was it done, than you washed your lips clean with plenty of water, and wiped them with all your fingers, that no contagion from my mouth might remain. . . . Besides that, you made haste to deliver your unhappy lover to angry Love, and to torture him in every manner, so that that kiss, changed from ambrosia, was now more bitter than bitter hellebore. Since then you impose this penalty on my unlucky love, henceforth I will never steal any kisses.

### C

CAELIVS AVFILENVM et Quintius Aufilenam
  flos Veronensum depereunt iuvenum,
hic fratrem, ille sororem.   hoc est, quod dicitur, illud
  fraternum vere dulce sodalitium.
cui faveam potius ?   Caeli, tibi : nam tua nobis
  perspecta egregiest unica amicitia,
cum vesana meas torreret flamma medullas.
  sis felix, Caeli, sis in amore potens.

### CI

MVLTAS per gentes et multa per aequora vectus
  advenio has miseras, frater, ad inferias,
ut te postremo donarem munere mortis
  et mutam nequiquam alloquerer cinerem,
quandoquidem fortuna mihi tete abstulit ipsum,
  heu miser indigne frater adempte mihi.
nunc tamen interea haec, prisco quae more parentum
  tradita sunt tristi munere ad inferias,
accipe fraterno multum manantia fletu,
  atque in perpetuum, frater, ave atque vale.          10

### CII

Si quicquam *tacite [1] commissumst fido †ab amico,
  cuius sit penitus nota fides animi,
meque esse invenies illorum iure sacratum,
  Corneli, et factum me esse puta Harpocratem.

  [1] tacito *codd.* : tacite *M.* : si quoi quid tacito commissumst
fido et amico *P.*, "*a silent and trusty friend*" ; *or* (taciti)
"*any secret.*"

## C

CAELIUS is mad for Aufilenus and Quintius for Aufilena, one for the brother, one for the sister, both the fine flower of Veronese youth. Here's the sweet brotherhood of the proverb! Which shall I vote for? You, Caelius; your friendship to me was excellently shown—it was unique! when a mad flame scorched my vitals. Luck to you, Caelius! success to your loves!

## CI

*ơ, K*

WANDERING through many countries and over many seas I come, my brother, to these sorrowful obsequies, to present you with the last guerdon of death, and speak, though in vain, to your silent ashes, since fortune has taken your own self away from me—alas, my brother, so cruelly torn from me! Yet now meanwhile take these offerings, which by the custom of our fathers have been handed down—a sorrowful tribute—for a funeral sacrifice; take them, wet with many tears of a brother, and for ever, O my brother, hail and farewell!

## CII

IF ever any secret whatsoever was entrusted in confidence by a faithful friend, the loyalty of whose heart was fully known, you will find that I am consecrated by their rite,[1] Cornelius, and you may think that I am become a very Harpocrates.[2]

---

[1] Or (comma after *illorum*) "one of them, duly consecrate," M. *meque,* or "that I too"; *cf.* M.'s note.
[2] Or (*putum* P.) "a very Harpocrates."

## CIII

Avt, sodes, mihi redde decem sestertia, Silo,
  deinde esto quamvis saevus et indomitus:
aut, si te nummi delectant, desine quaeso
  leno esse atque idem saevus et indomitus.

## CIV

Credis me potuisse meae maledicere vitae,
  ambobus mihi quae carior est oculis?
non potui, nec si possem tam perdite amarem:
  sed tu cum Tappone omnia monstra facis.

## CV

Mentvla conatur Pipleum scandere montem:
  Musae furcillis praecipitem eiciunt.

## CVI

Cvm puero bello praeconem qui videt esse,
  quid credat, nisi se vendere discupere?

## CVII

Sicvi quid cupido optantique optigit umquam
  insperanti, hoc est gratum animo proprie.
quare hoc est gratum nobis quoque, †carius auro,
  quod te restituis, Lesbia, mi cupido,

## CIII

Prithee, Silo, either give me back the ten sestertia, and then you may be as violent and overbearing as you like; or, if the money gives you pleasure, don't try, I beg, to ply your trade and be at the same time violent and overbearing.

## CIV

Do you think that I ever could have spoken ill of my life, of her who is dearer to me than both my eyes? No, I could never have done it; nor, if I could help it, would I be so ruinously in love. But you and Tappo make out everything to be prodigious.

## CV

Mentula strives to climb the Piplean mount: the Muses with pitchforks drive him out headlong.

## CVI

If one sees a pretty boy in company with an auctioneer, what is one to think but that he wants to sell himself?

## CVII

If anything ever happened to any one who eagerly longed and never hoped, that is a true pleasure to the mind. And so to me too this is a pleasure more precious than gold,[1] that you, Lesbia, restore yourself to me who longed for you, restore to me who longed,

---

[1] Or *carior auro*, referring to Lesbia, P.

restituis cupido atque insperanti, ipsa refers te
    nobis : o lucem candidiore nota !
quis me uno vivit felicior, aut magis hac rem
    optandam in vita dicere quis poterit ?

## CVIII

Si, Comini, populi arbitrio tua cana senectus
    spurcata impuris moribus intereat,
non equidem dubito quin primum inimica bonorum
    lingua execta avido sit data vulturio,
effossos oculos voret atro gutture corvus,
    intestina canes, cetera membra lupi.

## CIX

Ivcvndvm, mea vita, mihi proponis amorem
    hunc nostrum inter nos perpetuumque fore.
di magni, facite ut vere promittere possit,
    atque id sincere dicat et ex animo,
ut liceat nobis tota perducere vita
    aeternum hoc sanctae foedus amicitiae.

## CX

Avfilena, bonae semper laudantur amicae :
    accipiunt pretium quae facere instituunt.
tu, quod promisti mihi quod mentire,[1] inimica's :
    quod nec das et fers, turpe facis facinus.
aut facere ingenuae est aut non promisse pudicae,
    Aufilena, fuit : sed data corripere
fraudando officium est [2] plus quam meretricis avarae,
    quae sese toto corpore prostituit.

[1] mentire *P. for* mentita *of codd.*      [2] est *P.*

176

but never hoped, yes, you yourself give yourself back to me. O happy day, blessed with the whiter mark! What living wight is more lucky than I; or who can say that any fortune in life is more desirable than this?

## CVIII

IF, Cominius, your gray old age, soiled as it is by an impure life, should be brought to an end by the choice of the people, I for my part do not doubt that first of all your tongue, the enemy of all good people, would be cut out and quickly given to the greedy vulture, your eyes torn out and swallowed down the raven's black throat, while the dogs would devour your bowels, the rest of your members the wolves.

## CIX

You promise to me, my life, that this love of ours shall be happy and last for ever between us. Ye great gods, grant that she may be able to keep this promise truly, and that she may say it sincerely and from her heart, so that it may be our lot to extend through all our life this eternal compact of hallowed friendship.

## CX

AUFILENA, kind mistresses are always well spoken of; they get their price for what they purpose to do. You are no true mistress, for you promised and now you break faith; you take and do not give, and that is a scurvy trick. To comply were handsome, not to promise were to be chaste; but to take all you can get and cheat one of his due shows a woman more greedy than the most abandoned harlot.

## CXI

AVFILENA, viro contentam vivere solo,
    nuptarumst laus e laudibus eximiis:
sed quoivis quamvis potius succumbere par est,
    quam matrem fratres ex patruo parere.

## CXII

MVLTVS homo es, Naso, neque tecum multus homost
    qui
descendit: Naso, multus es et pathicus.

## CXIII

CONSVLE Pompeio primum duo, Cinna, solebant
    Maeciliam: facto consule nunc iterum
manserunt duo, sed creverunt milia in unum
    singula.    fecundum semen adulterio.

## CXIV

FIRMANO saltu non falso Mentula dives
    fertur, qui tot res in se habet egregias,
aucupia omne genus, piscis, prata, arva ferasque.
    nequiquam: fructus sumptibus exuperat.
quare concedo sit dives, dum omnia desint.
    *saltus laudemus commoda, dum ipse egeat.*

## CXI

Aufilena, to live content with one her husband and
no other husband is a glory for brides one of the
most excellent: but 'tis better to be company for
every one, than that a mother with an uncle should
conceive brothers.

## CXII

You are many men's man, Naso, but not many men
go down town with you: Naso, you are many men's
man and minion.

## CXIII

When Pompey first was consul, Cinna, there were two
that had Maecilia's favours: now he is consul again,
there are still two, but three noughts have grown
up beside each one. A fruitful seed has adultery.

## CXIV

Mentula is truly said to be rich in the possession of
the grant of land at Firmum, which has so many fine
things in it, fowling of all sorts, fish, pasture, corn-
land, and game. All to no purpose; he outruns the
produce of it by his expenses. So I grant that he is
rich, if you will allow that he lacks everything. Let
us admire the advantages of his estate, so long as he
himself is in want.[1]

[1] The reading of the MSS. *saltum laudemus dum modo ipse
egeat* is probably corrupt. M. accepts it, taking *modo* as abl. :
"so long as he himself has no standard of moderation," with
a reference to cxv. 5, 6. The reading in the text is Dr. Post-
gate's (*Journal of Philology*, xxii. 261). Rd. suggests *modio.*

## CXV

Mentvla habet †instar triginta iuginta prati,
  quadraginta arvi : cetera sunt maria.
cur non divitiis Croesum superare potis sit
  uno qui in saltu †totmoda [1] possideat,
prata, arva, ingentis silvas †saltusque paludesque
  usque ad Hyperboreos et mare ad Oceanum ?
omnia magna haec sunt ; tamen ipsest maximus, alter [2]
  non homo sed vero mentula magna minax.

## CXVI

Saepe tibi studioso animo venante requirens
  carmina uti possem mittere Battiadae,
qui te lenirem nobis, neu conarere
  tela infesta * mihi mittere in usque * caput, [3]
hunc video mihi nunc frustra sumptum esse laborem,
  Gelli, nec nostras hic valuisse preces.
contra nos tela ista tua * evitamus amictu * : [4]
  at fixus nostris tu dabi' supplicium.

---

[1] tot bona (*P. from Avant.*), *or* tot qui in saltu uno commoda
*M. :* tot modia opsideat *Rd.*
[2] alter (*P.*) *for* altor, ultro, *of codd.*
[3] *So P. reads for* telis infesta mitteremusque *of codd.*
[4] *Possibly* levi evitamus amictu.

## CXV

MENTULA has something like [1] thirty acres of grazing land, forty of plough-land : [2] the rest is salt water. How can he fail to surpass Croesus in wealth, who occupies so many good things in one estate, pasture, arable, vast woods and cattle-ranges and lakes as far as the Hyperboreans and the Great Sea ?  All this is wonderful : but he himself is the greatest wonder of all, not a man like the rest of us, but a monstrous menacing Mentula.

## CXVI

I HAVE often cast about with busy questing mind [3] how I could send to you some poems of Callimachus with which I might make you placable to me, and that you might not try to send a shower of missiles to reach my head ; but now I see that this labour has been taken by me in vain, Gellius, and that my prayers have here availed nothing.  Now in return I will parry those missiles of yours by wrapping my cloak round my arm ; but you shall be pierced by mine and punished.

---

[1] Or *iuxta* (Scal.) "nearly," or *vester* (P.) "your [Caesar's] friend."  Rd. suggests *transi*, "go and explore for yourself."
[2] Or (*nemoris* M.) "woodland."
[3] Or (*studiose*) "eagerly searching"; or *studioso* may be taken as dative, "at your desire."

# GAI VALERI CATVLLI LIBER

## FRAGMENTA

1.  At non effugies meos iambos.


2.  Hunc lucum tibi dedico consecroque Priape,
    qua domus tua Lampsacist quaque [silva],
        Priape,[1]
    nam te praecipue in suis urbibus colit ora
    Hellespontia ceteris ostreosior oris.


3.  – 0 – 0 0 de meo ligurrire libidost.


4.  [0 – 0 – et Lario imminens Comum.]


5.  Lucida qua splende[n]t [summi] carchesia mali.


[1] quaque propria sedes, *Garrod conj.* silva *added by the Italian editors.*

## FRAGMENTS

1. But you shall not escape my iambics.

2. This inclosure I dedicate and consecrate to thee, O Priapus, at Lampsacus, where is thy house and sacred grove, O Priapus. For thee specially in its cities the Hellespontian coast worships, more abundant in oysters than all other coasts.

3. It is my fancy to taste on my own account.

4. And Comum built on the shore of Lake Larius.

5. With which shines the bright top of the mast.

# TIBULLUS
## TRANSLATED BY
## J. P. POSTGATE

# INTRODUCTION

THE poems which have come down to us under the name of Tibullus consist of three books, the first two of which, published before his death in 19 B.C., were known to antiquity under the titles of *Delia* and *Nemesis*, the mistresses whom they celebrated. The third book (divided by the Renaissance scholars into two), which may be called the Messalla collection, and consisting of pieces by different hands, was added at some later time. Among its contents may be distinguished six elegies by one Lygdamus dedicated to a "Neaera," a panegyric of Messalla in hexameter verse, five short and graceful poems on the love of Sulpicia, a kinswoman of Messalla, for a certain Cerinthus, and possibly written by Tibullus, followed by six very brief pieces by the lady herself, upon which they appear to have been founded, and, lastly, two poems of doubtful authorship, though the first (III. XIX.) claims to be by Tibullus. On these questions, and on that of the name of the poet, generally said to be Albius Tibullus, see Postgate, *Selections from Tibullus* (ed. 2, 1910), pp. xxxiv–li and 179–184.

# INTRODUCTION

The best of the complete extant MSS. is the Ambrosianus (A.), the only one cited in this edition. For the others and the lost or imperfect sources of the text and their values reference should be made to the *praefationes* of the critical editions, or to the Critical Appendix in *Selections from Tibullus,* pp. 200 *sqq.*

The first two editions of Tibullus are that with Catullus, Propertius, and the *Silvae* of Statius by Vindelin de Spira (Venice, 1472), and one of Tibullus alone by Florentius de Argentina, probably published in the same year.

The chief commentaries on Tibullus still of value are Heyne's (4th ed., 1819), Huschke's (1819), and Dissen's (1835), all in Latin. So also Némethy's (1905–6). There is no complete English commentary. Postgate's *Selections* contain the larger half. Modern critical editions are those of Baehrens (1878), Hiller (1885, with Index Verborum, a later recension in the new *Corpus Poetarum Latinorum*), Postgate (Oxford Classical Texts, 1905), Cartault's *Tibulli,* &c. (Paris, 1909). Cartault's *À propos du Corpus Tibullianum* (1906) gives a valuable account of recent contributions. The articles on the poet in Schanz's *Geschichte der römischen Litteratur* (1911) and Teuffel's corresponding history (1910), and Marx's article "Albius" in Pauly-Wissowa's *Realencyclopädie,* may be recommended.

The Latin text here translated is based upon the text and *apparatus criticus* already published in the

# INTRODUCTION

Oxford Classical Texts, and is printed with the permission of the Delegates of the Clarendon Press. Only such notes are appended as are needful to save the reader from misunderstanding.

Square brackets in the translation are used to enclose matter which is not from Tibullus, whether it is a translation of a corrupt original or a conjectural supplement for a gap in the text. In the textual notes $\psi$ indicates a reading found in the inferior manuscripts and probably due to conjecture.

J. P. POSTGATE

*June* 12, 1912

SINCE the above was written there has appeared *The Elegies of Albius Tibullus*, by Kirby Flower Smith (American Book Co., 1913), containing the *Corpus Tibullianum*, Latin text with Introduction and an ample commentary on Books I., II., and IV. II.–XIV. (= III. VIII.-end).

*May* 17, 1914            J. P. POSTGATE

# BOOK I

# TIBVLLI

## LIBER PRIMVS

### 1

Dɪᴠɪᴛɪᴀs alius fulvo sibi congerat auro
    et teneat culti iugera multa soli,
quem labor adsiduus vicino terreat hoste,
    Martia cui somnos classica pulsa fugent:
me mea paupertas vita traducat inerti,
    dum meus adsiduo luceat igne focus.       6
iam mihi, iam possim contentus vivere parvo    25
    nec semper longae deditus esse viae,
sed Canis aestivos ortus vitare sub umbra
    arboris ad rivos praetereuntis aquae.
nec tamen interdum pudeat tenuisse bidentem
    aut stimulo tardos increpuisse boves;     30
non agnamve sinu pigeat fetumve capellae
    desertum oblita matre referre domum.     32
ipse seram teneras maturo tempore vites     7
    rusticus et facili grandia poma manu:
nec Spes destituat sed frugum semper acervos
    praebeat et pleno pinguia musta lacu.     10
nam veneror, seu stipes habet desertus in agris
    seu vetus in trivio florida serta lapis;

192

# TIBULLUS

## THE FIRST BOOK

### I

#### *The Poet's Ideal*

LET others heap up their treasure of yellow gold; let theirs be many acres of well-tilled ground; let them live in constant fighting and alarms with the foeman at their gates, their slumbers routed by the outburst of the signal for the fray. But let the humble fortune that is mine lead me along a quiet path of life, so my hearth but shine with an unfailing fire.

<sup>25</sup> May it now be mine to live for myself, to live contented with my little, and no more be ever vowed to distant marchings; but when the Dog-star rises, to escape its heat beneath some tree's shade with a rill of water fleeting past, nor think it shame to grasp the hoe at times or chide the laggard oxen with the goad, nor a trouble to carry homewards in my arms a ewe lamb or youngling goat forgotten by its dam and left alone.

<sup>7</sup> When the time is ripe, let me plant the tender vines and the stout orchard trees with my own deft hands, a countryman indeed. Nor let Hope disappoint me, but ever vouchsafe the heaped-up corn and rich new wine to fill my vat. For I bend in worship wherever flowery garlands lie on deserted tree-stock in the fields or old stone at a crossway, and

et quodcumque mihi pomum novus educat annus,
    libatum agricolae ponitur ante deo.
flava Ceres, tibi sit nostro de rure corona
    spicea, quae templi pendeat ante fores;
pomosisque ruber custos ponatur in hortis
    terreat ut saeva falce Priapus aves.
vos quoque, felicis quondam, nunc pauperis agri
    custodes, fertis munera vestra, Lares.    20
tunc vitula innumeros lustrabat caesa iuvencos :
    nunc agna exigui est hostia parva soli.
agna cadet vobis, quam circum rustica pubes
    clamet "io, messes et bona vina date."    24
at vos exiguo pecori, furesque lupique,    33
    parcite : de magno praeda petenda grege.
hinc ego pastoremque meum lustrare quot annis
    et placidam soleo spargere lacte Palem.
adsitis, divi, neu vos e paupere mensa
    dona nec e puris spernite fictilibus.—
fictilia antiquus primum sibi fecit agrestis
    pocula, de facili composuitque luto.—    40
non ego divitias patrum fructusque requiro,
    quos tulit antiquo condita messis avo :
parva seges satis est; satis est, requiescere lecto
    si licet et solito membra levare toro.
quam iuvat immites ventos audire cubantem
    et dominam tenero continuisse sinu
aut, gelidas hibernus aquas cum fuderit Auster,
    securum somnos imbre [1] iuvante sequi !
hoc mihi contingat : sit dives iure, furorem
    qui maris et tristes ferre potest pluvias.    50
o quantum est auri pereat potiusque smaragdi,
    quam fleat ob nostras ulla puella vias.

[1] igne *A.*, *which is possible.*

of all my fruit that the fresh season ripens I set the first before the country's guardian god. Ceres of the yellow hair, let my farm produce the spiky wreath to hang before thy temple doors. And in the fruit-laden garden be red Priapus set as watch, to scare the birds with cruel billhook.

19 Ye too, my Lares, who watch over an estate, now poor though thriving once, receive your gifts. Then a slain heifer was peace-offering for uncounted beeves; a lamb is now the humble victim for my narrow plot of ground. A lamb shall fall for you, and round it the country youth shall shout: "Huzza! Send us good crops and wine!"

33 But ye, ye thieves and wolves, have mercy on my scanty flocks; from great herds must ye take your spoil. Here is all I have to make the yearly expiation for my herdsman, and to sprinkle over Pales the milk that makes her kind. Be with me, Gods: nor scorn gifts from a humble board and on clean earthenware. Earthen were the drinking-cups which the ancient yokel made himself, modelling them from pliant clay.

41 I ask not for the riches of my sires or the gains which garnered harvests brought to my ancestors of yore. A small field's produce is enough—enough if I may sleep upon my bed and the mattress ease my limbs as heretofore. What delight to hear the winds rage as I lie and hold my love safe in my gentle clasp; or, when the stormy South Wind sheds the chilling showers, to follow the road of untroubled sleep, the rain my lullaby! This be my lot; let him be rightly rich who can bear the rage of the sea and the dreary rain. Ah, sooner let all the gold and all the emeralds perish from the world than any maiden weep for my departings.

te bellare decet terra, Messalla, marique,
    ut domus hostiles praeferat exuvias :
me retinent vinctum [1] formosae vincla puellae,
    et sedeo duras ianitor ante fores.
non ego laudari curo, mea Delia ; tecum
    dum modo sim, quaeso segnis inersque vocer.
te spectem, suprema mihi cum venerit hora,
    et teneam moriens deficiente manu.        60
flebis et arsuro positum me, Delia, lecto,
    tristibus et lacrimis oscula mixta dabis.
flebis : non tua sunt duro praecordia ferro
    vincta, nec in tenero stat tibi corde silex.
illo non iuvenis poterit de funere quisquam
    lumina, non virgo sicca referre domum.
tu manes ne laede meos, sed parce solutis
    crinibus et teneris, Delia, parce genis.
interea, dum fata sinunt, iungamus amores :
    iam veniet tenebris Mors adoperta caput ;    70
iam subrepet iners aetas, nec amare decebit,
    dicere nec cano blanditias capite.
nunc levis est tractanda venus, dum frangere postes
    non pudet et rixas inseruisse iuvat.
hic ego dux milesque bonus : vos, signa tubaeque,
    ite procul, cupidis vulnera ferte viris,
ferte et opes : ego composito securus acervo
    dites despiciam despiciamque famem.

---

[1] victum ψ, "*defeated,*" *and captive may be right.*

[53] 'Tis right for thee, Messalla, to campaign on land and sea that on thy house's front may show the spoils of foemen: I am a captive fast bound in the bonds of a lovely girl; I sit a janitor before her stubborn doors. I care not for glory, Delia dear; let me only be with thee, and I will pray folk call me sluggard and idler.

[59] May I look on thee when my last hour comes; may I hold thy hand, as I sink, in my dying clasp. Thou wilt weep for me, Delia, when I am laid on the bed that is to burn; thou wilt give me kisses mingled with bitter tears. Thou wilt weep: thy breast is not cased in iron mail; in thy soft heart there is no stubborn flint. From that burial none, neither youth nor maiden, will return with dry eyes home. Do thou hurt not my spirit; but spare thy loosened hair and spare thy soft cheeks, Delia.

[69] Meantime, while Fate allows, let us be one in love. Soon will Death be here with his head cowled in dark. Soon will steal on us the inactive age, nor will it be seemly to play the lover or utter soft speeches when the head is hoar. Now let gay love be my pursuit while it is no shame to break a door down and a joy to plunge into a brawl. 'Tis here I am brave captain and private. Begone, ye trumpets and ensigns! take wounds to the men of greed, and take them wealth. I, safe on my garnered heap, will look down on hunger as I look down on wealth.

# TIBVLLVS

## II

Adde merum vinoque novos compesce dolores,
  occupet ut fessi lumina victa sopor ;
neu quisquam multo percussum tempora baccho
  excitet, infelix dum requiescit amor.
nam posita est nostrae custodia saeva puellae,
  clauditur et dura ianua firma sera.
ianua difficilis domini te verberet imber,
  te Iovis imperio fulmina missa petant.
ianua, iam pateas uni mihi victa querellis,
  neu furtim verso cardine aperta sones.                    10
et mala si qua tibi dixit dementia nostra,
  ignoscas ; capiti sint precor illa meo.
te meminisse decet quae plurima voce peregi
  supplice cum posti florida serta darem.
tu quoque ne timide custodes, Delia, falle.
  audendum est : fortes adiuvat ipsa Venus.
illa favet seu quis iuvenis nova limina temptat
  seu reserat fixo dente puella fores ;
illa docet molli furtim derepere lecto,
  illa pedem nullo ponere posse sono,                       20
illa viro coram nutus conferre loquaces
  blandaque compositis abdere verba notis.
nec docet hoc omnes, sed quos nec inertia
    tardat
  nec vetat obscura surgere nocte timor.
en ego cum tenebris tota vagor anxius urbe,                 25

    .        .        .        .        .        .

nec sinit occurrat quisquam qui corpora ferro            25a
  vulneret aut rapta praemia veste petat.

198

## II

### *To Delia*

MORE wine; let the liquor master these unwonted pains, that on my wearied eyes may fall triumphant sleep; and when the wine god's copious fumes have mounted to my brain, let none awake me from unhappy love's repose. For a cruel watch has been set upon my girl, and the door is shut and bolted hard against me. Door of a stubborn master, may the rain lash thee, and bolts flying at Jupiter's command make thee their mark. Door, now yield to my complaining and open only unto me, and make no sound as thy hinge turns stealthily to let me in. And if my frenzy has ever called ill upon thee, have pardon; let that fall, I pray, on my own head. 'Tis right thou shouldst remember all that I rehearsed in suppliant tones when on thy posts I laid my flowery garlands.

¹⁵ Do thou too, Delia, trick the guard with no faint spirit. Be bold: Venus herself aids the stouthearted. She helps when a lad tries a strange threshold or a lass pushes in the prong to lift the bar from the door. She shows how to creep down stealthily from the pillowed bed; how so to set the foot that it makes no sound; how in the husband's presence to exchange the speaking nods and hide love's language under a code of signs. Nor shows she this to all, but to them whom neither indolence delays nor fear forbids to rise in the murk of night.

²⁵ Lo, I in my wanderings in distress through all the city in the dark [meet with no harm. The goddess shields me] and lets no one cross my path to wound my body with his steel or seize my garments for his

quisquis amore tenetur, eat tutusque sacerque
    qualibet; insidias non timuisse decet.
non mihi pigra nocent hibernae frigora noctis,
    non mihi cum multa decidit imber aqua.     30
non labor hic laedit, reseret modo Delia postes
    et vocet ad digiti me taciturna sonum.
parcite luminibus, seu vir seu femina fias
    obvia: celari vult sua furta Venus.
neu strepitu terrete pedum neu quaerite nomen
    neu prope fulgenti lumina ferte face.
si quis et imprudens aspexerit, occulat ille
    perque deos omnes se meminisse neget:
nam fuerit quicumque loquax, is sanguine natam,
    is Venerem e rapido sentiet esse mari.     40
nec tamen huic credet coniunx tuus, ut mihi verax
    pollicita est magico saga ministerio.
hanc ego de caelo ducentem sidera vidi;
    fluminis haec rapidi carmine vertit iter.
haec cantu finditque solum manesque sepulcris
    elicit et tepido devocat ossa rogo;
iam tenet infernas magico stridore catervas,
    iam iubet aspersas lacte referre pedem.
cum libet, haec tristi depellit nubila caelo:
    cum libet, aestivo convocat orbe nives.     50
sola tenere malas Medeae dicitur herbas,
    sola feros Hecatae perdomuisse canes.
haec mihi composuit cantus, quis fallere posses:
    ter cane, ter dictis despue carminibus.
ille nihil poterit de nobis credere cuiquam,
    non sibi, si in molli viderit ipse toro.

prize. Whosoe'er hath love in his heart may pass in heaven's keeping where he will; no ambush should he fear. The numbing cold of winter's night brings me no hurt, no hurt the heavy downpour of the rain. My sufferings here will harm me not, if Delia but unbar the door and summon me silently with a finger's snap.

[33] Be not busy with your eyes, be you man or woman that we meet. Love's goddess wills her thefts should not be seen. Nor frighten us with noisy feet nor seek our names, nor bring the flashing torch-lights near us. And if any have beheld us unawares, let him hide the knowledge and aver by all the gods that he remembers not. For if any man turn prater, he shall find that Venus is the child of blood and whirling seas.

[41] And yet none such will thy spouse believe, as the honest witch has promised me from her magic rites. I have seen her drawing stars from the sky. Her spells turn the course of the hurrying stream. Her chaunting cleaves the ground, lures the spirit from its tomb, and down from the warm pyre summons the bony frame. Now with magic shrillings she keeps the troops of the grave before her; now she sprinkles them with milk and commands them to retreat. At will she chases the clouds from the frowning heavens; at will she musters the snow in the summer skies. Only she, men say, holds the secret of Medea's deadly herbs, only she has tamed the wild hounds of Hecate.

[53] She framed me a charm to enable thee to deceive: chaunt it thrice and spit thrice when the spell is done. Then will he never trust any one in aught that is said about us, nay, not even his own eyes if he see us on the pillowed bed. Yet from

tu tamen abstineas aliis: nam cetera cernet
  omnia: de me uno sentiet ille nihil.
"quid credam?"[1]  nempe haec eadem se dixit
  amores
  cantibus aut herbis solvere posse meos,               60
et me lustravit taedis, et nocte serena
  concidit ad magicos hostia pulla deos.
non ego totus abesset amor, sed mutuus esset,
  orabam, nec te posse carere velim.
ferreus ille fuit qui, te cum posset habere,
  maluerit praedas stultus et arma sequi.
ille licet Cilicum victas agat ante catervas,
  ponat et in capto Martia castra solo,
totus et argento contextus, totus et auro,
  insideat celeri conspiciendus equo;
ipse boves mea si tecum modo Delia possim
  iungere et in solito pascere monte pecus,
et te dum liceat teneris retinere lacertis,
  mollis et inculta sit mihi somnus humo.
quid Tyrio recubare toro sine amore secundo
  prodest cum fletu nox vigilanda venit?
nam neque tunc plumae nec stragula picta soporem
  nec sonitus placidae ducere possit aquae.
num Veneris magnae violavi numina verbo,
  et mea nunc poenas impia lingua luit?           80
num feror incestus sedes adiisse deorum
  sertaque de sanctis deripuisse focis?
non ego, si merui, dubitem procumbere templis
  et dare sacratis oscula liminibus,
non ego tellurem genibus perrepere supplex
  et miserum sancto tundere poste caput.
at tu, qui laetus rides mala nostra, caveto
  mox tibi: non uni saeviet usque deus.

[1] quin credam? *Baehrens, which is not necessary if the text
is punctuated as above.*

others thou must keep away; since all else will he perceive; only to me will he be blind.

59 "Why should I trust her?" Surely it was she, none other, said that by spells or herbs she could unbind my love. She cleansed me with the torch rite, and in the clear night a dusky victim fell to the gods of sorcery. But my prayer was not that my love might pass entirely, but that it might be shared. I would not choose to be without thee if I could. That man was iron who, when thou mightest have been his, chose rather to follow war and plunder. Let him chase Cilicia's routed troops before him, and pitch his martial camp upon captured ground; let folk gaze upon him as he sits his swift charger, from head to foot a tissue of silver and gold, if only with thee, my Delia, I may put the oxen in the yoke and feed my flock on the familiar hill; and, so my young arms may hold thee fast, I shall find soft slumber even on the rugged earth.

75 What gain is it to lie on Tyrian cushions with Love untoward, when night must pass in waking and weeping? For then can neither pillows of feathers nor broidered coverlets nor the sound of purling waters bring us sleep.

79 Have I wronged the godhead of Venus by aught that I have said, and does my tongue now pay the penalty of sin? Can they say of me that I have wickedly invaded an abode of gods and plucked the garland from the sacred altar? Am I guilty, then I will not shrink to fall prone before her temple and to press kisses on its hallowed threshold, nor to crawl on suppliant knees along the earth and strike my head against the sacred door-posts.

87 Yet thou who dost now rejoice and laugh at my woes must look to thyself ere long; the god will

vidi ego qui iuvenum miseros lusisset amores
    post Veneris vinclis subdere colla senem      90
et sibi blanditias tremula componere voce
    et manibus canas fingere velle comas;
stare nec ante fores puduit caraeve puellae
    ancillam medio detinuisse foro.
hunc puer, hunc iuvenis turba circumterit arta,
    despuit in molles et sibi quisque sinus.
at mihi parce, Venus: semper tibi dedita servit
    mens mea: quid messes uris acerba tuas?


# III


IBITIS Aegaeas sine me, Messalla, per undas,
    o utinam memores ipse cohorsque mei!
me tenet ignotis aegrum Phaeacia terris:
    abstineas avidas Mors modo nigra manus.
abstineas, Mors atra, precor: non hic mihi mater
    quae legat in maestos ossa perusta sinus,
non soror, Assyrios cineri quae dedat odores
    et fleat effusis ante sepulcra comis,
Delia non usquam quae, me quam mitteret urbe,
    dicitur ante omnes consuluisse deos.      10
illa sacras pueri sortes ter sustulit: illi
    rettulit e trinis omnia certa puer.
cuncta dabant reditus: tamen est deterrita
        numquam
    quin fleret nostras respiceretque vias.
ipse ego solator, cum iam mandata dedissem,
    quaerebam tardas anxius usque moras.

not always persecute but one. I have seen the man that had mocked the hapless loves of the young, in later time put his aged neck in the halter of Venus and make soft speeches for himself in quavering tones and turn his hands to dressing his hoary hair: nor did he blush to stand before the doors of the beloved or to stop her maid in the middle of the forum. Round him boys and young men pressed in a jostling crowd, and spat each into his own soft bosom.

**97** Be gentle with me, Venus: my soul is ever thy loyal slave. Why burn thine own corn in thy passion?

## III ×

### *The Poet Sick—To Messalla*

WITHOUT me will ye go, Messalla, across the Aegean wave, yet thinking, oh, I pray, both chief and staff of me. Phaeacia holds me back, sick in a foreign land. Keep off thy greedy hands, I pray, black Death.[1] Black Death, I pray thee keep them off. No mother have I here to gather the burned bones to her grieving bosom; no sister to lavish Assyrian perfumes on my ashes and weep with hair dishevelled by my tomb. Nor any Delia, who, ere from the city she let me go, inquired, they say, of every god. From the boy's hands thrice did she lift a sacred lot, and from the three did the boy make answer to her that all was sure.

**13** All promised a return; yet did nothing stay her from looking back in tears and terror on my journey. Yea, even I her comforter, after I had given my parting charge, sought still in my disquiet

---

[1] The general sense is given. The Latin is corrupt.

aut ego sum causatus aves aut omina dira
    Saturnive sacram me tenuisse diem.
o quotiens ingressus iter mihi tristia dixi
    offensum in porta signa dedisse pedem !       20
audeat invito ne quis discedere Amore,
    aut sciet [1] egressum se prohibente deo.
quid tua nunc Isis mihi, Delia, quid mihi prosunt
    illa tua totiens aera repulsa manu,
quidve, pie dum sacra colis, pureque lavari
    te, memini, et puro secubuisse toro?
nunc, dea, nunc succurre mihi (nam posse mederi
    picta docet templis multa tabella tuis)
ut mea votivas persolvens Delia noctes [2]
    ante sacras lino tecta fores sedeat       30
bisque die resoluta comas tibi dicere laudes
    insignis turba debeat in Pharia.
at mihi contingat patrios celebrare Penates
    reddereque antiquo menstrua tura Lari.
quam bene Saturno vivebant rege, priusquam
    tellus in longas est patefacta vias!
nondum caeruleas pinus contempserat undas,
    effusum ventis praebueratque sinum,
nec vagus ignotis repetens compendia terris
    presserat externa navita merce ratem.       40
illo non validus subiit iuga tempore taurus,
    non domito frenos ore momordit equus,
non domus ulla fores habuit, non fixus in agris,
    qui regeret certis finibus arva, lapis.
ipsae mella dabant quercus, ultroque ferebant
    obvia securis ubera lactis oves.

---

[1] sciet *Doering :* sciat *A.*       [2] noctes *Scaliger :* voces *A.*

for reasons to linger and delay. Either birds or
words of evil omen were my pretexts, or there was
the holy-day of Saturn to detain me. How often,
when my foot was on the road, said I that, stumbling
at the gate, it had warned me of disaster! Let no
man venture to depart when Love says nay; else
shall he learn that a god forbade his going.

<sup>23</sup> What help is there now for me in thy Isis, Delia?
what help in the bronze that was clashed so often in
thy hands? Or what avails it that in thy dutiful ob-
servance of her rites, as I remember well, thou didst
bathe in clean water and sleep apart in a clean bed?

<sup>27</sup> Now aid me, goddess, now—that thou canst heal
saith a crowd of painted panels [1] in thy temples—that
my Delia may pay the nightly vigils of her vow, sitting
all swathed in linen before thy holy door, and twice
in the day be bound to chaunt thy praise with loosened
tresses for all to mark amid the Pharian throng. And
be it mine many times to stand before the shrine of
my sires' Penates and offer incense, as the months
come round, to the old Lar of my home.

<sup>35</sup> How well lived folk in olden days when Saturn
was the king, before the earth was opened out for
distant travel! Not as yet had the pine-tree learned
to swim the blue sea wave or surrendered the spread-
ing sail to belly before the wind; nor, seeking gain in
unknown lands, had the vagrant seaman loaded his
bark with foreign wares. That was a time when the
sturdy bull had not bent his neck to the yoke, nor
the tamed horse champed the bit. No house had
doors; no stone was planted on the land to set fixed
boundaries to men's estates. The very oaks gave
honey; and with milky udders came the ewes un-
bidden to meet the careless swain. Then were no

---

[1] Pictures on slabs of wood, representing the cures.

non acies, non ira fuit, non bella, nec ensem
  immiti saevus duxerat arte faber.
nunc Iove sub domino caedes et vulnera semper,
  nunc mare, nunc leti mille repente viae.          50
parce, pater.   timidum non me periuria terrent,
  non dicta in sanctos impia verba deos.
quod si fatales iam nunc explevimus annos,
  fac lapis inscriptis stet super ossa notis:
HIC IACET IMMITI CONSVMPTVS MORTE TIBVLLVS,
  MESSALLAM TERRA DVM SEQVITVRQVE MARI.
sed me, quod facilis tenero sum semper Amori,
  ipsa Venus campos ducet in Elysios.
hic choreae cantusque vigent, passimque vagantes
  dulce sonant tenui gutture carmen aves;          60
fert casiam non culta seges, totosque per agros
  floret odoratis terra benigna rosis;
ac iuvenum series teneris immixta puellis
  ludit, et adsidue proelia miscet amor.
illic est, cuicumque rapax Mors venit amanti,
  et gerit insigni myrtea serta coma.
at scelerata iacet sedes in nocte profunda
  abdita, quam circum flumina nigra sonant:
Tisiphoneque impexa feros pro crinibus angues
  saevit et huc illuc impia turba fugit;          70
tum niger in porta serpentum Cerberus ore
  stridet et aeratas excubat ante fores.
illic Iunonem temptare Ixionis ausi
  versantur celeri noxia membra rota;
porrectusque novem Tityos per iugera terrae
  adsiduas atro viscere pascit aves.
Tantalus est illic, et circum stagna: sed acrem
  iam iam poturi deserit unda sitim;

marshalled hosts, no lust of blood, no battles; no
swords had been forged by the cruel armourer's
ruthless skill. But now that Jupiter is lord, there
are wounds and carnage without cease; now the sea
slays, and a thousand ways of sudden death.

⁵¹ Spare me, Sire. No broken oaths make me to
fear and tremble, no wicked speech against the holy
gods. But if even now I have fulfilled my destined
span, let a stone be set above my bones, graven with
this legend:

HERE LIES TIBULLUS, RAVISHED BY DEATH'S HAND,
MESSALLA COMRADING O'ER SEA AND LAND.

⁵⁷ But me, for I have been ever pliable to gentle
Love, shall Venus' self escort to the Elysian fields.
There never flags the dance. The birds fly here and
there, fluting sweet carols from their slender throats.
Untilled the field bears cassia, and through all the land
with scented roses blooms the kindly earth. Troops
of young men meet in sport with gentle maidens, and
Love never lets his warfare cease. There are all, on
whom Death swooped because of love; on their hair
are myrtle garlands for all to see.

⁶⁷ But the Wicked Place lies buried in the gulf of
night; and round it black rivers roar. There storms
Tisiphone, wild snakes her unkempt hair; and this
way and that way flees the godless crowd. Then at
the gate upon black Cerberus hiss his wide-mouthed
snakes as he keeps his sentry-watch before the doors
of bronze. There is Ixion, who dared to offer force to
Juno: on the swift wheel whirl his guilty limbs. And
there is Tityos stretched over nine roods of land; on
his black vitals feed the birds that never tire. There
too is Tantalus, and pools around him; but on the
instant, ere he drinks, the wave flies from his raging

o

et Danai proles, Veneris quod numina laesit,
    in cava Lethaeas dolia portat aquas.        80
illic sit quicumque meos violavit amores,
    optavit lentas et mihi militias.
at tu casta precor maneas, sanctique pudoris
    adsideat custos sedula semper anus.
haec tibi fabellas referat positaque lucerna
    deducat plena stamina longa colu;
at circa gravibus pensis adfixa puella
    paulatim somno fessa remittat opus.
tunc veniam subito, nec quisquam nuntiet ante,
    sed videar caelo missus adesse tibi.       90
tunc mihi, qualis eris longos turbata capillos,
    obvia nudato, Delia, curre pede.
hoc precor, hunc illum nobis Aurora nitentem
    Luciferum roseis candida portet equis.

## IV

" Sic umbrosa tibi contingant tecta, Priape,
    ne capiti soles, ne noceantque nives :
quae tua formosos cepit sollertia?  certe
    non tibi barba nitet, non tibi culta coma est ;
nudus et hibernae producis frigora brumae,
    nudus et aestivi tempora sicca Canis."
sic ego : tum Bacchi respondit rustica proles
    armatus curva sic mihi falce deus.
" o fuge te tenerae puerorum credere turbae :
    nam causam iusti semper amoris habent.      10

thirst. And the offspring of Danaus for slighting the godhead of Venus carry the waters of Lethe [1] into leaking butts. There let all be who have profaned my love and who have wished me lingering campaigns.

83 But thou, I pray, continue chaste. Let the aged dame sit ever by thy side to keep thy honour true. She shall tell thee stories when the lamp is in its place, as she draws the long yarn from the loaded distaff, while all around the maids bend over the toilsome task till sleep steals upon them and the work drops from the tired hand. Then of a sudden let me come, and no one bring the news of me; but may I seem to have come from heaven to thy side. Then, just as thou art, with long hair all disordered and feet unsandalled, run to meet me, Delia. For this I pray; thus may that radiant Day-star bless my sight, borne by the rosy horses of the shining Dawn.

## IV

### *To Priapus*

" PRIAPUS, tell me—so may the sheltering shade be thine, nor thy head be harmed by sun or snows— what cunning of thine captures the handsome lads? Sure thou hast no glossy beard nor well-kept hair. Naked thou art all through the cold of stormy winter, naked through the parching season of the Dog-star's heats."

7 Thus I; and thus to me replied the country child of Bacchus, the god armed with the curving billhook:

9 "O beware of trusting thyself to the gentle band of boys; for they furnish always some valid ground for love. One pleases, for he keeps a

[1] Here. and elsewhere a general term for the world below.

hic placet, angustis quod equum compescit habenis ;
  hic placidam niveo pectore pellit aquam ;
hic, quia fortis adest audacia, cepit ; at illi
  virgineus teneras stat pudor ante genas.
sed ne te capiant, primo si forte negabit,
  taedia ; paulatim sub iuga colla dabit.
longa dies homini docuit parere leones,
  longa dies molli saxa peredit aqua ;
annus in apricis maturat collibus uvas,
  annus agit certa lucida signa vice.                     20
nec iurare time : veneris periuria venti
  inrita per terras et freta summa ferunt.
gratia magna Iovi : vetuit Pater ipse valere,
  iurasset cupide quidquid ineptus amor ;
perque suas impune sinit Dictynna sagittas
  adfirmes, crines perque Minerva suos.
at si tardus eris errabis.  transiit [1] aetas
  quam cito !  non segnis stat remeatve dies.
quam cito purpureos deperdit terra colores,
  quam cito formosas populus alta comas.                  30
quam iacet, infirmae venere ubi fata senectae,
  qui prior Eleo est carcere missus equus.
vidi iam iuvenem premeret cum serior aetas
  maerentem stultos praeteriisse dies.
crudeles divi !  serpens novus exuit annos :
  formae non ullam fata dedere moram.
solis aeterna est Baccho Phoeboque iuventas :
  nam decet intonsus crinis utrumque deum.
tu, puero quodcumque tuo temptare libebit,
  cedas : obsequio plurima vincit amor.                   40
neu comes ire neges, quamvis via longa paretur
  et Canis arenti torreat arva siti,

----

[1] transiet *A.*, *a doubtful form.*

tight hand on his horse's rein; another drives the
calm water before a breast of snow. This one takes
you with his brave assurance, that one by the maiden
shame that guards his cheeks.

15 " Perchance at first he will refuse thee; but let
not this dishearten thee. Little by little his neck
will pass beneath the yoke. Length of time teaches
lions to submit to man; with length of time weak
water eats through rock. The year's flight ripens
the grapes on the sunny hillside; the year's flight
carries the radiant signs along their round of change.

21 " Be not afraid to swear. Null and void are the
perjuries of love; the winds bear them over land and
the face of the sea. Great thanks to Jove! The Sire
himself has decreed no oath should stand that love has
taken in the folly of desire. Dictynna lets thee with-
out harm assever by her arrows, Minerva by her hair.

27 " But if thou art slow, thou wilt be lost. Youth
is gone how quickly! Time stands not idle, nor returns.
How quickly does the earth lose its purple hues! how
quickly the tall poplar its beauteous leaves! How
neglected is the horse, when the lot of weak age
overtakes him, that once [1] shot free from the barriers
of Elis! I have seen a young man on whom later
years were closing round mourning for his folly in the
days that had fled. Cruel gods! The snake sheds his
years, and is young: but the Fates grant no respite to
beauty. Only Bacchus and Phoebus have youth ever-
lasting; of either god are unshorn tresses the glory.

39 " Do thou yield to thy lad in aught that he is
minded to attempt: love wins most by compliance.
Nor refuse to go with him, though far be his purposed
journey and the Dog-star bake the land with parching

[1] *prior* seems to be adverbial, rather than adjectival,
" conquering."

# TIBVLLVS

quamvis praetexat [1] picta ferrugine caelum
  venturam minitans imbrifer [1] arcus aquam.
vel si caeruleas puppi volet ire per undas,
  ipse levem remo per freta pelle ratem.
nec te paeniteat duros subiisse labores
  aut opera insuetas atteruisse manus ;
nec, velit insidiis altas si claudere valles,
  dum placeas, umeri retia ferre negent.                    50
si volet arma, levi temptabis ludere dextra ;
  saepe dabis nudum, vincat ut ille, latus.
tunc tibi mitis erit, rapias tum cara licebit
  oscula : pugnabit, sed tibi rapta [2] dabit.
rapta dabit primo, post adferet ipse roganti,
  post etiam collo se implicuisse velit.
heu male nunc artes miseras haec saecula tractant :
  iam tener adsuevit munera velle puer.
at tua, qui venerem docuisti vendere primus,
  quisquis es, infelix urgeat ossa lapis.                   60
Pieridas, pueri, doctos et amate poetas,
  aurea nec superent munera Pieridas.
carmine purpurea est Nisi coma ; carmina ni sint,
  ex umero Pelopis non nituisset ebur.
quem referent Musae, vivet, dum robora tellus,
  dum caelum stellas, dum vehet amnis aquas.
at qui non audit Musas, qui vendit amorem,
  Idaeae currus ille sequatur Opis,
et tercentenas erroribus expleat urbes
  et secet ad Phrygios vilia membra modos.                  70
blanditiis vult esse locum Venus ipsa : querellis
  supplicibus, miseris fletibus illa favet.''

---

[1] praetexens . . . amiciat imbrifer  *A.  The correction,*
*Rigler's is uncertain.*
  [2] sed tamen apta *A.*

drought, though, fringing the sky with hues of purple, the rain-charged bow threaten the coming storm. Should he wish to fly over the blue waves in a boat, take the oar thyself and drive the light bark through the sea. Nor grieve to undergo rough labour or if thy hands are chafed by tasks to which they are strange. If round the deep glen he would place the ambush, then, so thou canst pleasure him, let thy shoulders not refuse to bear the hunting nets. If he would fence, thou wilt try thy light hand at the sport, and often leave thy side unguarded, that he may win.

53 " Then will he be gentle with thee; then thou mayst snatch the precious kiss: he will struggle, but let thee snatch it. He will let thee snatch at first; but later will he bring it for the asking, and presently even he will be fain to hang upon thy neck.

57 " But now, alas! our perverse age plies wretched crafts. Now gentle lads have learned to look for gifts. Whoever thou art that first didst teach the sale of love, may an unhallowed stone weigh heavy on thy bones.

61 " Love the Pierid maidens, lads, and gifted poets; to no golden presents let the Pierian maids succumb. Verse keeps the lock of Nisus [1] purple. Were verses not, no ivory would have shone on Pelops' shoulder. He whom the Muses tell of shall live, while earth bears oaks, sky stars, and rivers water. But he who has no ear for the Muses, who sells his love—let him follow the car of Ops of Ida and traverse, a vagabond, three hundred towns and slash the parts he slights to Phrygian measures. Venus herself allows love's blandishments their play. She sides with piteous weeping and suppliant complaints."

[1] The father of Scylla, whom she betrayed to Minos by severing his purple lock.

haec mihi, quae canerem Titio, deus edidit ore:
    sed Titium coniunx haec meminisse vetat.
pareat ille suae: vos me celebrate magistrum,
    quos male habet multa callidus arte puer.
gloria cuique sua est: me, qui spernentur, amantes
    consultent; cunctis ianua nostra patet.
tempus erit, cum me Veneris praecepta ferentem
    deducat iuvenum sedula turba senem.     80
eheu quam Marathus lento me torquet amore!
    deficiunt artes, deficiuntque doli.
parce, puer, quaeso, ne turpis fabula fiam,
    cum mea ridebunt vana magisteria.

# V

Asper eram et bene discidium me ferre loquebar:
    at mihi nunc longe gloria fortis abest.
namque agor ut per plana citus sola verbere turben
    quem celer adsueta versat ab arte puer.
ure ferum et torque, libeat ne dicere quicquam
    magnificum post haec; horrida verba doma.
parce tamen, per te furtivi foedera lecti,
    per venerem quaeso compositumque caput.
ille ego cum tristi morbo defessa iaceres
    te dicor votis eripuisse meis;
ipseque te circum lustravi sulpure puro,     10
    carmine cum magico praecinuisset anus;
ipse procuravi, ne possent saeva nocere,
    somnia, ter sancta deveneranda mola;

⁷³ These things did the god's voice utter for me to sing to Titius; but them doth Titius' wife forbid him to remember. So let *him* listen to his dear; but do ye throng to my school whom some crafty lad with many wiles treats ill. Each of us has his proper glory. Let slighted lovers seek advice from me; to all my doors are open. A time shall come when round the master of the lore of Venus shall crowd the attentive young and take the old man home.

⁸¹ Alas! what lingering torture is this love for Marathus: helpless is my skill, and helpless all my cunning. Spare me, I pray thee, boy, lest I become a byword, when folk shall laugh at my useless teaching.

## V

### *To Delia*

I WAS angry. I vowed I could bear our severance well. But now my proud vaunting has left me far and far away. For I am driven as a top that springs before the lash over the level ground, whirled by a quick boy's practised art.

⁵ Bring brands and tortures for the untamed creature, that he may have no love of talking loud hereafter: quell his wild utterances.

⁷ Yet spare me, by the bonds of our stealthy union, I entreat thee, by our love and the head that has lain by mine. It was I, they say, whose vows snatched thee from peril when thou layest exhausted in sickness' gloomy hold. It was I that scattered all about thee the cleansing sulphur, the beldame first chaunting her magic spell. I appeased the cruel Dreams that had thrice to be propitiated with offering of holy meal, that they might work no harm.

ipse ego velatus filo tunicisque solutis
  vota novem Triviae nocte silente dedi.
omnia persolvi : fruitur nunc alter amore,
  et precibus felix utitur ille meis.
at mihi felicem vitam, si salva fuisses,
  fingebam, demens, et renuente deo.                    20
" rura colam, frugumque aderit mea Delia custos,
  area dum messes sole calente teret,
aut mihi servabit plenis in lintribus uvas
  pressaque veloci candida musta pede.
consuescet numerare pecus ; consuescet amantis
  garrulus in dominae ludere verna sinu.
illa deo sciet agricolae pro vitibus uvam,
  pro segete spicas, pro grege ferre dapem.
illa regat cunctos, illi sint omnia curae :
  at iuvet in tota me nihil esse domo.                  30
huc veniet Messalla meus, cui dulcia poma
  Delia selectis detrahat arboribus ;
et, tantum venerata decus,[1] hunc sedula curet,
  huic paret atque epulas ipsa ministra gerat."
haec mihi fingebam quae nunc Eurusque Notusque
  iactat odoratos vota per Armenios.
saepe ego temptavi curas depellere vino :
  at dolor in lacrimas verterat omne merum.
saepe aliam tenui : sed iam cum gaudia adirem,
  admonuit dominae deseruitque Venus.                   40
tunc me discedens devotum femina dixit,
  a pudet, et narrat scire nefanda meam.
non facit hoc verbis, facie tenerisque lacertis
  devovet et flavis nostra puella comis.

---

[1] decus *editor :* virum *A. against the metre ; see "Classical
Quarterly,"* VI. *40.*

In woollen headdress and ungirdled tunic I made nine vows to Trivia in the stilly night. All have I paid; but another hath now my love. He is the fortunate one, and reaps the fruit of all my prayers. Yet I used to dream that, if thou wert spared, there would be a happy life for me. Madman! a god said No.

21 "In the country," I said, "I will live. My Delia shall be there to keep watch upon the grain, while the threshing-floor winnows the harvest in the blazing sun; or she shall watch the grapes in the brimming trough when the quick feet tread the gleaming must. She shall learn to count the flock; she shall teach the prattling serf-child to play on a loving mistress' lap. To the god that tends the country she will know what gifts to offer—for vines a cluster, spiked ears for cornfield, drink offering for flock. All folk shall she direct, and all things be her care. I shall love to be but a cipher in the house. Hither shall come my own Messalla. From chosen trees shall Delia pull him down sweet fruit. In homage to his greatness she shall give him zealous tendance, and prepare and carry him the repast, herself his waiting-maid."

35 Such were my dreams and prayers, now tost from East Wind unto South over all Armenia's scented land.

37 Often have I sought to banish love's troubles with strong drink; but pain turned all the wine to tears. Often have I held another in my arms; but on the very brink of delight Love bade me think of my mistress and forsook me. Then the woman, departing, declared me bewitched, and spread the tale (oh, shame!) that my love was versed in unholy arts. Not by charms does my lass do this. 'Tis her beauty, soft arms and golden hair bewitch me. Such was

talis ad Haemonium Nereis Pelea quondam
    vecta est frenato caerula pisce Thetis.
haec nocuere mihi.   quod adest huic dives amator,
    venit in exitium callida lena meum.
sanguineas edat illa dapes atque ore cruento
    tristia cum multo pocula felle bibat;          50
hanc volitent animae circum sua fata querentes
    semper, et e tectis strix violenta canat;
ipsa fame stimulante furens herbasque sepulcris
    quaerat et a saevis ossa relicta lupis;
currat et inguinibus nudis ululetque per urbes,
    post agat e triviis aspera turba canum.
eveniet; dat signa deus: sunt numina amanti,
    saevit et iniusta lege relicta Venus.
at tu quam primum sagae praecepta rapacis
    desere: nam donis vincitur omnis amor.      60
pauper erit praesto tibi semper; pauper adibit
    primus et in tenero fixus erit latere;
pauper in angusto fidus comes agmine turbae
    subicietque manus efficietque viam;
pauper †ad occultos furtim deducet amicos,†[1]
    vinclaque de niveo detrahet ipse pede.
heu canimus frustra nec verbis victa patescit
    ianua sed plena est percutienda manu.
at tu, qui potior nunc es, mea fata[2] timeto:
    versatur celeri Fors levis orbe rotae.      70
non frustra quidam iam nunc in limine perstat
    sedulus ac crebro prospicit ac refugit

---

[1] *Corrupt.* adhuc luteos suris deducet amictus *editor*—i.e.,
"*will draw the still muddy coverings* ["*fasciae* quibus crura
*vestiuntur,*" *Quint.* XI. 3, 143] *from thy calves.*"
[2] furta *A., which means* "*intriguing on my part.*" *Then* qui-
dam *71 would mean* "*I.*"

Thetis, the sea-blue Nereid, when in old days she rode on her bridled fish to Peleus of Haemonia.

⁴⁷ These charms have been my bane. A rich lover waits for the lass. So the crafty bawd is bent on my undoing. May the hag's food be mixed with blood. May the cup she puts to her gory lips be bitterly charged with gall. May ghosts flit round her always, bemoaning their fate, and the fierce vampire bird shrill from her roof; and she herself, frantic from hunger's goad, hunt for weeds upon the graves and for bones which the wild wolves have left, and with middle bare run and shriek through the towns, and a savage troop of dogs from the crossways chase her from behind.

⁵⁷ Thus shall it be. A god gives the sign. There are powers to guard the lover, and Love shows no ruth, when left for a lawless tie.

⁵⁹ But do thou, Delia, with all speed leave the school of the grasping witch. There is no love that gifts will not master. The poor man will ever be at hand for thy service; he will come to thee first and cleave to thy tender side. The poor man, a trusty companion in the trooping crowds, will push below with his hands and make thee a way. The poor man [will take thee privately to the abodes of his friends] and himself unlace the boots from thy snowy feet.

⁶⁷ Alas! in vain do I sing; no words will win her door to open. Nay, the hand that knocks upon it must be filled.

⁶⁹ But thou who art victor now must fear that my fate awaits thee. Chance turns lightly on her swift-rolling wheel. Not without reason even now some one stands patient on the threshold, looks oft in front, retreats, feigns to pass by the house, but

221

et simulat transire domum, mox deinde recurrit
  solus et ante ipsas exscreat usque fores.
nescio quid furtivus amor parat.  utere, quaeso,
  dum licet: in liquida nam [1] tibi linter aqua.


## VI


SEMPER ut inducar blandos offers mihi vultus,
  post tamen es misero tristis et asper, Amor.
quid tibi, saeve, rei mecum est?  an gloria magna
    est
  insidias homini composuisse deum?
nam mihi tenduntur casses; iam Delia furtim
  nescio quem tacita callida nocte fovet.
illa quidem iurata negat, sed credere durum est:
  sic etiam de me pernegat usque viro.
ipse miser docui, quo posset ludere pacto
  custodes: heu heu nunc premor arte mea.      10
fingere tunc didicit causas ut sola cubaret,
  cardine tunc tacito vertere posse fores;
tunc sucos herbasque dedi quis livor abiret
  quem facit impresso mutua dente venus.
at tu, fallacis coniunx incaute puellae,
  me quoque servato, peccet ut illa nihil,
neu iuvenes celebret multo sermone caveto
  neve cubet laxo pectus aperta sinu,
neu te decipiat nutu, digitoque liquorem
  ne trahat et mensae ducat in orbe notas.      20
exibit cum [2] saepe, time, seu visere dicet
  sacra Bonae maribus non adeunda Deae.

[1] nam *A.*, nat *ψ vulg.*
[2] cum *corrected MSS. :* quam *A.*

soon runs back again alone, and hawks without cease
before the very door. Stealthy Love has some scheme
afoot. Take thy good, I beg, while thou mayst; for
in calm [1] waters is thy shallop.


# VI

## *To Delia*

Love, thou dost always meet me with smiling visage
to draw me on; but after that, poor wretch, I find
thee frowning and angry. What hast thou to do
with me, cruel boy? Is there great glory to a god
in laying snares for a man?

5 For the net is spread to take me; now cunning
Delia clasps a gallant covertly in the hush of night.
She denies it, indeed, and on oath; but 'tis hard to
believe her. Thus touching me, too, she denies every
hour to her husband. Poor wretch, it was I who taught
her the ways of tricking her watchers, and now alas!
by my own craft am I sore bestead. Then learned she
how to frame excuses for lying alone, and then how to
turn the door without a sound from the hinges. Then I
gave her juices and herbs to efface the dark signs which
the teeth in love's communion imprint upon the flesh.

15 And thou, the unwary mate of a faithless wife,
watching me with the rest that she may never sin,
take care that she talk not much or oft with young
men, nor use nods to deceive thee, or recline with loose
robe and bosom bare; and see she take not wine on
her fingers and trace signs on the table's round.
Have thy fears when she goes out often, or if she say
that she would witness the rites of the Good Goddess
which no male must go nigh.

---

[1] *liquida*, literally "clear," "transparent."

at mihi si credas, illam sequar unus ad aras;
    tunc mihi non oculis sit timuisse meis.
saepe, velut gemmas eius signumque probarem,
    per causam memini me tetigisse manum;
saepe mero somnum peperi tibi, at ipse bibebam
    sobria supposita pocula victor aqua.
non ego te laesi prudens: ignosce fatenti:
    iussit Amor.  contra quis ferat arma deos?     30
ille ego sum, nec me iam dicere vera pudebit,
    instabat tota cui tua nocte canis.
quid tenera tibi coniuge opus?  tua si bona nescis
    servare, frustra clavis inest foribus.
te tenet, absentes alios suspirat amores
    et simulat subito condoluisse caput.
at mihi servandam credas: non saeva recuso
    verbera, detrecto non ego vincla pedum.
tum procul absitis, quisquis colit arte capillos,
    et fluit effuso cui toga laxa sinu;     40
quisquis et occurret, ne possit crimen habere,
    † stet procul aut alia stet procul ante via.†
sic fieri iubet ipse deus, sic magna sacerdos
    est mihi divino vaticinata sono.
haec, ubi Bellonae motu est agitata, nec acrem
    flammam, non amens verbera torta timet;
ipsa bipenne suos caedit violenta lacertos
    sanguineque effuso spargit inulta deam,
statque latus praefixa veru, stat saucia pectus,
    et canit eventus quos dea magna monet.     50

²³ But trust her to my keeping; and I, I only, will attend her to that altar. Then for my eyes need I have no fear.¹

²⁵ Many a time on the plea of judging her gem and its image can I remember how I touched her hand. Many a time my neat wine has put thee to sleep whilst *I* drank in triumph the sober cup of substituted water. I did not wrong thee of purpose—forgive me, now I own it—'twas at Love's bidding. And who may fight against a god? It was I—nor will I blush to speak the truth—whom thy dog was menacing the whole night through!

³³ What good is a gentle wife to thee? If thine own treasures thou canst not guard, the key is vainly turned in the door. Her arms are round thee; but her sighs are for another, an absent love. And of a sudden she feigns the throes of headache.

³⁷ Thou shouldst trust her to *my* keeping. Then I recoil not from torturing stripes, nor shrink from shackles on my feet. Then far be ye all who dress your hair with art and whose togas fall slack with copious folds. And let whosoever meets us, that no sin may be his, [stand aloof or pass by another road.]

⁴³ That this be done doth God himself command; and this hath the great priestess revealed to me with voice inspired. She, when Bellona's impulse drives her, fears in that frenzy neither searching flames nor twisted scourge. Fiercely with axe in hand she hacks at her own arms. With the gushing blood is the goddess sprinkled; but she goes without scathe. Erect with wounds on her breast, erect with the spit standing out from her side, she chaunts the words of fate that the great goddess prompts. "See to it that

¹ "It will be no profanation"—the penalty for which was blindness.

" parcite quam custodit Amor violare puellam,
    ne pigeat magno post didicisse malo.
attigerit, labentur opes, ut vulnere nostro
    sanguis, ut hic ventis diripiturque cinis."
et tibi nescio quas dixit, mea Delia, poenas :[1]
    si tamen admittas, sit precor illa levis.
non ego te propter parco tibi, sed tua mater
    me movet atque iras aurea vincit anus.
haec mihi te adducit tenebris multoque timore
    coniungit nostras clam taciturna manus ;            60
haec foribusque manet noctu me adfixa proculque
    cognoscit strepitus me veniente pedum.
vive diu mihi, dulcis anus : proprios ego tecum,
    sit modo fas, annos contribuisse velim.
te semper natamque tuam te propter amabo :
    quidquid agit, sanguis est tamen illa tuus.
sit modo casta, doce, quamvis non vitta ligatos
    impediat crines nec stola longa pedes.
et mihi sint durae leges, laudare nec ullam
    possim ego quin oculos appetat illa meos ;         70
et si quid peccasse putet, ducarque capillis
    immerito pronas proripiarque vias.
non ego te pulsare velim, sed, venerit iste
    si furor, optarim non habuisse manus.
nec saevo sis casta metu, sed mente fideli ;
    mutuus absenti te mihi servet amor.

     •      •      •      •      •

at quae fida fuit nulli, post victa senecta
    ducit inops tremula stamina torta manu
firmaque conductis adnectit licia telis
    tractaque de niveo vellere ducta putat.           80
hanc animo gaudente vident iuvenumque catervae
    commemorant merito tot mala ferre senem ;

---

[1] nescio quam ... poenam Baehrens, *which is easier.*

ye do no despite to the maid whom love doth guard,
lest hereafter a great mischief lesson you to your woe.
If any touch her, his fortune shall waste as the blood
doth from my wound, and as these ashes are scattered
by the wind."

55 And for thee, my Delia, she named a punish-
ment. If notwithstanding thou shouldst sin, I pray
let her be merciful. Not for thyself do I spare thee.
It is thy aged mother moves me; before her golden
nature sinks my wrath. She brings me to thee in
the dark, and in fear and trembling secretly and
silently she joins our hands. Fast by the door at
night she waits for me and knows afar the noise of
my coming feet. Long life to thee still, dear
dame. Did but heaven allow, to thy stock of years
would I add my own. I will love thee always,
and thy daughter for thy sake; whatever she does,
she is of thy blood after all. Only teach her to be
chaste, though no band of the matrons' fillets con-
fines her hair, nor their long robe her feet.

69 And for me let there be hard terms; let me
never praise a woman without *her* flying at my eyes,
and if she should think I have done her wrong, let
me be taken by the hair, though I be guiltless, and
pitched forward down the steep. I would not wish
to strike thee, Delia, but if such madness come to me,
I would pray to have no hands. Yet be not chaste
through cruel fear, but by loyal heart; and when
absent, let love on thy side keep thee safe for me. . . .

77 [The faithful have their reward.] But she whom
no one has found true, thereafter poor and bowed
with age draws out the twisted yarn with shaking
hand and for hire fastens firm the leashes to the loom
and pulls and cleans the handfuls of snowy wool. The
troops of young are glad at heart to see her plight,
and declare that she deserves to suffer so many woes in

# TIBVLLVS

hanc Venus ex alto flentem sublimis Olympo
    spectat et infidis quam sit acerba monet.
haec aliis maledicta cadant: nos, Delia, amoris
    exemplum cana simus uterque coma.

## VII

Hvnc cecinere diem Parcae fatalia nentes
    stamina, non ulli dissoluenda deo:
hunc fore,[1] Aquitanas posset qui fundere gentes,
    quem tremeret forti milite victus Atax.[2]
evenere: novos pubes Romana triumphos
    vidit et evinctos bracchia capta duces:
at te victrices lauros, Messalla, gerentem
    portabat nitidis currus eburnus equis.
non sine me est tibi[3] partus honos: Tarbella Pyrene
    testis et Oceani litora Santonici,      10
testis Arar Rhodanusque celer magnusque Garunna,
    Carnutis et flavi caerula lympha Liger.
an te, Cydne, canam, tacitis qui leniter undis
    caeruleus placidis per vada serpis aquis,
quantus et aetherio contingens vertice nubes
    frigidus intonsos Taurus alat Cilicas?
quid referam ut volitet crebras intacta per urbes
    alba Palaestino sancta columba Syro,
utque maris vastum prospectet turribus aequor
    prima ratem ventis credere docta Tyros,    20
qualis et, arentes cum findit Sirius agros,
    fertilis aestiva Nilus abundet aqua?

---

[1] *Or* hoc fore.

[2] *As Atax is a river of the Roman Province, probably either* quom [cum] tremeret (*ed.*) *should be read, or else* Atur (*a river of Aquitania, modern Adour*) *with Scaliger. See "Classical Review," XXII. pp. 112 seq.*

[3] non sine marte ibi *Baehrens;* cf. *"Pan." 107.*

228

age. Venus from her throne on high Olympus looks upon her weeping, and bids us mark how sharp she is with the faithless. Upon others, Delia, let these curses fall: but let us twain still be pattern lovers when our hair is white.

## VII

### *The Triumph of Messalla*

Of this day sang the Parcae as they span the thread of doom which no god can untwist—that this should be the day to put the folk of Aquitaine to rout, to make the Aude to tremble, by a valiant soldiery overpowered. So hath it come about. The men of Rome have seen new triumphs, and chiefs with shackles on their captive arms, whilst thou, Messalla, wearing the conqueror's bays, wast borne in ivory car by steeds of shining white.

⁹ Not without me was thy glory won: witness Tarbellian Pyrenees and the shores of Ocean by Saintonge; witness Saône and swift-running Rhône and great Garonne, with Loire, blue stream of the blonde tribes of Chartres.

¹³ Or, Cydnus, shall I sing of thee whose silent wave steals bluely through the waters of the still lagoon? Or how with head that reaches to the clouds extends chill Taurus, the feeder of Cilicia's long-haired sons? Why should I recount how from town to town unharmed flies the white dove that the Syrians of Palestine revere? How Tyre, first town that learned to trust the ship to the mercy of the wind, looks out from her towers across the vast sea-plain? Or how, when Sirius splits the parching fields, through all the heats life-giving Nile is full in flood?

Nile pater, quanam possim te dicere causa
    aut quibus in terris occuluisse caput?
te propter nullos tellus tua postulat imbres,
    arida nec pluvio supplicat herba Iovi.
te canit atque suum pubes miratur Osirim
    barbara, Memphiten plangere docta bovem.
primus aratra manu sollerti fecit Osiris
    et teneram ferro sollicitavit humum,       30
primus inexpertae commisit semina terrae
    pomaque non notis legit ab arboribus.
hic docuit teneram palis adiungere vitem,
    hic viridem dura caedere falce comam;
illi iucundos primum matura sapores
    expressa incultis uva dedit pedibus.
ille liquor docuit voces inflectere cantu,
    movit et ad certos nescia membra modos:
Bacchus et agricolae magno confecta labore
    pectora laetitiae [1] dissoluenda dedit;     40
Bacchus et adflictis requiem mortalibus adfert,
    crura licet dura compede pulsa sonent.
non tibi sunt tristes curae nec luctus, Osiri,
    sed chorus et cantus et levis aptus amor,
sed varii flores et frons redimita corymbis,
    fusa sed ad teneros lutea palla pedes
et Tyriae vestes et dulcis tibia cantu
    et levis occultis conscia cista sacris.
huc ades et Genium ludis centumque choreis
    concelebra et multo tempora funde mero;     50
illius et nitido stillent unguenta capillo,
    et capite et collo mollia serta gerat.

---

[1] laetitiae *Muretus:* tristitiae *A. vulg.*

²³ For what cause, Father Nile, or in what lands may I declare that thou hast hid thy head? Because of thee thy Egypt never sues for showers, nor does the parched blade bow to Jove the Rain-giver. Thou art sung and worshipped, as their own Osiris, by the barbarous folk brought up to wail the ox of Memphis.

²⁹ It was Osiris' cunning hand that first made ploughs and vexed the young earth with the iron share. He first entrusted seed to the untried earth, and gathered fruits from unknown trees. He showed how to join the young vine and the pole, he how to lop its green leaves with the stern pruning-hook. For him the ripe grape-clusters, which rugged feet had crushed, first yielded up their pleasant tastes; their juice taught men to guide the voice through changing strains, and bade untutored limbs move to a measure true.

³⁹ When the breast of the countryman is crushed with his heavy toil, it is the wine-god makes it over to gladness to be loosened from its bonds; 'tis the wine-god brings relief to mortals in distress, though cruel shackles clank upon their legs.

⁴³ Harsh cares and grief are not for thee, Osiris, but dance and songs and lightsome love. Yea, flowers of many hues and brows with the berried ivy circled, and robe of saffron flowing over youthful feet, raiment of Tyre and sweet-singing pipe and the light basket with its mystery of holy things.

⁴⁹ Then hither come, and with a hundred sports and dances do honour to the Birth-sprite, and let wine in plenty bathe his temples. From his glistening hair let the ointment drip, and on his head and neck let soft garlands hang. Thus come to us to-day, Birth-spirit; and I will bring thee offering

sic venias hodierne Geni;[1] tibi turis honores,
  liba et Mopsopio dulcia melle feram.
at tibi succrescat proles quae facta parentis
  augeat et circa stet veneranda senem.
nec taceat monumenta viae, quem Tuscula tellus
  candidaque antiquo detinet Alba Lare.
namque opibus congesta tuis hic glarea dura
  sternitur, hic apta iungitur arte silex.     60
te canet agricola, a magna cum venerit urbe
  serus, inoffensum rettuleritque pedem.
at tu, Natalis multos celebrande per annos,
  candidior semper candidiorque veni.


# VIII


Non ego celari possum, quid nutus amantis
  quidve ferant miti lenia verba sono.
nec mihi sunt sortes nec conscia fibra deorum,
  praecinit eventus nec mihi cantus avis:
ipsa Venus magico religatum bracchia nodo
  perdocuit multis non sine verberibus.
desine dissimulare; deus crudelius urit,
  quos videt invitos succubuisse sibi.
quid tibi nunc molles prodest coluisse capillos
  saepeque mutatas disposuisse comas,     10
quid fuco splendente genas ornare, quid ungues
  artificis docta subsecuisse manu?
frustra iam vestes, frustra mutantur amictus
  ansaque compressos colligit arta pedes.

---

[1] hodierne Geni; tibi *editor :* hodierne tibi; dem *A. vulg.*

of incense and cakes sweetened with honey from the
land of Mopsopus.[1]

55 But for thee, my friend, let a progeny spring up
to add fresh exploits to their sire's, and stand in their
distinctions about the old man's chair.

57 And let *him* not be silent on the great work
of thy road [2] whom the fields of Tusculum or white
Alba's ancient homesteads keep from the city. For,
heaped up through thy bounty, here is laid hard
gravel, and there are flint blocks featly joined. The
dweller in the country shall sing thy praise when he
has come at night from the great city and brought
his foot home without tripping.

63 But thou, Birth-spirit, come to thy honours for
many a year—come ever brighter and brighter still.

## VIII

### *To Pholoe on Marathus*

No one can hide from me the meaning of a lover's
nod, nor the message of gentle tones and whispered
words. Yet no lots help me, no liver with heaven's
will acquainted, nor do birds' notes tell me of the
things to come. 'Twas Venus' self that tied my arms
with magic knots and taught me all with many stripes.

7 Have done with concealments. God has fiercer
fires for those that he sees have fallen to him against
their will.

9 What advantage hast thou now in dressing the
soft hair or shifting continually the arrangement of
the tresses, what in beautifying cheeks with lustrous
pigment, in having the nails pared by an artist's
cunning hand? In vain thy gowns, thy shawls
are changed, and the tight loop squeezes the feet

---

[1] An old king of Attica.   [2] A section of the *Via Latina*.

illa placet, quamvis inculto venerit ore
  nec nitidum tarda compserit arte caput.
num te carminibus, num te pallentibus herbis
  devovit tacito tempore noctis anus ?
cantus vicinis fruges traducit ab agris,
  cantus et iratae detinet anguis iter,    20
cantus et e curru Lunam deducere temptat,
  et faceret, si non aera repulsa sonent.
quid queror heu misero carmen nocuisse, quid
    herbas ?
  forma nihil magicis utitur auxiliis :
sed corpus tetigisse nocet, sed longa dedisse
  oscula, sed femori conseruisse femur.
nec tu difficilis puero tamen esse memento :
  persequitur poenis tristia facta Venus.
munera ne poscas : det munera canus amator,
  ut foveat molli frigida membra sinu.    30
carior est auro iuvenis, cui levia fulgent
  ora nec amplexus aspera barba terit.
huic tu candentes umero suppone lacertos,
  et regum magnae despiciantur opes.
at Venus inveniet puero concumbere furtim,
  dum timet et teneros conserit usque sinus,
et dare anhelanti pugnantibus umida linguis
  oscula et in collo figere dente notas.
non lapis hanc gemmaeque iuvant, quae frigore
    sola
  dormiat et nulli sit cupienda viro.    40
heu sero revocatur amor seroque iuventas
  cum vetus infecit cana senecta caput.
tum studium formae est ; coma tum mutatur, ut
    annos
  dissimulet viridi cortice tincta nucis ;
tollere tum cura est albos a stirpe capillos
  et faciem dempta pelle referre novam.

still in its flowering springtide see that thou use it.
Not slow are its feet as it glides away.

⁴⁹ Nor torture Marathus. What glory is there in
discomfiting a boy? Be hard, my lass, to the effete
old. Spare the tender shoot, I pray. Naught ails
him gravely; 'tis from excess of passion comes the
yellow stain upon his skin. See again, poor wretch,
how often he heaps his piteous reproaches on the
absent and all around is flooded with his tears.

⁵⁵ "Why dost thou slight me?" he complains.
"The watch might have been baffled. Heaven itself
gives the lovesick skill to cozen. I know the secret
ways of love, how the breath may be taken gently,
and how kisses may be snatched and make no sound.
I can steal up e'en in the dead of night, and unseen
unbar the door without a sound. But what do arts
avail if the girl spurn the hapless swain and, cruel,
fly from the very couch of love? Then again when
she promises and suddenly plays false, I must wake
through a night of many woes. While I fondly
think that she will come to me, in every stir I hear
her footfall sounding."

⁶⁷ Shed tears no more, lad. Her heart is stone, and
thy eyes are already worn and swelled with weeping.
The gods, I warn thee, Pholoe, abhor disdain. 'Twill
be vain to offer incense to their holy fires. This is the
Marathus that once made mock of wretched lovers,
unwitting that behind him stood the god of ven-
geance. Often, too, we have heard, he laughed at
the tears of anguish and kept a lover waiting with
pretences for delay. Now he abhors all coyness;
now he hates every door that is bolted fast against
him. But for thee, girl, unless thou cease to be proud,
there is punishment in store. Then how wilt thou
long that prayers might bring thee back to-day!

## IX

Qvid mihi, si fueras miseros laesurus amores,
    foedera per divos, clam violanda, dabas ?
a miser, et si quis primo periuria celat,
    sera tamen tacitis Poena venit pedibus.
parcite, caelestes : aequum est impune licere
    numina formosis laedere vestra semel.
lucra petens habili tauros adiungit aratro
    et durum terrae rusticus urget opus ;
lucra petituras freta per parentia ventis
    ducunt instabiles sidera certa rates.        10
muneribus meus est captus puer.   at deus illa
    in cinerem et liquidas munera vertat aquas.
iam mihi persolvet poenas, pulvisque decorem
    detrahet et ventis horrida facta coma ;
ureter facies, urentur sole capilli,
    deteret invalidos et via longa pedes.
admonui quotiens "auro ne pollue formam :
    saepe solent auro multa subesse mala.
divitiis captus si quis violavit amorem,
    asperaque est illi difficilisque Venus.        20
ure meum potius flamma caput et pete ferro
    corpus et intorto verbere terga seca.
nec tibi celandi spes sit peccare paranti :
    scit deus, occultos qui vetat esse dolos.
ipse deus tacito permisit †lene† [1] ministro
    ederet ut multo libera verba mero ;

---

[1] *Corrupt.*  vina (*editor*) *is taken for the version*

## IX

### *To Marathus*

WHY, if thou wast to wrong my helpless love, didst thou pledge thy faith to me before the gods but to break it privily? Unhappy! even if at first we hide the perjury, yet in the end comes Punishment on noiseless feet. Still spare him, powers above. 'Tis not unjust if for *one* sin against your godhead beauty should pay no forfeit.

⁷ 'Tis in quest of gain the countryman yokes his bulls to his good plough and plies his hard work on the land; it is gain that the swaying ships pursue when the sure stars guide them through seas that the winds control. And by gifts has my lad been captured. But may God turn them to ashes and running water.

¹³ Ere long he will make me full amends; his comeliness will be lost amid the dust and the winds that roughen his hair; his face, his curls will be burned by the sun, and long travel will disable his tender feet.

¹⁷ How many times have I warned him: "Let not gold sully beauty; under gold there often lurks a multitude of ills. Whosoever has let wealth tempt him to outrage love, with him is Venus fierce and obdurate. Rather burn my head with fire, stab my body with steel, and cut my back with the twisted scourge. And have no hope of concealment when thou art planning wrong. God knows of it, and lets no treachery stay hid. God himself has set [wine] within the reach of a tongue-tied servant, that with much strong drink his speech might flow free.

ipse deus somno domitos emittere vocem
    iussit et invitos facta tegenda loqui.''
haec ego dicebam : nunc me flevisse loquentem,
    nunc pudet ad teneros procubuisse pedes.      30
tunc mihi iurabas nullo te divitis auri
    pondere, non gemmis vendere velle fidem,
non tibi si pretium Campania terra daretur,
    non tibi si Bacchi cura Falernus ager.
illis eriperes verbis mihi sidera caeli
    lucere et pronas fluminis esse vias.
quin etiam flebas : at non ego fallere doctus
    tergebam umentes credulus usque genas.
quid faciam, nisi et ipse fores in amore puellae ?
    sit precor, exemplo sit levis illa tuo.      40
o quotiens, verbis ne quisquam conscius esset,
    ipse comes multa lumina nocte tuli !
saepe insperanti venit tibi munere nostro
    et latuit clausas post adoperta fores.
tum miser interii, stulte confisus amori : [1]
    nam poteram ad laqueos cautior esse tuos.
quin etiam attonita laudes tibi mente canebam :
    at me nunc nostri Pieridumque pudet.
illa velim rapida Vulcanus carmina flamma
    torreat et liquida deleat amnis aqua.      50
tu procul hinc absis, cui formam vendere cura
    est
et pretium plena grande referre manu.
at te qui puerum donis corrumpere es ausus
    rideat adsiduis uxor inulta dolis,
et cum furtivo iuvenem lassaverit usu,
    tecum interposita languida veste cubet.

[1] amori *the corrected MSS. :* amari *A.*

Heaven itself has bidden the lips that slumber had
sealed to open and to speak unwillingly of deeds
that should have lain in the dark."

**29** So used I to say to thee. Now I am ashamed
that I wept as I spoke, that I fell at thy tender feet.
Then thou wouldst swear to me that for no weight
of precious gold or for pearls wouldst thou sell thy
faith, nay, not if Campania's land were given thee
as the price, or Falernum's fields that Bacchus tends.
Such words could have robbed me of my certainty that
stars shine in skies and that rivers run downward.
Nay, more, thou wouldst weep; but I unversed in
deceit would ever fondly wipe the water from thy
cheeks.

**39** What should I have done hadst thou not thyself
been in love with a maid? May she be fickle—
fickle, I pray, taking pattern by thee. Oh, how
oft in the late night, that none should be privy
to thy wooing, did I myself attend thee with the
light in my hand! Often, when thou didst not hope
for her, she came through my good offices, and stood
hid, a veiled figure, behind the fast shut door. Then,
poor wretch, was my undoing; I fondly trusted to
Love: I might have been warier of thy snares. Nay,
in my craze of mind I made verses in thy honour;
but now I am ashamed for myself and the Muses.
May the Fire-god shrivel those verses with devouring
flame, or the river wash them out in its running
waters. Go thou far hence whose aim is to sell thy
beauty and to return with a great wage filling thy
hand.

**53** And thou who durst corrupt the boy with thy
gifts, may thy wife unpunished make a constant jest
of thee by her intrigues; and when the gallant is
spent with her furtive dalliance, let her lie by thee lax

semper sint externa tuo vestigia lecto
  et pateat cupidis semper aperta domus;
nec lasciva soror dicatur plura bibisse
  pocula vel plures emeruisse viros.          60
illam saepe ferunt convivia ducere baccho,
  dum rota Luciferi provocet orta diem;
illa nulla queat melius consumere noctem
  aut operum varias disposuisse vices.
at tua perdidicit; nec tu, stultissime, sentis,
  cum tibi non solita corpus ab arte movet.
tune putas illam pro te disponere crines
  aut tenues denso pectere dente comas?
istane persuadet facies, auroque lacertos
  vinciat et Tyrio prodeat apta sinu?         70
non tibi sed iuveni cuidam vult bella videri,
  devoveat pro quo remque domumque tuam.
nec facit hoc vitio, sed corpora foeda podagra
  et senis amplexus culta puella fugit.
huic tamen accubuit noster puer: hunc ego credam
  cum trucibus venerem iungere posse feris.
blanditiasne meas aliis tu vendere es ausus,
  tune aliis demens oscula ferre mea?
tum flebis, cum me vinctum puer alter habebit
  et geret in regno regna superba tuo.        80
at tua tum me poena iuvet, Venerique merenti
  fixa notet casus aurea palma meos:
HANC TIBI FALLACI RESOLVTVS AMORE TIBVLLVS
  DEDICAT ET GRATA SIS DEA MENTE ROGAT.

with the coverlet between. Let there be always
stranger tracks upon thy bed, and thy house be always
free and open to the amorous. Nor let it be said that
her wanton sister can drain more cups or exhaust
more gallants. She, folk say, prolongs her wine-
bibbing revels till the wheels of the Light-bringer
rise to summon forth the day. Than she could none
lay out the night hours better, or arrange the different
modes of love.

⁶⁵ But thy spouse has learned it all, and yet thou,
poor fool, dost notice naught when she moves her
limbs with an unaccustomed art. Dost thou think
that it is for thee that she arranges her hair and
through her fine tresses passes the close-toothed
comb? Is it *thy* beauty prompts her to clasp gold
on her arms and come forth arrayed in Tyrian
drapery? Not thee, but a certain youth would she
have find her charming. For him she would consign
to ruin thee and all thy house. Nor does she this out
of depravity; but the dainty girl shrinks from limbs
that gout disfigures and an old man's arms.

⁷⁵ Yet by him has my own lad lain. I could believe
that he would mate with a savage beast. Didst thou
dare, mad youth, to sell caresses that belonged to me
and to take to others the kisses that were mine? Thou
wilt weep, then, when another lad has made me his
captive and shall proudly reign in thy realm.

⁸¹ In that hour of thy punishment I shall rejoice,
and a golden palm-branch shall be put up to Venus
for her goodness, with this record of my fortunes:

TIBULLUS WHOM FROM TREACHEROUS LOVE, GODDESS,
    THOU DIDST UNBIND
OFFERS THEE THIS AND BEGS THEE KEEP FOR HIM A
    THANKFUL MIND.

# TIBVLLVS

## X

Qvis fuit, horrendos primus qui protulit enses?
  quam ferus et vere ferreus ille fuit!
tum caedes hominum generi, tum proelia nata,
  tum brevior dirae mortis aperta via est.
an nihil ille miser meruit, nos ad mala nostra
  vertimus, in saevas quod dedit ille feras?
divitis hoc vitium est auri, nec bella fuerunt,
  faginus astabat cum scyphus ante dapes.
non arces, non vallus erat, somnumque petebat
  securus varias dux gregis inter oves.          10
tunc mihi vita foret †vulgi† nec tristia nossem
  arma nec audissem corde micante tubam.
nunc ad bella trahor, et iam quis forsitan hostis
  haesura in nostro tela gerit latere.
sed patrii servate Lares: aluistis et idem,
  cursarem vestros cum tener ante pedes.
neu pudeat prisco vos esse e stipite factos:
  sic veteris sedes incoluistis avi.
tunc melius tenuere fidem, cum paupere cultu
  stabat in exigua ligneus aede deus.            20
hic placatus erat, seu quis libaverat uvam
  seu dederat sanctae spicea serta comae;
atque aliquis voti compos liba ipse ferebat
  postque comes purum filia parva favum.
at nobis aerata, Lares, depellite tela,

  hostiaque e plena rustica porcus hara.

## X

*Against War*

Who was the first discoverer of the horrible sword? How savage was he and literally iron! Then slaughter and battles were born into the world of men: then to grisly death a shorter road was opened.

5 But perhaps, poor wretch, he is to blame in nothing, but we turn to our mischief what he gave us to use against the savage wild beast. This is the curse of precious gold; nor were there wars when the cup of beechwood stood beside men's food. There were no citadels, no palisades, and void of care the flock's commander courted sleep with his sheep of divers hue around him.

11 In that age would I have lived nor known grim warfare or heard the trumpet-call with beating heart. Now am I dragged to war; and some foeman, maybe, already bears the weapon that is to be buried in my side.

15 Yet save me, Lares of my fathers! Ye too did rear me when I ran, a little child, before your feet. And feel it not a shame that ye are made of but an ancient tree-stock. Such were ye when ye dwelt in the home of my grandsire long ago. Then faith was better kept, when a wooden god stood poorly garbed in a narrow shrine. His favour was won when a man had offered a bunch of grapes as first fruits, or laid the spiky garland on the holy hair. And one who had gained his prayer would with his own hands bring the honey-cake, his little daughter following with the pure honeycomb in hers.

25 O Lares, turn the bronze javelins away from me [and as thankoffering for my safe return shall

hanc pura cum veste sequar myrtoque canistra
 vincta geram, myrto vinctus et ipse caput.
sic placeam vobis : alius sit fortis in armis,
 sternat et adversos Marte favente duces,    30
ut mihi potanti possit sua dicere facta
 miles et in mensa pingere castra mero.
quis furor est atram bellis accersere Mortem ?
 imminet et tacito clam venit illa pede.
non seges est infra, non vinea culta, sed audax
 Cerberus et Stygiae navita turpis aquae ;
illic pertussisque [1] genis ustoque capillo
 errat ad obscuros pallida turba lacus.
quin potius laudandus hic est quem prole parata
 occupat in parva pigra senecta casa !    40
ipse suas sectatur oves, at filius agnos,
 et calidam fesso comparat uxor aquam.
sic ego sim, liceatque caput candescere canis
 temporis et prisci facta referre senem.
interea pax arva colat. pax candida primum
 duxit araturos sub iuga curva boves ;
pax aluit vites et sucos condidit uvae,
 funderet ut nato testa paterna merum ;
pace bidens vomerque nitent, at tristia duri
 militis in tenebris occupat arma situs.—[2]    50
rusticus e lucoque vehit, male sobrius ipse,
 uxorem plaustro progeniemque domum.—
sed veneris tunc bella calent, scissosque capillos
 femina, perfractas conqueriturque fores ;
flet teneras subtusa genas : sed victor et ipse
 flet sibi dementes tam valuisse manus.
at lascivus Amor rixae mala verba ministrat,
 inter et iratum lentus utrumque sedet.

    [1] pertusisque *Livineius :* percussisque *A.*
    [2] *Something appears to be lost here.*

fall . . .] and a hog from the full sty, a farmer's victim.
With it will I follow in clean apparel, and bear the
basket bound with myrtle, even as the myrtle binds
my hair. Thus may I find favour in your eyes. Let
another be stout in war and, Mars to aid him, lay
the hostile chieftains low, that, while I drink, he
may tell me of his feats in fighting and draw the
camp in wine upon the table.

**33** What madness is it to call black Death to us
by warfare! It is ever close upon us: it comes un-
seen on silent feet. Below there are neither corn-
lands nor well-kept vineyards; only wild Cerberus
and the ill-favoured mariner of the stream of Styx.
There wanders a sallow throng beside the dusky
pools with eyeless sockets and fire-ravaged hair.

**39** Nay, the hero is he whom, when his children are
begotten, old age's torpor overtakes in his humble
cottage. He follows his sheep, his son the lambs,
while the good wife heats the water for his weary
limbs. So let me live till the white hairs glisten on
my head and I tell in old man's fashion of the days
gone by. Let Peace in the meantime tend our fields.
Bright Peace first led the oxen under curved yoke to
plough. Peace made the vine plants grow and stored
the grape juice that from the father's jars might
pour wine for the son. In peace shine hoe and
ploughshare; but the grisly arms of the rugged
soldier rust preys on in the dark.

**51** Then the yeoman drives back from the grove,
himself half sober, with wife and offspring in his wain.

**53** Then love's war rages hotly; and women
lament that hair is torn and doors are broken.
The fair weeps for the buffets on her tender cheek;
but the conqueror weeps too that his mad hands were
so strong; while freakish Love feeds the feud with

a lapis est ferrumque, suam quicumque puellam
    verberat : e caelo deripit ille deos.         60
sit satis e membris tenuem rescindere vestem,
    sit satis ornatus dissoluisse comae,
sit lacrimas movisse satis ; quater ille beatus
    quo tenera irato flere puella potest.
sed manibus qui saevus erit, scutumque sudemque
    is gerat et miti sit procul a Venere.
at nobis, Pax alma, veni spicamque teneto,
    profluat et pomis candidus ante sinus.

bitter speeches, and sits in unconcern between the
angry pair. Ah, he is stone and iron who would beat
his lass : this is to drag the gods down from the sky.
Be it enough to tear the light robe from her limbs,
and to disorder the fair arrangement of her hair :
enough to cause her tears to flow. Thrice happy he
whose anger can make a soft lass weep! But he
whose hands are cruel should carry shield and stake
and keep afar from gentle Venus.

[67] Then come to us, gracious Peace; grasp the
cornspike in thy hand, and from the bosom of thy
white robe let fruits pour out before thee.

# BOOK II

# LIBER SECVNDVS

## I

Qvisqvis adest, faveat: fruges lustramus et agros,
    ritus ut a prisco traditus extat avo.
Bacche, veni, dulcisque tuis e cornibus uva
    pendeat, et spicis tempora cinge, Ceres.
luce sacra requiescat humus, requiescat arator,
    et grave suspenso vomere cesset opus.
solvite vincla iugis; nunc ad praesepia debent
    plena coronato stare boves capite.
omnia sint operata deo; non audeat ulla
    lanificam pensis imposuisse manum.          10
vos quoque abesse procul iubeo, discedat ab aris,
    cui tulit hesterna gaudia nocte Venus.
casta placent superis: pura cum veste venite
    et manibus puris sumite fontis aquam.
cernite, fulgentes ut eat sacer agnus ad aras
    vinctaque post olea candida turba comas.
di patrii, purgamus agros, purgamus agrestes:
    vos mala de nostris pellite limitibus,

# THE SECOND BOOK

## I

### *The Country Festival*[1]

ALL present hush. We purify the crops and lands in the fashion handed down from our ancestors of old. Come to us, Bacchus, with the sweet grape cluster hanging from thy horns, and, Ceres, wreathe thy temples with the corn-ears.

5 Upon this holy day let earth, let ploughman rest. Hang up the share and let the heavy labour cease. Loose from the yokes their straps; now by the well-filled manger must the oxen stand with garlands round their heads. Let all things be at the service of the god; let no spinner choose to set her hand to the task of wool. Ye too I bid stand far away—let none be nigh the altar to whom Love's goddess gave her pleasures yesternight. The powers above ask purity. Clean be the raiment that ye come in, and clean the hands to take the waters from the spring. Mark how to the shining altar goes the holy lamb, and behind the white procession; the olive binds their hair.

17 Gods of our sires, we cleanse the farms, we cleanse the farming folk. Do ye outside our boundaries drive all evil things. Let not our sown fields

1 The *Ambarvalia*, celebrated in late spring or early summer, at different times in different places. See *Classical Quarterly*, III. (1909), pp. 127 *sqq.*

neu seges eludat messem fallacibus herbis,
   neu timeat celeres tardior agna lupos.       **20**
tunc nitidus plenis confisus rusticus agris
   ingeret ardenti grandia ligna foco,
turbaque vernarum, saturi bona signa coloni,
   ludet et ex virgis extruet ante casas.
eventura precor : viden ut felicibus extis
   significet placidos nuntia fibra deos ?
nunc mihi fumosos veteris proferte Falernos
   consulis et Chio solvite vincla cado.
vina diem celebrent; non festa luce madere
   est rubor, errantes et male ferre pedes.     **30**
sed "bene Messallam" sua quisque ad pocula dicat,
   nomen et absentis singula verba sonent.
gentis Aquitanae celeber Messalla triumphis
   et magna intonsis gloria victor avis,
huc ades aspiraque mihi, dum carmine nostro
   redditur agricolis gratia caelitibus.
rura cano rurisque deos.   his vita magistris
   desuevit querna pellere glande famem ;
illi compositis primum docuere tigillis
   exiguam viridi fronde operire domum ;     **40**
illi etiam tauros primi docuisse feruntur
   servitium et plaustro supposuisse rotam.
tum victus abiere feri, tum consita pomus,
   tum bibit inriguas fertilis hortus aquas,
aurea tum pressos pedibus dedit uva liquores
   mixtaque securo est sobria lympha mero.

mock the reaping with defaulting blade. Let not our slow lambs fear the swifter wolves. Then[1] the sleek rustic, full of trust in his teeming fields, will heap huge logs upon his blazing hearth; and a young troop of home-born slaves, fair signs that show a lusty yeoman, will play about and build them huts of sticks before the fire. My prayers are heard. See in the favouring entrails how the liver-markings bear a message that the gods are gracious.

[27] Now from the old bin bring me out the smoked Falernians and loose the bands of the Chian jar.[2] Let drinking be the order of the day. Now we keep holiday, and to be tipsy is no shame, nor to carry ill our unsteady feet. But let each one, as he drinks, cry, "Health to Messalla!" and in every utterance be the name of the absent heard.

[33] Messalla, now the talk of all for thy triumph over the race of Aquitaine, whose victories cover thy unshorn ancestors with glory, hither come and breathe upon me while with my song I pay thanksgiving to the powers that tend the fields.

[37] I sing the country and the country's gods. They were the guides when man first ceased to chase his hunger with the acorns from the oak. They taught him first to put the planks together and cover his humble dwelling with green leaves. They too, 'tis told, trained bulls to be his slaves, and placed the wheel beneath the wain. Then savage habits passed away; then was the fruit-tree planted, and the thriving garden drank the water from the rills. Then the golden grapes gave up their juices to the trampling feet, and sober water was mixed with cheering wine.

---

[1] In the cold weather, after the autumn sowing.

[2] The heady Falernian and the light Chian were a favourite blend. The consul's name on the label showed the year. *Falernos*, sc. *cados*.

rura ferunt messes, calidi cum sideris aestu
  deponit flavas annua terra comas.
rure levis verno flores apis ingerit alveo,
  compleat ut dulci sedula melle favos.         50
agricola adsiduo primum satiatus aratro
  cantavit certo rustica verba pede,
et satur arenti primum est modulatus avena
  carmen, ut ornatos diceret ante deos;
agricola et minio suffusus, Bacche, rubenti
  primus inexperta duxit ab arte choros.
huic datus a pleno memorabile munus ovili
  dux pecoris curtas auxerat hircus opes.
rure puer verno primum de flore coronam
  fecit et antiquis imposuit Laribus.        60
rure etiam teneris curam exhibitura puellis
  molle gerit tergo lucida vellus ovis.
hinc et femineus labor est, hinc pensa colusque,
  fusus et adposito pollice versat opus;
atque aliqua adsiduae textrix operata minervae [1]
  cantat, et a pulso [2] tela sonat latere.
ipse quoque inter agros interque armenta Cupido
  natus et indomitas dicitur inter equas.
illic indocto primum se exercuit arcu:
  ei mihi, quam doctas nunc habet ille manus!   70
nec pecudes, velut ante, petit: fixisse puellas
  gestit et audaces perdomuisse viros.
hic iuveni detraxit opes, hic dicere iussit
  limen ad iratae verba pudenda senem;
hoc duce custodes furtim transgressa iacentes
  ad iuvenem tenebris sola puella venit,

---

[1] assidue minervam . . . *A.*, *which requires the change of*
textrix *to* textis.

[2] a pulso *Muretus:* appulso *A.*

From the country comes our harvest, when in heaven's glowing heat the earth is yearly shorn of her shock of yellow hair. Through the country flits the bee in spring-time, heaping the hive with flowers in her zeal to fill the combs with the honey sweet.

51 Then first the countryman, sated with ploughing without cease, sang rustic words in time and tune; and, full of meat, first composed a song on the dry oat-pipes to chaunt before the gods that his hands had dressed. And, Bacchus, it was a countryman that first dyed his skin with red vermilion and wound through the dance with unpractised art. It was he too that, offering from all his fold a gift to tell about, the he-goat, leader of the flock, gained increase for his scanty wealth.

59 In the country the lad first made a circlet from the flowers of spring and placed it on the ancient Lares' head. Of the country too is the sheep that will ere long make trouble for gentle girls with the soft fleece it wears upon its glistening back. Thence comes the toil of women's hands, the weighed wool and the distaff, and the spindle that twists its work 'twixt thumb and finger; and weaving women in unremitting service to Minerva sing while the loom clatters as the clay weights swing.

67 Desire too himself, they say, was born amid the fields, amid the cattle and the unbridled mares. There first he practised with prentice bow. Ah, me! what expert hands has he now! Nor are beasts his mark as heretofore. His joy is to pierce maids' hearts and make the bold man bite the dust. He strips the young of their wealth; the old he forces to shameful speech at the threshold of an angry fair. He guides the girl who stealthily steps by prostrate watchers and comes alone to her lover in

R                                                          257

et pedibus praetemptat iter suspensa timore,
   explorat caecas cui manus ante vias.
a miseri, quos hic graviter deus urget ! at ille
   felix, cui placidus leniter adflat Amor.      80
sancte, veni dapibus festis ; sed pone sagittas
   et procul ardentes hinc precor abde faces.
vos celebrem cantate deum pecorique vocate
   voce ; palam pecori, clam sibi quisque vocet.
aut etiam sibi quisque palam : nam turba iocosa
   obstrepit et Phrygio tibia curva sono.
ludite : iam Nox iungit equos, currumque sequuntur
   matris lascivo sidera fulva choro,
postque venit tacitus furvis circumdatus alis
   Somnus et incerto Somnia nigra pede.      90

## II

Dicamvs bona verba : venit Natalis ad aras :
   quisquis ades, lingua, vir mulierque, fave.
urantur pia tura focis, urantur odores
   quos tener e terra divite mittit Arabs.
ipse suos Genius adsit visurus honores,
   cui decorent sanctas mollia serta comas.
illius puro destillent tempora nardo,
   atque satur libo sit madeatque mero,
adnuat et, Cornute, tibi, quodcumque rogabis.
   en age (quid cessas ? adnuit ille) roga.      10

the night, high strung with fear, her feet feeling her path before her while her hand is advanced to find passage through the dark.

79 Ah, wretched they upon whom our god bears hardly; and happy is he on whom Love in his graciousness breathes gently. Come to our festal cheer, holy lord. But, prithee, lay aside thy arrows, and far from us put away thy burning torch.

83 Do ye chaunt the god whom all adore, and loudly call him for your herd. Let each one call him for the herd aloud, but in a whisper for himself. Or aloud too for himself: for the merriment of the throng and the bent pipe's Phrygian note will drown the prayer. So take your sport. Now Night is yoking her team; and on their mother's car follow the golden Stars, a capering troupe, while behind comes Sleep the silent, enwrapped in dusky wings, and black Visions of the night with wavering steps.

## II ✓

### To Cornutus on his Birthday

LET naught but good words pass our lips : the Birth-sprite cometh to the altar. Whoso art with us, man or woman, peace ! Let its fire burn the holy incense, burn the spices which the soft Arabian sends us from his wealthy land. Let the Genius come to view the offering to himself. Soft garlands must deck his hallowed locks ; his temples must drop with spikenard pure ; he must be filled with honey-cake and tipsy with neat wine. And to whatsoever thou askest, Cornutus, must he bow assent. See, quick ! Why laggest thou ? He bows, and thou must ask. I

auguror, uxoris fidos optabis amores;
   iam reor hoc ipsos edidicisse deos.
nec tibi malueris, totum quaecumque per orbem
   fortis arat valido rusticus arva bove,   ✓
nec tibi, gemmarum quidquid felicibus Indis
   nascitur, Eoi qua maris unda rubet.
vota cadunt: viden ut [1] strepitantibus advolet alis
   flavaque coniugio vincula portet Amor,
vincula quae maneant semper dum tarda senectus
   inducat rugas inficiatque comas.     20
eveniat,[2] Natalis, avis prolemque ministret,
   ludat et ante tuos turba novella pedes.

# III

Rvra meam, Cornute, tenent villaeque puellam:
   ferreus est, heu heu, quisquis in urbe manet.
ipsa Venus latos iam nunc migravit in agros,
   verbaque aratoris rustica discit Amor.
o ego, cum [3] aspicerem dominam, quam fortiter illic
   versarem valido pingue bidente solum
agricolaeque modo curvum sectarer aratrum,
   dum subigunt steriles arva serenda boves!
nec quererer quod sol graciles exureret artus,
   laederet et teneras pussula rupta manus.     10
pavit et Admeti tauros formosus Apollo;
   nec cithara intonsae profueruntve comae,
nec potuit curas sanare salubribus herbis:
   quidquid erat medicae vicerat artis amor.     14

---

[1] viden ut *the corrected MSS.:* utinam *A.*   *The correction is*
*uncertain.*      [2] eveniat *Housman:* hic veniat *A.*
[3] dum, *"provided that," Heyne, is not improbable.*

divine that thou wilt pray for thy wife's true love:
by now methinks the gods have learnt this well.
Thou wouldst not have rather for thine own all the
fields in the whole world that stout yeomen plough
with sturdy steers, nor for thine own all pearls soever
that grow for India the blest by the red waters of the
Eastern sea.

[17] 'Tis done as thou dost pray.[1] See, on rustling
wings Love flies to thy side with yellow bands to
bind thy spouse—bands never to be loosed till
dragging age bring wrinkles to her brow and bleach
her hair. May the sign come true, Birth-spirit, and
bring them offspring, and may a troop of younglings
play before thy feet.

## III

### Nemesis is taken to the Country

In country and farmhouse bides my girl, Cornutus.
Ah, me! he is iron who can stay in town. Venus
herself has moved into the spreading fields and Love is
learning the rustic speech of ploughmen. Oh, when I
looked upon my mistress, how stoutly there with my
sturdy hoe would I turn the fertile soil and follow
the curved plough as a tiller of the fields, while the
barren oxen forced the clods up for the sowing! Nor
would I murmur that the sun burned my slender
limbs or that broken blisters hurt my delicate
hands.

[11] Apollo, too, the beautiful, fed the bulls of
Admetus; nor did his lute and hair unshorn avail
him aught, nor could he cure his trouble by health-
giving herbs. Love had triumphed o'er all resources

---

[1] *cadunt*, "fall," "happen," a metaphor from dice.

ipse deus solitus stabulis expellere vaccas     14*a*
    *dicitur* . . .

et miscere novo docuisse coagula lacte,     14*b*
    lacteus et mixtis obriguisse liquor.     14*c*

tunc fiscella levi detexta est vimine iunci,
    raraque per nexus est via facta sero.

o quotiens illo vitulum gestante per agros
    dicitur occurrens erubuisse soror !

o quotiens ausae, caneret dum valle sub alta,
    rumpere mugitu carmina docta boves !     20

saepe duces trepidis petiere oracula rebus,
    venit et a templis inrita turba domum ;

saepe horrere sacros doluit Latona capillos,
    quos admirata est ipsa noverca prius.

quisquis inornatumque caput crinesque solutos
    aspiceret, Phoebi quaereret ille comam.

Delos ubi nunc, Phoebe, tua est, ubi Delphica Pytho ?
    nempe Amor in parva te iubet esse casa.

felices olim, Veneri cum fertur aperte
    servire aeternos non puduisse deos.     30

fabula nunc ille est : sed cui sua cura puella est,
    fabula sit mavult quam sine amore deus.

at tu, quisquis is es, cui tristi fronte Cupido
    imperat ut nostra sint tua castra domo

. . . . .

ferrea non venerem sed praedam saecula laudant :
    praeda tamen multis est operata malis.

praeda feras acies cinxit discordibus armis ;
    hinc cruor, hinc caedes mors propiorque venit.

of the healer's art. The god became accustomed
to drive the kine from the byre, ['tis said] . . . and
taught the way of mixing rennet with new milk, and
the milky stream curdled at its touch. Then was the
cheese-basket woven from the bulrushes' light stems,
and here and there through their interlacings a passage
left for the whey. Oh, how often as he went through
the fields, a calf in his arms, do they say, his sister
met him and blushed! Oh, how often, while he was
singing deep in the valley, did the kine with their
lowings rudely break in on the artistic verse! Often
did chiefs seek oracles from him in times of trouble
and the company go home in disappointment from
his temple. Often did Latona grieve for the un-
kemptness of the sacred hair which before had been a
marvel to his stepmother herself. Whoever had seen
his head undecked and hair all loose would have asked
indeed where were the locks of Phoebus. Where,
Phoebus, is thy Delos now, and where thy Delphian
Pytho? Why, Love bids thee house in a humble cot.

29 Happy the men of olden days, when they tell
that gods eternal were not ashamed to be the open
slaves of passion. Now is he the talk of all. But one
that loves his girl would liefer be the talk of all than
a god without a love.

32 And thou, whosoever thou art, whom frowning
Love now bids make warfare in my house . . .[1]

35 It is not love but booty that this iron age
applauds. Yet booty is concerned in a multitude of
ills. Booty buckles the armour of strife on the raging
hosts; hence bloodshed comes, hence slaughter, and
death approaches nigher than before. Booty bade

---

[1] The sense of the lost lines was probably, "Beware, my
successful rival, of reverses in your turn. A richer lover may
supplant you."

praeda vago iussit geminare pericula ponto,
  bellica cum dubiis rostra dedit ratibus.                    40
praedator cupit immensos obsidere campos,
  ut multa innumera iugera pascat ove ;
cui lapis externus curae est, urbisque tumultu
  portatur validis mille columna iugis,
claudit et indomitum moles mare, lentus ut intra
  neglegat hibernas piscis adesse minas.
at mihi laeta trahant Samiae convivia testae
  fictaque Cumana lubrica terra rota.
heu heu divitibus video gaudere puellas:
  iam veniant praedae, si Venus optat opes :        50
ut mea luxuria Nemesis fluat utque per urbem
  incedat donis conspicienda meis.
illa gerat vestes tenues, quas femina Coa
  texuit, auratas disposuitque vias ;
illi sint comites fusci, quos India torret
  Solis et admotis inficit ignis equis ;
illi selectos certent praebere colores
  Africa puniceum purpureumque Tyros.
nota loquor.   regnum ipse tenet, quem saepe coegit
  barbara gypsatos ferre catasta pedes.              60
at tibi, dura seges, Nemesim quae abducis ab urbe,
  persolvat nulla semina Terra fide.
et tu, Bacche tener, iucundae consitor uvae,
  tu quoque devotos, Bacche, relinque lacus.
haud impune licet formosas tristibus agris
  abdere ; non tanti sunt tua musta, pater.

men double the perils on the surging deep when it
fitted the beaks of war to the rocking ships. 'Tis the
freebooter who longs to seize upon the measureless
plains, that on many an acre he may graze his count-
less sheep. His fancy turns to foreign marbles, and
through the quaking city his column is carried by a
thousand sturdy teams. For him the mole confines
the tameless sea, that unconcerned inside the fish
may reck naught of the storm that blusters near.
But in *my* feast's happy course let there be only the
pottery of Samos or the slippery clay that Cumae's
wheels have shaped.

⁴⁹ Alas! I see that maidens' hearts are set upon
the rich. Then come booty, if Love desires wealth,
that my Nemesis may float in finery and step it
through the city, in bravery a gift from me! Let
her wear the gossamer robe which some woman of
Cos has woven and laid it out in golden tracks.¹
Let hers be the dusky pages that India scorches and
the Sun's fire tans as he drives so near. Let the
lands vie to give her their choicest dyes, Afric the
crimson and Tyre the purple.

⁵⁹ What I say all know. That very man has now
a kingdom who on the barbarians' platform has oft
been forced to move his gypsumed feet.²

⁶¹ For thee, cruel field, that drawest Nemesis away
from town, may Earth fail utterly to pay the grain
she owes thee. And thou, soft Bacchus, planter of
the pleasant grape-vine, do thou too, Bacchus, leave
the vats that we have cursed. No one may bury
fair maids 'mid dreary fields without a punishment.
Thy new wine, Sire, is not worth this price. Oh, let

¹ The *viae* are the stripes or bands woven into the cloth.
² Slaves were exposed for sale on a platform (*catasta*) with
their feet smeared with gypsum.

o valeant fruges, ne sint modo rure puellae;
  glans alat et prisco more bibantur aquae.
glans aluit veteres, et passim semper amarunt;
  quid nocuit sulcos non habuisse satos?      70
tunc, quibus aspirabat Amor, praebebat aperte
  mitis in umbrosa gaudia valle Venus.
nullus erat custos, nulla exclusura dolentes
  ianua.   si fas est, mos precor ille redi.

      .      .      .      .

  horrida villosa corpora veste tegant.
nunc si clausa mea est, si copia rara videndi,
  heu miserum, laxam quid iuvat esse togam?
ducite: ad imperium dominae sulcabimus agros;
  non ego me vinclis verberibusque nego.      80


## IV

Hic mihi servitium video dominamque paratam:
  iam mihi, libertas illa paterna, vale.
servitium sed triste datur, teneorque catenis,
  et numquam misero vincla remittit Amor,
et seu quid merui seu nil peccavimus, urit.
  uror, io, remove, saeva puella, faces.
o ego, ne possem tales sentire dolores,
  quam mallem in gelidis montibus esse lapis,
stare vel insanis cautes obnoxia ventis,
  naufraga quam vasti tunderet unda maris!    10
nunc et amara dies et noctis amarior umbra est;
  omnia nam tristi tempora felle madent.

the corn go, so there are no lasses in the country; let
acorns be our fare and water our drink in the olden
way. Acorns were the food of the ancients, and
they had love always wherever they were. What
hurt to them if they had no furrows sown with seed?

71 Then to those on whom Love's god breathed
kindly did gentle Venus bring open pleasures in the
shady vales. No watchers were there, nor door to
close against the anguished. If it be not wrong, old
custom, I pray thee to return. [Then . . . and let]
rough limbs be clad in shaggy raiment. Now, if my
love is under bolt and bar, if but seldom I can see
her, poor wretch, what comfort is there in a flowing
toga? Take me away; I will plough the fields at
a mistress's command. From chains and stripes my
body shall not shrink.

# IV

## *Female Covetousness.   To Nemesis*

HERE see I slavery and mistress waiting for me.
Now, ancient freedom of my fathers, fare thee well.
Yea, harsh slavery is my lot—chains to hold me and
Love that never slackens the wretched prisoner's
bonds, and burns me whether I have deserved to
suffer or have done no wrong. Ah, how I burn!
Take the torch away, thou cruel girl.

7 Oh, not to feel such pangs as these, would I were
rather a stone on the bleak hills or cliff exposed to
the frenzy of the winds on which beats the ship-
wrecking wave of the desolate sea. Now bitter is
the day and bitterer still the shades of night, for
every moment is steeped in acrid gall.

nec prosunt elegi nec carminis auctor Apollo;
  illa cava pretium flagitat usque manu.
ite procul, Musae, si non prodestis amanti;
  non ego vos, ut sint bella canenda, colo,
nec refero Solisque vias et qualis, ubi orbem
  complevit, versis Luna recurrit equis.
ad dominam faciles aditus per carmina quaero;
  ite procul, Musae, si nihil ista valent.                    20
at mihi per caedem et facinus sunt dona paranda,
  ne iaceam clausam flebilis ante domum;
aut rapiam suspensa sacris insignia fanis;
  sed Venus ante alios est violanda mihi.
illa malum facinus suadet dominamque rapacem
  dat mihi; sacrilegas sentiat illa manus.
o pereat quicumque legit viridesque smaragdos
  et niveam Tyrio murice tingit ovem.
addit avaritiae causas et Coa puellis
  vestis et e rubro lucida concha mari.                       30
haec fecere malas; hinc clavim ianua sensit
  et coepit custos liminis esse canis.
sed pretium si grande feras, custodia victa est
  nec prohibent claves et canis ipse tacet.
heu quicumque dedit formam caelestis avarae,
  quale bonum multis attulit ille malis!
hinc fletus rixaeque sonant, haec denique causa
  fecit ut infamis nunc deus erret Amor.
at tibi, quae pretio victos excludis amantes,
  eripiant partas ventus et ignis opes.                       40
quin tua tunc iuvenes spectent incendia laeti,
  nec quisquam flammae sedulus addat aquam.
seu veniet tibi mors, nec erit qui lugeat ullus
  nec qui det maestas munus in exsequias

¹³ Nor doth elegy help or Apollo, inspirer of my song. Her hollowed palm is ever stretched out for gold. Away, ye Muses, if ye have no aid for the lover; I court you not that I may sing of wars. Nor tell I of the goings of the Sun, nor how when she has accomplished her circuit the Moon wheels her horses and returns. Easy access to my lady is all I seek by song. Off with ye, Muses, if the song is of no avail.

²¹ Yet by crime and slaughter must I get gifts, that I may not lie lamenting before closed doors. Or I must seize the ornaments that hang in holy temples. But Venus must I pillage first. 'Tis she that prompts the evil deed, 'tis she that gives me a grasping mistress; so let her feel my sacrilegious hands.

²⁷ Ah, ruin to all who gather the emeralds green or with Tyrian purple dye the snowy sheepskin. The stuffs of Cos and the bright pearl from out of the red seas sow greed in lasses. 'Tis these have made them evil. From these hath the door learned to feel the key, and the dog been set to guard the threshold. But if thou comest with a great fee, the watch is worsted, keys turn in vain, and the very dog is mute. Ah, that god who gave beauty to the covetous girl, what a pearl did he bring to a herd of mischiefs! From this comes the noise of weeping and of bickering. This, in brief, is the cause that Love now roams the earth dishonoured.

³⁹ But thou, that dost shut out lovers whom gold has vanquished, may wind and fire sweep off the wealth that thou hast gained. Nay, may the young then see thy house ablaze, and none bestir himself to put water on the fire. Or, if 'tis death that comes to thee, let there be none to mourn thee or come with offering to

at bona quae nec avara fuit, centum licet annos
    vixerit, ardentem flebitur ante rogum;
atque aliquis senior veteres veneratus amores
    annua constructo serta dabit tumulo,
et "bene" discedens dicet "placideque quiescas,
    terraque securae sit super ossa levis."         50
vera quidem moneo, sed prosunt quid mihi vera ?
    illius est nobis lege colendus amor.
quin etiam, sedes iubeat si vendere avitas,
    ite sub imperium sub titulumque, Lares.
quidquid habet Circe, quidquid Medea veneni,
    quidquid et herbarum Thessala terra gerit,
et quod, ubi indomitis gregibus Venus adflat amores,
    hippomanes cupidae stillat ab inguine equae,
si modo me placido videat Nemesis mea vultu,
    mille alias herbas misceat illa, bibam.      60

## V

Phoebe, fave ; novus ingreditur tua templa sacerdos ;
    huc age cum cithara carminibusque veni.
nunc te vocales impellere pollice chordas,
    nunc precor ad laudes flectere verba pias.
ipse triumphali devinctus tempora lauro,
    dum cumulant aras, ad tua sacra veni.
sed nitidus pulcherque veni ; nunc indue vestem
    sepositam, longas nunc bene pecte comas,

thy woful burial. But she that has been kind and free from greed, though she live a hundred years, shall be wept by the burning pyre. And some aged man in homage to his ancient love will yearly place a garland on her mounded tomb, and, as he goes, will say: "Sleep well and peacefully, and above thy untroubled ashes let the earth be light."

⁵¹ 'Tis a true warning; but of what help is the truth to me? I must ply my love as she ordains. Yea, if she bid me sell the home of my forefathers, then, gods of the household, ye must stoop to be labelled at her word.[1] All Circe's, all Medea's potions, all the herbs that the land of Thessaly bears, even the hippomanes which drips from the yearning mare when Venus breathes passion into unbridled herds, yea, a thousand herbs beside may my Nemesis mingle in the draught, and, so she look kindly on me, I will drink.

## V

### *The Installation of Messalinus* [2]

BE gracious, Phoebus; a new priest sets foot within thy temple. Hither I bid thee come with lyre and song. Now, I prithee, let thy fingers sweep the singing strings; now tune thy song to a loyal paean. And while they heap the altar, come to thy rites thyself, thy brows encircled with triumphal bay. Come bright and beautiful; now don thy treasured raiment; now duly comb thy flowing locks. Be as

[1] The *titulus* was the label affixed to objects for sale by auction.

[2] As one of the *quindecimviri sacris faciundis*, who had the custody of the Sibylline books.

qualem te memorant Saturno rege fugato
    victori laudes concinuisse Iovi.          10
tu procul eventura vides, tibi deditus augur
    scit bene quid fati provida cantet avis;
tuque regis sortes, per te praesentit haruspex,
    lubrica signavit cum deus exta notis;
te duce Romanos numquam frustrata Sibylla,
    abdita quae senis fata canit pedibus.
Phoebe, sacras Messalinum sine tangere chartas
    vatis, et ipse precor quid canat illa doce.
haec dedit Aeneae sortes, postquam ille parentem
    dicitur et raptos sustinuisse Lares        20
nec fore credebat Romam, cum maestus ab alto
    Ilion ardentes respiceretque deos.
(Romulus aeternae nondum formaverat urbis
    moenia, consorti non habitanda Remo;
sed tunc pascebant herbosa Palatia vaccae
    et stabant humiles in Iovis arce casae.
lacte madens illic suberat Pan ilicis umbrae
    et facta agresti lignea falce Pales,
pendebatque vagi pastoris in arbore votum,
    garrula silvestri fistula sacra deo,        30
fistula cui semper decrescit harundinis ordo;
    nam calamus cera iungitur usque minor.
at qua Velabri regio patet, ire solebat
    exiguus pulsa per vada linter aqua.
illa saepe gregis diti placitura magistro
    ad iuvenem festa est vecta puella die,
cum qua fecundi redierunt munera ruris,
    caseus et niveae candidus agnus ovis.)

men tell thou wast when, Saturn driven from his throne, thou sangest a paean for victorious Jove.

11 Thou seest from afar the things to come. The augur whose soul is given up to thee knows well what means the note of the bird that foresees what is to be. 'Tis thou dost guide the lots; through thee divines the reader of the inward parts, whensoever a god has set his marks on the glistening entrails.

15 With thee her guide, the Sibyl who sings Fate's hidden will in six-foot measure hath never played the Romans false. Phoebus, grant leave to Messalinus to touch the seeress' holy scroll, and teach him thyself the meaning of her strains.

19 'Twas she that gave responses to Aeneas after the hour when, as story tells, he bore away in his arms his sire and household gods, never dreaming that a Rome would be, when from the deep he turned his eyes in sorrow on Ilion and its gods ablaze.

23 (Not yet had Romulus traced the walls of the Eternal City wherein was no abiding for his brother Remus. But still on a grassy Palatine browsed the kine, and lowly cabins stood upon the heights of Jove. There, drenched with milk, was Pan beneath the holm-oak's shade, and Pales shaped from wood by rustic knife; and on the tree, in quittance of the roving shepherd's vow, the prattling pipe hung sacred to the woodland god—the pipe with its ever-dwindling rows of reeds, whose wax joins stalks each lesser than the last. But where now spreads the quarter of Velabrum, a small skiff stirred the waters as it plied across the shallows. There oft a lass who would please some rich keeper of a herd was ferried on holidays to her swain, and with her came back the gifts of a thriving farm, cheese and the white lamb of a snowy ewe.)

" Impiger Aenea, volitantis frater Amoris,
    Troica qui profugis sacra vehis ratibus,        **40**
iam tibi Laurentes adsignat Iuppiter agros,
    iam vocat errantes hospita terra Lares.
illic sanctus eris cum te veneranda Numici
    unda deum caelo miserit indigetem.
ecce super fessas volitat Victoria puppes;
    tandem ad Troianos diva superba venit.
ecce mihi lucent Rutulis [1] incendia castris;
    iam tibi praedico, barbare Turne, necem.
ante oculos Laurens castrum murusque Lavini est
    Albaque ab Ascanio condita Longa duce.        50
te quoque iam video, Marti placitura sacerdos
    Ilia, Vestales deseruisse focos,
concubitusque tuos furtim vittasque iacentes
    et cupidi ad ripas arma relicta dei.
carpite nunc, tauri, de septem montibus herbas
    dum licet; hic magnae iam locus urbis erit.
Roma, tuum nomen terris fatale regendis,
    qua sua de caelo prospicit arva Ceres,
quaque patent ortus et qua fluitantibus undis
    Solis anhelantes abluit amnis equos.        60
Troia quidem tunc se mirabitur et sibi dicet
    vos bene tam longa consuluisse via.
vera cano : sic usque sacras innoxia laurus
    vescar, et aeternum sit mihi virginitas."
haec cecinit vates et te sibi, Phoebe, vocavit,
    iactavit fusas et caput ante comas.—
quidquid Amalthea, quidquid Marpesia dixit
    Herophile, Phyto Graia quod admonuit,
quaeque Aniena sacras Tiburs per flumina sortes
    portarat sicco pertuleratque sinu—        70

---

[1] Rutulis *the corrected MSS.* : rutilis *A.,* " *flcry red.* "

[39] "Aeneas never-resting, brother of Cupid ever on the wing, whose exiled barks carry the holy things of Troy, now doth Jove allot to thee the fields of Laurentum, now doth a hospitable land invite thy wandering gods. There shall divinity be thine when Numicius' ever-worshipped waters pass thee to heaven, a god of the native-born. See, o'er the weary ships is Victory hovering. At last the haughty goddess comes to the men of Troy. Lo, I see the fire blaze from the Rutule camp.[1] Now, savage Turnus, I foretell thy fall. Before my eyes is Laurentum's fortress and Lavinium's wall, and Long Alba, which Ascanius leads his host to found. Now thee too, Ilia, priestess whom Mars is to find fair, I see departed from the Vestal hearth. I see thy secret bridal, thy snood cast upon the ground, and, left upon the banks, the arms of the eager god. Now, while ye may, bulls, crop the grass of the Seven Hills. Ere long this will be a great city's site. Thy nation, Rome, is fated to rule the earth wherever Ceres looks from heaven upon the fields she tends, both where the gates of dawn are opened and where in tossing waters the Ocean river bathes the Sun-god's panting team. Then shall old Troy be a marvel to herself, and own that in this far journey ye did well for her. 'Tis truth I sing; so may I ever eat the holy bay unharmed and everlasting maidenhood be mine."

[65] So sang the seeress, and called thee to her, Phoebus, and tossed before her face her streaming hair.

[67] All that Amalthea,[2] all that Herophile[2] of Marpessos foretold, all the warnings of Grecian Phyto[2] and hers of Tibur who carried her holy scrolls of destiny through the stream of Anio and in dry bosom

[1] The allusion is obscure.
[2] Names of various Sibyls. The Sibyl of Tibur was Albunea.

haec fore dixerunt belli mala signa cometen,
   multus ut in terras deplueretque lapis.
atque tubas atque arma ferunt strepitantia caelo
   audita et lucos praecinuisse fugam :
et simulacra deum lacrimas fudisse tepentes     77
   fataque vocales praemonuisse boves.     78
ipsum etiam Solem defectum lumine vidit     75
   iungere pallentes nubilus annus equos.     76
haec fuerant olim : sed tu iam mitis, Apollo,
   prodigia indomitis merge sub aequoribus,     80
et succensa sacris crepitet bene laurea flammis,
   omine quo felix et sacer[1] annus erit.
laurus ubi bona signa dedit, gaudete coloni ;
   distendet spicis horrea plena Ceres,
oblitus et musto feriet pede rusticus uvas,
   dolia dum magni deficiantque lacus ;
ac madidus baccho sua festa Palilia pastor
   concinet : a stabulis tunc procul este lupi.
ille levis stipulae sollemnis potus acervos
   accendet, flammas transilietque sacras.     90
et fetus matrona dabit, natusque parenti
   oscula comprensis auribus eripiet ;
nec taedebit avum parvo advigilare nepoti
   balbaque cum puero dicere verba senem.
tunc operata deo pubes discumbet in herba,
   arboris antiquae qua levis umbra cadit,
aut e veste sua tendent umbracula sertis
   vincta, coronatus stabit et ipse calix.
at sibi quisque dapes et festas extruet alte
   caespitibus mensas caespitibusque torum.     100

[1] satur (*Cornelissen*), "*rich*," "*fruitful*," would give a better sense.

bore them home. . . . These told that a comet should
appear, the evil sign of war, and how that thick on
earth should fall the stony shower. And they say
that trumpets and the clash of arms were heard in
heaven, and sacred groves rang with the coming rout.
From the images of the gods poured the warm tears;
and kine found tongue and spake of the coming
doom. Yea, from the very Sun ebbed the light, and
the clouded year saw him yoke dim horses to his
car.

79 So was it once; but thou, Apollo, kind at last,
whelm monstrous things beneath the savage deep.
Let the bay crackle loud as it kindles in the holy
flames, an omen telling that the season shall be
blest and holy. When the bay has given propitious
sign, rejoice, ye farmers: Ceres will fill with ears
your straining barns. And smeared with must the
countryman will stamp above the grapes till the
great tanks and butts can hold no more. And
drenched in wine the shepherd will chaunt the feast
of Pales, the shepherd's holiday. Ye wolves, be ye
then far from the fold. Full of drink, he will fire
the light straw heaps in the appointed way, and leap
across the sacred flames. Then shall his dame bear
offspring, and the child take hold of his father's ears
to snatch the kiss; nor shall the grandsire find it
irksome to watch by his little grandson's side, nor,
for all his years, to lisp in prattle with the child.

95 Then in the god's service the folk shall recline
upon the grass where fall the flickering shadows of
some ancient tree, or of their garments spread out
canopies and tie them up with garlands, wreaths
also round the goblets where they stand. Then each
for himself will pile high the feast and festal board,
cut sods the table and cut sods the couch. Here the

ingeret hic potus iuvenis maledicta puellae,
  postmodo quae votis inrita facta velit;
nam ferus ille suae plorabit sobrius idem
  et se iurabit mente fuisse mala.
pace tua pereant arcus pereantque sagittae,
  Phoebe, modo in terris erret inermis Amor.
ars bona: sed postquam sumpsit sibi tela Cupido,
  heu heu quam multis ars dedit ista malum!
et mihi praecipue, iaceo cum saucius annum
  et (faveo morbo cum iuvat ipse dolor)                     110
usque cano Nemesim, sine qua versus mihi nullus
  verba potest iustos aut reperire pedes.
at tu, nam divum servat tutela poetas,
  praemoneo, vati parce, puella, sacro,
ut Messalinum celebrem, cum praemia belli
  ante suos currus oppida victa feret,
ipse gerens laurus: lauro devinctus agresti
  miles "io" magna voce "triumphe" canet.
tunc Messalla meus pia det spectacula turbae
  et plaudat curru praetereunte pater.                      120
adnue: sic tibi sint intonsi, Phoebe, capilli,
  sic tua perpetuo sit tibi casta soror.


# VI

Castra Macer sequitur: tenero quid fiet Amori?
  sit comes et collo fortiter arma gerat?
et seu longa virum terrae via seu vaga ducent
  aequora, cum telis ad latus ire volet?
ure, puer, quaeso, tua qui ferus otia liquit
  atque iterum erronem sub tua signa voca.

tipsy lad will heap curses on his lass, such as ere long
he will hope and pray may turn to naught. Aye, he
who is now so savage with his dear will weep when
he is sober, and swear that his wits had gone astray.

105 Phoebus, by thy good leave, let bows and
arrows perish, so Love may rove unarmed upon the
earth. 'Tis an honest craft; but since Cupid took to
carrying arrows, how many, ah me, has that honest
craft made smart! And me beyond the rest. For a
year have I been afflicted from his stroke, and, siding
with my malady (for the pain itself is pleasure), I sing
unceasingly of Nemesis, apart from whom no verse
of mine can find its words or proper feet.

113 But do thou, damsel (for guardian gods watch
over poets), be warned in time, and spare thy sacred
bard, that I may tell of Messalinus when before *his*
chariot he shall bear the conquered towns, the prize
of war, wearing the bay wreath, while his soldiery,
with wild bay round their brows, loudly chaunt the cry
of triumph. Then let my dear Messalla afford the
throng the sight of a father's love, and clap his hands
as his son's car passes by. Phoebus, grant this; and
so be thy locks for aye unshorn, and thy sister ever
a maiden pure.

# VI

## To Macer

For the camp is Macer bound. What shall become
of gentle Love? Must he go with him and stoutly
bear his arms about his neck? And, weapons in hand,
will he be at the gallant's side whether his path
lie over the distant mainland or the tossing seas?
Young sir, I prithee, brand the rebel that has left thy
haunts of peace: call back the truant to thy banners.

quod si militibus parces, erit hic quoque miles,
   ipse levem galea qui sibi portet aquam.
castra peto, valeatque Venus valeantque puellae ;
   et mihi sunt vires et mihi laeta tuba est.          10
magna loquor, sed magnifice mihi magna locuto
   excutiunt clausae fortia verba fores.
iuravi quotiens rediturum ad limina numquam !
   cum bene iuravi, pes tamen ipse redit.
acer Amor, fractas utinam tua tela sagittas,
   si licet, extinctas aspiciamque faces !
tu miserum torques, tu me mihi dira precari
   cogis et insana mente nefanda loqui.
iam mala finissem leto, sed credula vitam
   spes fovet et fore cras semper ait melius.      20
spes alit agricolas, spes sulcis credit aratis
   semina quae magno faenore reddat ager ;
haec laqueo volucres, haec captat harundine pisces,
   cum tenues hamos abdidit ante cibus ;
spes etiam valida solatur compede vinctum :
   crura sonant ferro, sed canit inter opus ;
spes facilem Nemesim spondet mihi, sed negat illa.
   ei mihi, ne vincas, dura puella, deam.
parce, per immatura tuae precor ossa sororis :
   sic bene sub tenera parva quiescat humo.     30
illa mihi sancta est ; illius dona sepulcro
   et madefacta meis serta feram lacrimis ;
illius ad tumulum fugiam supplexque sedebo
   et mea cum muto fata querar cinere.
non feret usque suum te propter flere clientem :
   illius ut verbis, sis mihi lenta veto,

⁷ But if thou art merciful to soldiers, here is one will be a soldier too, and bring himself refreshing water in his helm. I am off to the camp. Farewell to Love, farewell to lasses. I too am stout of limb; in my ears too the trumpet's note is sweet.

¹¹ Brave is my speech; but when I have uttered the brave bravado, the shutting of a door strikes the bold words from my lips. How often have I sworn that to its threshold I would return no more! For all my valiant swearing, my foot comes back itself. Fierce Love, oh, if this could be, I would see thine arms destroyed, the arrows broken and the torches quenched. Thou rackest me with anguish: thou forcest me to curse myself and in impious speech to vent the frenzy of my soul. Ere now I would have ended my miseries in death; but fond Hope keeps the spark alive, whispering ever that to-morrow things will mend.

²¹ 'Tis Hope sustains the farmer; to ploughed furrows Hope entrusts the seed for fields to render back with heavy usury. She takes the fowl in noose, the fish with rod, the slender hook first hidden by the bait. Hope comforts, too, the slave whom stout fetters bind. The iron clanks upon his legs, but still he sings at his task. Hope promises me that Nemesis shall be kind; but she says Nay. Ah me! worst not the goddess, cruel girl.

²⁹ Mercy, I pray thee, by the bones of thy sister, dead before her time; so may the child sleep well beneath the gentle earth. For me she is divine; to her tomb I will bring offerings and garlands wetted with my tears. To her grave will I fly and, sitting suppliant there, bewail my fate to her silent dust. Not forever will she bear with thee for making her votary weep. In her name I bid thee, be not cold

ne tibi neglecti mittant mala somnia manes,
    maestaque sopitae stet soror ante torum,
qualis ab excelsa praeceps delapsa fenestra
    venit ad infernos sanguinolenta lacus.         40
desino, ne dominae luctus renoventur acerbi :
    non ego sum tanti, ploret ut illa semel.
nec lacrimis oculos digna est foedare loquaces :
    lena nocet nobis, ipsa puella bona est.
lena necat miserum Phryne furtimque tabellas
    occulto portans itque reditque sinu.
saepe, ego cum dominae dulces a limine duro
    agnosco voces, haec negat esse domi ;
saepe, ubi nox mihi promissa est, languere puellam
    nuntiat aut aliquas extimuisse minas.        50
tunc morior curis, tunc mens mihi perdita fingit,
    quisve meam teneat, quot teneatve modis ;
tunc tibi, lena, precor diras : satis anxia vivas,
    moverit e votis pars quotacumque deos.

to me, lest the slighted spirit send thee evil dreams
and in thy slumbers thy mournful sister stand before
thy bed, such as she was, when from the high case-
ment she fell headlong down and passed blood-
spattered to the lakes below. I cease, lest I stir
again my lady's bitter woe. I am not worth one
cry of grief from her.

[43] Nor is it well that tears should mar those speak-
ing eyes. 'Tis the bawd that is my bane; the girl
herself is good. Phryne, the bawd, is killing me,
alas, as stealthily she passes to and fro with tablets
hidden in her bosom. Many times, when from the
hard threshold I recognise my mistress's sweet voice,
Phryne denies she is at home. Often, when the night
has been pledged to me, she brings message that the
girl is sick or has been affrighted by some warning.
Then I die with distress, and desperate fancy figures
to itself in what and whose embraces my love is
held. Then I call curses on thee, bawd. Thy life
should be full enough of fears, if any part of what
I pray is heard in heaven.

# BOOK III

# LIBER TERTIVS

## (LYGDAMI ALIORVMQVE)

### LYGDAMI ELEGIAE

### I

Martis Romani festae venere kalendae
  (exoriens nostris hic fuit annus avis),
et vaga nunc certa discurrunt undique pompa
  perque vias urbis munera perque domos.
dicite, Pierides, quonam donetur honore
  seu mea, seu fallor, cara Neaera tamen.
"carmine formosae, pretio capiuntur avarae:
  gaudeat, ut digna est, versibus illa novis.
lutea sed niveum involvat membrana libellum,
  pumex et canas tondeat ante comas,          10
summaque praetexat tenuis fastigia chartae
  indicet ut nomen littera facta tuum,
atque inter geminas pingantur cornua frontes:
  sic etenim comptum mittere oportet opus."
per vos, auctores huius mihi carminis, oro
  Castaliamque umbram Pieriosque lacus,
ite domum cultumque illi donate libellum,
  sicut erit; nullus defluat inde color.
illa mihi referet, si nostri mutua cura est,
  an minor, an toto pectore deciderim.        20

# THE THIRD BOOK

## ELEGIES OF LYGDAMUS

### I

#### *Dedication to Neaera*

THE festal Calends of Mars of Rome are come. This for our ancestors was the year's dawning. And on all sides, travelling in order due, presents are speeding this way and that along the city's streets and houses. Tell me, Pierian maids, with what tribute shall I present Neaera, whether mine or, if she plays me false, dear to me still.

⁷ " Poetry is the lure for the beautiful, gold for the greedy : so let there be new verses to gladden her as she deserves. But first let yellow parchment wrap the snow-white roll and pumice shear its hoary locks, and letters traced to show thy name border the high top of the fine papyrus, and let the horned knobs 'mid both its fronts be painted. For in such trim guise must thy work be sent."

¹⁵ Inspirers of this my song, I entreat ye by the shade of Castaly and the Pierian springs go to the house, and give her the dainty book just as it is ; let none of its bloom be lost. She will send me answer if her love is still as mine, or if it is less, or if I have fallen wholly out of her heart. And first (she

sed primum meritam larga donate salute
  atque haec submisso dicite verba sono :
" haec tibi vir quondam, nunc frater, casta Neaera,
  mittit et accipias munera parva rogat,
teque suis iurat caram magis esse medullis,
  sive sibi coniunx sive futura soror :
sed potius coniunx : huius spem nominis illi
  auferet extincto pallida Ditis aqua."


## II


Qvi primus caram iuveni carumque puellae
  eripuit iuvenem, ferreus ille fuit.
durus et ille fuit, qui tantum ferre dolorem,
  vivere et erepta coniuge qui potuit.
non ego firmus in hoc, non haec patientia nostro
  ingenio : frangit fortia corda dolor.
nec mihi vera loqui pudor est vitaeque fateri,
  tot mala perpessae, taedia nata meae.
ergo cum tenuem fuero mutatus in umbram
  candidaque ossa supra nigra favilla teget,      10
ante meum veniat longos incompta capillos
  et fleat ante meum maesta Neaera rogum.
sed veniat carae matris comitata dolore :
  maereat haec genero, maereat illa viro.
praefatae ante meos manes animamque recentem [1]
  perfusaeque pias ante liquore manus,
pars quae sola mei superabit corporis, ossa
  incinctae nigra candida veste legent,

---

[1] recentem *editor :* rogate *A.:* precatae *vulg.*

has deserved it) bestow on her an ample greeting
and in subdued accents speak these words:

23 "Thy husband once, thy brother now, sends
these lines to thee, chaste Neaera, and prays thee to
accept the humble gift. He swears that thou art
dearer to him than his very marrow, whether thou
wilt be his sister or his wife. Better his wife: hope
of this title shall only Dis's wan waters take from him
when his life is quenched."

## II

### Lygdamus Deprived of Neaera

HE who first robbed a swain of his dear and a girl of
the youth she loved was a man of iron. And *he* was
hard too who could bear a grief so great and live
when his mate was taken. I am not stout in this:
in my strain is no such endurance. Pain makes the
brave heart break. I think it no shame to speak
the truth or to own that within me there is risen
loathing of a life that has suffered so much
sorrow.

9 So then when I am changed to a phantom shade
and above my white bones lies the black ashes' cover-
ing, let Neaera come to my pyre with her long hair
disordered and sadly weep beside it. Let her come
with her dear mother to share her grief, to mourn,
one for a husband, the other for a son.

15 First of all let them address my shade and fresh
departed spirit and in lustral water bathe their hands.
Then with black robes ungirdled shall they gather
the white bones, sole part remaining of my body,
and when they are gathered together sprinkle them

T

et primum annoso spargent collecta lyaeo,
 mox etiam niveo fundere lacte parent,    20
post haec carbaseis umorem tollere velis
 atque in marmorea ponere sicca domo.
illic quas mittit dives [1] Panchaia merces
 Eoique Arabes, dives [1] et Assyria,
et nostri memores lacrimae fundantur eodem :
 sic ego componi versus in ossa velim.
sed tristem mortis demonstret littera causam
 atque haec in celebri carmina fronte notet :
LYGDAMVS HIC SITVS EST. DOLOR HVIC ET CVRA NEAERAE
CONIVGIS EREPTAE CAVSA PERIRE FVIT.    30


## III


QVID prodest caelum votis implesse, Neaera,
 blandaque cum multa tura dedisse prece,
non ut marmorei prodirem e limine tecti,
 insignis clara conspicuusque domo,
aut ut multa mei renovarent iugera tauri
 et magnas messes terra benigna daret,
sed tecum ut longae sociarem gaudia vitae
 inque tuo caderet nostra senecta sinu,
tum cum permenso defunctus tempore lucis
 nudus Lethaea cogerer ire rate ?    10
nam grave quid prodest pondus mihi divitis auri,
 arvaque si findant pinguia mille boves ?
quidve domus prodest Phrygiis innixa columnis,
 Taenare sive tuis, sive Caryste tuis,

[1] *In one of these lines* dives *is corrupt and should probably be*
pinguis.

with old wine first and next proceed to drench them
with snowy milk likewise, and after this to remove
the moisture with linen cloths and place them dry in
a chamber of marble. There[1] let the merchandise
which rich Panchaia, Eastern Araby, and rich Assyria
send, and tears to my memory withal, be shed on the
same spot. Thus, when naught is left of me but bones,
would I be laid to rest.

[27] But the sad cause of my death let a legend show,
and on the stone's face which all may see let it set
out these lines:

> HERE LYGDAMUS IS LAID, BY GRIEVOUS PAIN
> AND LONGING FOR HIS LOST NEAERA SLAIN.

## III

### *What is Wealth to Lygdamus without Love?*

WHAT gain is it to have filled the heavens with vows,
Neaera, and offered bland incense with constant
prayer, not that I might step out from the threshold
of a marble dwelling, observed and noted for a
glorious house, or that bulls of mine might turn the
clods o'er many a rood and earth in her bounty give
me great harvests, but that through long years of
life I might share my joys with thee, and that in
thine arms might drop my aged frame in the hour
when my course of light was fully run and stripped
of all I was forced to voyage on the barque of Lethe?

[11] What good to me were heavy weight of precious
gold or a thousand oxen cleaving my rich fields?
what good a house that rests on pillars from Phrygian
quarries, or, Taenaros, from thine, or thine, Carystos,

---

[1] Or "Thereupon."

et nemora in domibus sacros imitantia lucos
    aurataeque trabes marmoreumque solum?
quidve in Erythraeo legitur quae litore concha
    tinctaque Sidonio murice lana iuvat,
et quae praeterea populus miratur?   in illis
    invidia est; falso plurima vulgus amat.        20
non opibus mentes hominum curaeque levantur;
    nam Fortuna sua tempora lege regit.
sit mihi paupertas tecum iucunda, Neaera:
    at sine te regum munera nulla volo.
o niveam quae te poterit mihi reddere lucem!
    o mihi felicem terque quaterque diem!
at si, pro dulci reditu quaecumque voventur,
    audiat aversa non meus aure deus,
nec me regna iuvant nec Lydius aurifer amnis
    nec quas terrarum sustinet orbis opes.       30
haec alii cupiant; liceat mihi paupere cultu
    securo cara coniuge posse frui.
adsis et timidis faveas, Saturnia, votis,
    et faveas concha, Cypria, vecta tua.
aut si fata negant reditum tristesque sorores,
    stamina quae ducunt quaeque futura neunt,[1]
me vocet in vastos amnes nigramque paludem
    dives in ignava luridus Orcus aqua.


IV


Di meliora ferant, nec sint mihi somnia vera,
    quae tulit hesterna pessima nocte quies.
ite procul, vani, falsumque avertite visum:
    desinite in nobis quaerere velle fidem.

    [1] canunt, "*sing*," *Heinsius, is a probable conjecture.*

woods within mansions mimicking the sacred groves,
or gilded cross-beams and a floor of marble? Or what
the pearl shell gathered on Erythraean shores, or wool
dipped in the purple dye of Sidon, and all besides that
the world admires? Here envy lodges: the crowd is
misguided in most that it adores. Wealth lightens
not the hearts and cares of men. For Fortune rules
their circumstances by ordinances of her own.

23 With thee, Neaera, would I welcome poverty
without thee I want nothing that the kings can give.
O snow-bright morn that shall give thee back to me!
O day that will bring me three- and four-fold bliss!

27 But if the unfriendly god should turn his ears
away from all that I vow for that dear return,
then no kingdoms please me, nor river of Lydia
charged with gold, nor all the wealth that the earth's
round bears. Let others long for these; but let me
live in humble style, if without misgivings I may
have my dear wife for my own.

33 Be with me, daughter of Saturn, and listen to
my timid prayers, and thou too listen, goddess of
Cyprus whose chariot is thy shell. But if Fate and
the dour sisters who draw the yarn and spin the
future deny returning, then let the voice of sallow
Orcus, the lord of treasures amidst sluggish waters,
call me to his desolate rivers and his black morass.

## IV

### *Lygdamus' Dream*

MAY the gods send better fortune, nor may the
dream prove true which an evil sleep brought me
yesternight. Depart from me, vain visions, take your
false show away; cease to seek credit at my cost.

divi vera monent, venturae nuntia sortis
 vera monent Tuscis exta probata viris:
somnia fallaci ludunt temeraria nocte
 et pavidas mentes falsa timere iubent?
et vanum metuens hominum genus omina noctis
 farre pio placant et saliente sale?     10
et tamen, utcumque est, sive illi vera moneri,
 mendaci somno credere sive solent,
efficiat vanos noctis Lucina timores
 et frustra immeritum pertimuisse velit,
si mea nec turpi mens est obnoxia facto
 nec laesit magnos impia lingua deos.
iam Nox aetherium nigris emensa quadrigis
 mundum caeruleo laverat amne rotas,
nec me sopierat menti deus utilis aegrae:
 Somnus sollicitas deficit ante domos.     20
tandem, cum summo Phoebus prospexit ab ortu,
 pressit languentis lumina sera quies.
hic iuvenis casta redimitus tempora lauro
 est visus nostra ponere sede pedem.
non illo quicquam formosius ulla priorum
 aetas, humanum ¹ nec videt ulla domus.
intonsi crines longa cervice fluebant,
 stillabat Syrio myrrhea rore coma.
candor erat qualem praefert Latonia Luna,
 et color in niveo corpore purpureus,     30
ut iuveni primum virgo deducta marito
 inficitur teneras ore rubente genas,
et cum contexunt amarantis alba puellae
 lilia et autumno candida mala rubent.
ima videbatur talis inludere palla;
 namque haec in nitido corpore vestis erat.

---

¹ heroum *Lachmann; but* humanum *is the gen. plur. of*
humanus, *"man." See " Classical Quarterly,"* VI. 41.

The warnings gods send are true, and true the warnings of the inward parts, approved by seers of Tuscany, announcing the fate to come. But dreams—do they sport at random in a deceiving night, filling affrighted souls with false alarms, and, vainly fearing, do mankind seek to propitiate the menaces of the night with offering of spelt and sputtering salt? And yet, howsoever it be, whether they are wont to receive true warnings or to give ear to lies of sleep, may Lucina frustrate the terrors of this night and ordain that the innocent shall have been alarmed in vain, if neither my soul be chargeable with ugly sin nor my tongue have wickedly profaned the holy gods.

17 Night's car of four black steeds had already traversed the firmament of ether and bathed its wheels in the dark blue stream. Yet on me the god who aids the sick spirit had laid no spell: Sleep vanishes before the house of care. At last, when Phoebus looked out above the dawn, late slumber closed the tired sufferer's eyes. Thereon a youth with holy bay encircling his brow, methought, set foot within my dwelling. Nothing more lovely than him did any age of our forerunners see, or any house of mortal folk. Down his long neck his unshorn hair was streaming. From his myrrh-laden tresses trickled dews of Syria. His radiance was such as the moon, daughter of Latona, spreads before her, and over his body's snow was a crimson flush, such as dyes the fair cheeks and blushing face of a maid when she is first escorted to her young husband's home, or like white lilies which flower-girls interweave with amaranths, or argent apples touched with autumn red. The hem of his palla seemed to play about his ankles. For this was the garment that

artis opus rarae, fulgens testudine et auro
  pendebat laeva garrula parte lyra.
hanc primum veniens plectro modulatus eburno
  felices cantus ore sonante dedit:               40
sed postquam fuerant digiti cum voce locuti,
  edidit haec dulci tristia verba modo:
"salue, cura deum: casto nam rite poetae
  Phoebusque et Bacchus Pieridesque favent:
sed proles Semelae Bocchus doctaeque sorores
  dicere non norunt quid ferat hora sequens:
at mihi fatorum leges aevique futuri
  eventura pater posse videre dedit.
quare ego quae dico non fallax accipe vates
  quamque [1] deus vero Cynthius ore ferar. [1]    50
tantum cara tibi quantum nec filia matri,
  quantum nec cupido bella puella viro,
pro qua sollicitas caelestia numina votis,
  quae tibi securos non sinit ire dies
et, cum te fusco Somnus velavit amictu,
  vanum nocturnis fallit imaginibus,
carminibus celebrata tuis formosa Neaera
  alterius mavult esse puella viri,
diversasque suas [2] agitat mens impia curas,
  nec gaudet casta nupta Neaera domo.      60
a crudele genus nec fidum femina nomen!
  a pereat, didicit fallere si qua virum.
sed flecti poterit; mens est mutabilis illis:
  tu modo cum multa bracchia tende prece.
saevus Amor docuit validos temptare labores,
  saevus Amor docuit verbera posse pati.
me quondam Admeti niveas pavisse iuvencas
  non est in vanum fabula ficta iocum.

---

[1] quamque, ferar *editor:* quique, ferat *A.:* quodque, feram
*vulg.*   *The Latin might also mean "how truly the Cynthian is
called a god."*     [2] tuis *Lipsius, which may be right.*

covered his gleaming limbs. On his 'eft side hung
his babbling lyre, wrought with rare skill, shining
with tortoise-shell and gold. On this, when first he
came, he played with ivory quill, and cheering music
sounded from his lips. But when fingers and voice
had spoken together, then to the tune of a sweet
measure he uttered these bitter words:

43 " Hail to thee, favourite of the gods—for to a
holy poet Phoebus, Bacchus, and the Pierid maids
are fitly friends. But Bacchus, offspring of Semele,
and the lettered sisters have no skill to say what
future hours shall bring. But to me my Sire has
granted the power to see the laws of Fate and what
shall issue in the time to come. Wherefore hearken
to what I say, no seer untrustworthy, and learn how
true are accounted the utterances of Cynthus' god.
She who is as precious to thee as is no daughter to
her mother nor maiden fair to her yearning husband,
for whom thy prayers give the powers of heaven no
rest, who never lets thy day pass without misgiving,
and when Sleep has wrapped thee in his dusky robe
baffles and mocks thee with her semblances in the
night, the beautiful Neaera whom thy songs have
made renowned, prefers to be the girl of another man.
Her unnatural heart pursues an alien fancy of its own,
and Neaera delights not to be a wife in a virtuous
home. O cruel sex! Woman a treacherous race!
Away with her who has learned to play her husband
false!

63 " But she may be turned: their minds are change-
able: but thou must stretch thy hands to her with
much beseeching. Tyrant Love has schooled us to
engage in stubborn labours, tyrant Love to endure the
lash. It is no story made for idle merriment that once
I fed the snow-white kine of Admetus. Then could

tunc ego nec cithara poteram gaudere sonora
 nec similes chordis reddere voce sonos,  70
sed perlucenti cantum meditabar avena
 ille ego Latonae filius atque Iovis.
nescis quid sit amor, iuvenis, si ferre recusas
 immitem dominam coniugiumque ferum.
ergo ne dubita blandas adhibere querellas;
 vincuntur molli pectora dura prece.
quod si vera canunt sacris oracula templis,
 haec illi nostro nomine dicta refer:
hoc tibi coniugium promittit Delius ipse;
 felix hoc alium desine velle virum.''  80
dixit, et ignavus defluxit corpore somnus.
 a ego ne possim tanta videre mala.
nec tibi crediderim votis contraria vota
 nec tantum crimen pectore inesse tuo.
nam te nec vasti genuerunt aequora ponti
 nec flammam volvens ore Chimaera fero
nec canis anguina redimitus terga caterva,
 cui tres sunt linguae tergeminumque caput,
Scyllaque virgineam canibus succincta figuram,
 nec te conceptam saeva leaena tulit,  90
barbara nec Scythiae tellus horrendave Syrtis;
 sed culta et duris non habitanda domus
et longe ante alias omnes mitissima mater
 isque pater quo non alter amabilior.
haec deus in melius crudelia somnia vertat
 et iubeat tepidos inrita ferre Notos.

I take no pleasure in the lyre's loud tones nor my
voice sing back in accord to its strings, but on the
unstopped reeds I practised, I, Latona's son and
Jove's. Young sir, thou knowest not what is love
if thou dost shrink to bear with a cruel mistress and
ungentle wife. So doubt not to use the gentle
arts of complaining : soft pleadings make the hard
heart melt. If oracles in holy temples utter truth,
then give her this message in my name : This is
the mate that the Delian himself awards to thee.
Happy in him, cease to desire another man.''

⁸¹ He said, and from my limbs slipped off the
lethargy of sleep. Ah, may I never live to see such
woe! I could not think that thou hast hopes thus
crossing hopes, or that sin so great is harboured in thy
breast. For thou wast not sprung from the waste sea's
fields, or from Chimaera rolling flames from savage
jaws, or from the dog with three tongues and a triple
head and back by a snaky troop encircled, or Scylla
with a girdle of hounds about her woman's body. No
cruel lioness conceived and bore thee, nor the bar-
barous land of Scythia or the fearful Syrtis, but a
humane home where the ungentle might not dwell
and a mother far kinder than all her sex, and a sire
than whom is none more lovable.

⁹⁵ May a god turn this cruel dream to good,
or bid the hot South Wind carry it away without
fulfilment!

# LYGDAMVS

## V

Vos tenet, Etruscis manat quae fontibus unda,
    unda sub aestivum non adeunda Canem,
nunc autem sacris Baiarum proxima lymphis,
    cum se purpureo vere remittit humus.
at mihi Persephone nigram denuntiat horam.
    immerito iuveni parce nocere, dea.
non ego temptavi nulli temeranda virorum
    audax laudandae sacra docere deae,
nec mea mortiferis infecit pocula sucis
    dextera nec cuiquam trita venena dedit,          10
nec nos sacrilegos templis admovimus ignes,
    nec cor sollicitant facta nefanda meum,
nec nos insanae meditantes iurgia mentis
    impia in adversos solvimus ora deos.
et nondum cani nigros laesere capillos,
    nec venit tardo curva senecta pede.
natalem primo nostrum videre parentes,
    cum cecidit fato consul uterque pari.
quid fraudare iuvat vitem crescentibus uvis
    et modo nata mala vellere poma manu ?          20
parcite, pallentes undas quicumque tenetis
    duraque sortiti tertia regna dei.
Elysios olim liceat cognoscere campos
    Lethaeamque ratem Cimmeriosque lacus,
cum mea rugosa pallebunt ora senecta
    et referam pueris tempora prisca senex.

300

# V

### *Lygdamus Sick to his Friends*

YE, my friends, stay by the stream that flows from
Etruscan source, stream not to be approached in the
Dog-star's heat, but now second only to the holy
waters of Baiae when the ground loosens in bright-
hued spring. But *I* have warning from Persephone
that the black hour is nigh.

6 Harm me not, goddess; I am young and have
done no wrong. I have not sought in recklessness
to make known the rites of the goddess whom folk
call Good, which no male must profane. My hand
has infused no deadly juices in men's cups or pounded
poison for the lips of any one. Nor have I sacrilegiously
set fire to temples, nor is my conscience vexed by
horrid crime, nor from the pent-up bitterness of a
frantic soul have I let my blaspheming tongue wag
in the very face of heaven.

15 Neither as yet has my black hair been harmed by
grey, nor bowed age come to me on halting feet. My
parents first beheld my birthday when both the con-
suls fell by the self-same fate.[1] What gain is it to rob
a vine of growing grapes or to pluck the fruit just
formed with brutal hand ? Spare me, ye gods in whose
sway are the wan waters and the stern realms, allotted
to you third.[2] Let the hour be far off when my eyes
shall see the Elysian plains, the barque of Lethe, and
the Cimmerian pools, when my cheeks are sallow with
wrinkled age and the old man tells the boys of the
days gone by.

1 Hirtius and Pansa, in B.C. 43.
2 An allusion to the casting of lots by which Jupiter,
Neptune, and Pluto determined their spheres of influence, the
lower world being the third.

atque utinam vano nequiquam terrear aestu!
  languent ter quinos sed mea membra dies.
at vobis Tuscae celebrantur numina lymphae
  et facilis lenta pellitur unda manu.             30
vivite felices, memores et vivite nostri,
  sive erimus seu nos fata fuisse velint.
interea nigras pecudes promittite Diti
  et nivei lactis pocula mixta mero.

# VI

CANDIDE Liber ades: sic sit tibi mystica vitis
  semper, sic hedera tempora vincta feras;
aufer et ipse meum patera medicante dolorem:
  saepe tuo cecidit munere victus Amor.
care puer, madeant generoso pocula baccho,
  et nobis prona funde Falerna manu.
ite procul durum curae genus, ite labores;
  fulserit hic niveis Delius alitibus.
vos modo proposito dulces faveatis amici,
  neve neget quisquam me duce se comitem;    10
aut si quis vini certamen mite recusat,
  fallat eum tecto cara puella dolo.
ille facit mites [1] animos deus, ille ferocem
  contudit et dominae misit in arbitrium;
Armenias tigres et fulvas ille leaenas
  vicit et indomitis mollia corda dedit.

---

[1] mites *the corrected MSS.*: dites *A.*

²⁷ And would it were no real fever, but some vain alarm! But for thrice five days their strength has left my limbs.

²⁹ But ye, my friends, resort to the haunts of Tuscan water sprites, and the stream parts lightly to the strokes of your leisurely arms. May ye live happy and with thoughts of me, whether I am here or destiny choose that I be no more. Meantime do ye promise black sheep to Dis and cups of snow-white milk mingled with wine

## VI

### *Lygdamus at the Feast*

FAIR Liber, come to me; so mayst thou ever have thy mystic vine, so bear the ivy bound about thy brows. And do thou take away my pain with healing chalice. Oft has Love fallen, vanquished by thy bounty. Dear lad, let the cups be flooded with noble wine; slant the hand that pours out our Falernian.

⁷ Go, far away go, toils and troubles, heartless tribe. Here let the Delian shine with his birds of snow. Only, dear friends, ye must approve my project, and none refuse his company if I lead the way. Or if any shrinks from wine's gentle bouts, let his dear lass play him false with covert treachery. Our god softens the heart, he crushes the proud spirits and sends them under the strict yoke of a mistress. He vanquishes the Armenian tiger and the tawny lioness and puts a tame heart in the tameless. These things,

haec Amor et maiora valet.  sed poscite Bacchi
  munera: quem vestrum pocula sicca iuvant?
convenit ex aequo nec torvus Liber in illis
  qui se quique una vina iocosa colunt:         20
nam [1] venit iratus nimium nimiumque severis:[2]
  qui timet irati numina magna, bibat.
quales his poenas qualis quantusque minetur,
  Cadmeae matris praeda cruenta docet.
sed procul a nobis hic sit timor, illaque, si qua est,
  quid valeat laesi sentiat ira dei.
quid precor a demens?  venti temeraria vota,
  aeriae et nubes diripienda ferant.
quamvis nulla mei superest tibi cura, Neaera,
  sis felix et sint candida fata tua.         30
at nos securae reddamus tempora mensae:
  venit post multas una serena dies.
ei mihi, difficile est imitari gaudia falsa,
  difficile est tristi fingere mente iocum,
nec bene mendaci risus componitur ore,
  nec bene sollicitis ebria verba sonant.
quid queror infelix?  turpes discedite curae:
  odit Lenaeus tristia verba pater.
Gnosia, Theseae quondam periuria linguae
  flevisti ignoto sola relicta mari:        40
sic cecinit pro te doctus, Minoi, Catullus
  ingrati referens impia facta viri.
vos ego nunc moneo: felix, quicumque dolore
  alterius disces posse cavere tuom.
nec vos aut capiant pendentia bracchia collo
  aut fallat blanda sordida lingua prece.

---

    [1] nam *editor* : non *A.*
    [2] severis *Livineius:* severus *A.*

and greater, can Love do. But do ye call for the
gifts of Bacchus. For which of you have chill[1]
draughts charms?

19 A mate and equal, with no front of menace,
doth Liber show himself to such as pay their court
to him and joyous wine at once; while without
bound or measure runs his wrath against the aus-
tere. Whoso fears a mighty god in anger, let him
drink. For such what chastisement he threatens,
what and how great the threatener, the bloody quarry[2]
of the Theban mother shows us well. But far from
us be this terror; let *her* feel all the anger of an
outraged god. Ah, what is this mad prayer? May
the winds and clouds of heaven bear off and scatter
all ways the reckless wish! And, Neaera, though
no thought of me survives in thy breast, mayst
thou be happy and thy lot be bright. But let us
devote these moments to the cheering board. After
many days a cloudless one has come.

33 Ah me! mock joys are hard to make; 'tis hard
to feign merriment when the heart is sad. Ill is it
to force a false smile to the face; ill is it when tipsy
accents are heard from the distressed. Unhappy,
what is this complaining? Away, ye ugly cares'
Father Lenaeus loathes the language of sorrow. In
old times, maid of Cnossos, thou wast left alone to
mourn the perjuries of Theseus' tongue to an alien sea.
So for thee, daughter of Minos, did accomplished
Catullus sing, recounting the wicked doings of thy
ingrate husband. And so I now warn you, friends.
Fortunate wilt thou be who art taught by another's
suffering to avoid thy own. Be not ye deceived by
arms flung round your necks, or cheated by a knavish
tongue with wheedling prayers. Though the beguiler

---

[1] Those of water-drinkers (*sicci*).          [2] Pentheus.

etsi perque suos fallax iuravit ocellos
   Iunonemque suam perque suam Venerem,
nulla fides inerit : periuria ridet amantum
   Iuppiter et ventos inrita ferre iubet.       **50**
ergo quid totiens fallacis verba puellae
   conqueror ?   ite a me, seria verba, precor.
quam vellem tecum longas requiescere noctes
   et tecum longos pervigilare dies,
perfida nec merito nobis † inimica merenti †
   perfida, sed, quamvis perfida, cara tamen !
Naida Bacchus amat : cessas, o lente minister ?
   temperet annosum Marcia lympha merum.
non ego, si fugit nostrae convivia mensae
   ignotum cupiens vana puella torum,       **60**
sollicitus repetam tota suspiria nocte.
   tu, puer, i, liquidum fortius adde merum.
iam dudum Syrio madefactus tempora nardo
   debueram sertis implicuisse comas.

## PANEGYRICVS MESSALLAE
### (TERTII LIBRI VII. = QVARTI I.)

TE, Messalla, canam, quamquam tua cognita virtus
terret.  ut infirmae nequeant subsistere vires,
incipiam tamen ac, meritas si carmina laudes
deficiant, humilis tantis sim conditor actis,
nec tua praeter te chartis intexere quisquam
facta queat, dictis ut non maiora supersint,
est nobis voluisse satis.  nec munera parva
respueris.  etiam Phoebo gratissima dona

swear by her eyes, by her Juno, by her Venus, there
will be no truth in her words. Jupiter laughs at
the false oaths of lovers, and bids the winds carry
them off without fulfilment. Then why do I com-
plain so oft of the words of a faithless girl? Away
from me, I pray, all serious talk! How I could wish
to pass with thee long nights of rest and spend
with thee long waking days, maid faithless, and for
no fault of mine—faithless, but, though faithless,
belovèd still.

⁵⁷ Bacchus loves the Naiad. Dost thou lag, my
slow attendant? Let Marcian water temper our
ancient wine. If a trustless girl, in her yearning
for a stranger's arms, has fled the entertainment
of my table, shall I be sighing in distress the whole
night through? Not I. Come, boy, and without
faltering pour in the bright wine. Long ago should
I have drenched my brows with nard of Syria and
twined a garland in my hair.


## EULOGY OF MESSALLA


Messalla, I will sing of thee albeit the knowledge
of thy worth affrights me. Though my feeble powers
may not bear the strain, still will I make beginning:
and, if my verse fall short of thy meed of praise and
I am but a poor chronicler for deeds so great, and if
none but thyself can so embroider the page with thy
achievements that what is left is not greater than
what is recounted, it is enough for me to have
shown the will. And do not thou reject the humble
offering. Even to Phoebus did the Cretan bring gifts

Cres tulit, et cunctis Baccho iucundior hospes
Icarus, ut puro testantur sidera caelo      10
Erigoneque Canisque, neget ne longior aetas.
quin etiam Alcides, deus ascensurus Olympum,
laeta Molorcheis posuit vestigia tectis,
parvaque caelestis placavit mica, nec illis
semper inaurato taurus cadit hostia cornu.
hic quoque sit gratus parvus labor, ut tibi possim
inde alios aliosque memor componere versus.

    alter dicat opus magni mirabile mundi,
qualis in immenso desederit aere tellus,
ɋualis et in curvum pontus confluxerit orbem,    20
et, vagus e terris qua surgere nititur aer,
huic ut [1] contextus passim fluat igneus aether,
pendentique super claudantur ut omnia caelo :
at quodcumque meae poterunt audere camenae,
seu tibi par poterunt seu, quod spes abnuit, ultra
sive minus (certeque canent minus), omne vovemus
hoc tibi, nec tanto careat mihi nomine charta.
nam quamquam antiquae gentis superant tibi laudes,
non tua maiorum contenta est gloria fama,
nec quaeris quid quaque index sub imagine dicat,  30

---

[1] ut *the corrected MSS.* : et *A.*

most welcome, and to Bacchus was Icarus [1] a host
more pleasing than all besides, as stars in the clear
sky witness, Erigone and the Hound, lest a distant
age deny the tale. Nay, more : Alcides, who was
to mount a god to Olympus, gladly set foot in the
dwelling of Molorchus. [2] A few grains [of salt] ap-
pease the powers above ; nor do they always claim as
their victim a bull with gilded horns. So may this
humble effort prove welcome also, that thereafter the
memory may give me strength to make yet other and
yet other verses in thy honour.

[18] Let another tell of the great world's wondrous
fabric, how the Earth sank down in the measureless
Air and how the Sea streamed over the round globe ;
and how, where the shifting Air strives to rise from
the Earth, conjoined to it closely far and wide undu-
lates the fiery Ether, and how all is shut in above by
the hanging Firmament. All efforts of my muses'
daring, whether they can reach thy level or whether
(but this Hope grants not) they rise above it or they
fall below (and below it surely will they fall), I dedi-
cate to thee ; nor must a name so great be wanting
to my page. For though thou hast distinctions abun-
dant in thy ancient family, *thy* thirst for fame is not
to be sated with the renown of ancestors, nor dost
thou ask what saith the scroll beneath each mask ;

---

[1] Icarius (Icarus), an Athenian, and his daughter Erigone
entertained Dionysus when he visited Attica. In return
Dionysus presented him with a skin of wine. The shepherds
whom Icarius regaled with the liquor, thinking that they
were poisoned, killed him. His corpse was discovered by his
dog Maera, who led Erigone to the spot. She hanged her-
self there, and the three were transformed by Dionysus into
constellations.

[2] A poor vine-dresser of Cleonae who entertained Heracles
when he went to kill the Nemean lion.

# PANEGYRICVS MESSALLAE

sed generis priscos contendis vincere honores,
quam tibi maiores maius decus ipse futuris :
at tua non titulus capiet sub nomine facta,
aeterno sed erunt tibi magna volumina versu,
convenientque tuas cupidi componere laudes
undique quique canent vincto pede quique soluto.
quis potior, certamen erit : sim victor in illis,
ut nostrum tantis inscribam nomen in actis.

    nam quis te maiora gerit castrisve forove ?
nec tamen hic aut hic tibi laus maiorve minorve,   40
iusta pari premitur veluti cum pondere libra,   41
qualis, inaequatum si quando onus urget utrimque, 43
instabilis natat alterno depressior orbe,   44
prona nec hac plus parte sedet nec surgit ab illa. 42

    nam seu diversi fremat inconstantia vulgi,   45
non alius sedare queat ; seu iudicis ira
sit placanda, tuis poterit mitescere verbis.
non Pylos aut Ithace tantos genuisse feruntur
Nestora vel parvae magnum decus urbis Vlixem,
vixerit ille senex quamvis, dum terna per orbem   50
saecula fertilibus Titan decurreret horis,
ille per ignotas audax erraverit urbes,
qua maris extremis tellus includitur undis.
nam Ciconumque manus adversis reppulit armis ;
nec valuit lotos captos avertere cursus ;
cessit et Aetnaeae Neptunius incola rupis

but thou strivest to surpass the olden honours of thy
line, thyself a greater lustre to posterity than ancestry
to thee. For thy exploits no legend underneath a
name has room. Thou shalt have great rolls of im-
mortal verse; and, in eagerness to write thy praises,
all will assemble who compose in rhythm, whether
bound or free.[1] They will strive who shall be first.
May I be the conqueror among them all, that I may
write my name above the great story of those deeds.

[39] For who doth greater things than thou, whether
in camp or forum? Yet neither here nor there hast
thou either greater or lesser praise. Just as when a
true pair of scales is loaded with equal weights—one
that, so often as it has to carry a balancing load on
either side, wavers unsteadily with each pan lower in
turn—it sinks no more on this side than it rises
on that.

[45] For whether it be the fickle populace roaring in
division, there will be none to appease it like thee;
or be it an angry juror to be soothed, thy words will
avail to make him mild. Neither Pylos nor Ithaca
can claim to have had sons as great in Nestor or in
Ulysses, high ornament of a humble town, though
the old man lived on while Titan ran for three
lifetimes [2] through his cycle of fruit-bringing seasons,
and the other roved fearlessly through unknown
cities where Earth is shut in by Ocean's bounding
waves. He faced the bands of Cicones in fight and
drave them back. The Lotus could not ensnare
and turn aside his course. No match for him was
Neptune's son that dwelt on the cliffs of Aetna

---

[1] *I.e.*, whether in verse or prose.
[2] It is not clear whether here and in 112 Nestor is sup-
posed to live through three *generations* (= 100 years) or three
*centuries*, *saeculum* having both meanings.

victa Maroneo foedatus lumina baccho;
vexit et Aeolios placidum per Nerea ventos;
incultos adiit Laestrygonas Antiphatenque,
nobilis Artacie gelida quos inrigat unda;       60
solum nec doctae verterunt pocula Circes,
quamvis illa foret Solis genus, apta vel herbis
†aptaque† vel cantu veteres mutare figuras;
Cimmerion etiam obscuras accessit ad arces,
quis numquam candente dies apparuit ortu,
seu supra terras Phoebus seu curreret infra;
vidit ut inferno Plutonis subdita regno
magna deum proles levibus ius diceret umbris;
praeteriitque cita Sirenum litora puppi.
illum inter geminae nantem confinia mortis     70
nec Scyllae seno [1] conterruit impetus ore,
cum canibus rabidas inter fera serperet undas,
nec violenta suo consumpsit more Charybdis,
vel si sublimis fluctu consurgeret imo,
vel si interrupto nudaret gurgite pontum.
non violata vagi sileantur pascua Solis,
non amor et fecunda Atlantidos arva Calypsus,
finis et erroris miseri Phaeacia tellus.
atque haec seu nostras inter sunt cognita terras,
fabula sive novum dedit his erroribus orbem,    80
sit labor illius, tua dum facundia, maior.

    nam te non alius belli tenet aptius artes,
qua deceat tutam castris praeducere fossam,
qualiter adversos hosti defigere cervos,
quemve locum ducto melius sit claudere vallo,
fontis ubi dulces erumpat terra liquores,

            [1] seno *editor:* sevo (*i.e.,* saevo) *A.*

whose eye was ravaged when the wine of Maron
made it close. He bore the winds of Aeolus o'er
the calmed realm of Nereus. He visited the savage
Laestrygonians and Antiphates, whose lands the cool
waters of renowned Artacie lave. Him only could the
cup of cunning Circe not transform, though she was
the offspring of the Sun and skilled to change man's
proper shape by herbs and spells. He came also to
the dark fastnesses of the Cimmerians, whose eyes
never saw the day dawn brightly, whether Phoebus
ran above or underneath the Earth. He saw how,
subjected to the nether rule of Pluto, the gods' great
sons laid down the law for flitting shades; and in
swift-rowed ship he passed the Sirens' coast. He
sailed a strait bordered by death on either hand;
yet neither did the swoop of Scylla's six mouths
dismay him when the monster stole out amid the
waves that her wild dogs infested, nor did raging
Charybdis destroy him after her wont, whether rising
aloft in surge from the abyss or baring the sea-bed
with the breach in her waters. I should not be mute
on the profaning of the pastures of the far-travelling
Sun, nor the passion and rich fields of Atlas' daughter
Calypso, nor Phaeacia's land, the term of his woful
wandering. And whether these adventures were
encountered amid the lands we know or report
has placed his wanderings in some new world, in
suffering he may be first, but thou must be first in
eloquence.

8² Again, than thou there is none with a surer
mastery of the arts of war: where should be drawn
a protecting fosse before a camp, after what fashion
chevaux de frise be driven in to stop the foe, round
what spots 'tis best to draw the enclosing earthwork
where the earth throws up a gush of sweet spring

ut facilisque tuis aditus sit et arduus hosti,
laudis ut adsiduo vigeat certamine miles
quis tardamve sudem melius celeremve sagittam
iecerit aut lento perfregerit obvia pilo,      90
aut quis equum celeremque arto compescere freno
possit et effusas tardo permittere habenas
inque vicem modo derecto contendere passu,
seu libeat, curvo brevius convertere gyro,
quis parma, seu dextra velit seu laeva, tueri,
sive hac sive illac veniat gravis impetus hastae,
amplior,[1] aut signata cita loca tangere funda.
iam simul audacis veniant certamina Martis
adversisque parent acies concurrere signis,
tum tibi non desit faciem componere pugnae,   100
seu sit opus quadratum acies consistat in agmen,
rectus ut aequatis decurrat frontibus ordo,
seu libeat duplicem seiunctim cernere martem,
dexter uti laevum teneat dextrumque sinister
miles sitque duplex gemini victoria casus.

  at non per dubias errant mea carmina laudes:
nam bellis experta cano.   testis mihi victae
fortis Iapydiae miles, testis quoque fallax
Pannonius, gelidas passim disiectus in Alpes,
testis Arupinis et pauper natus in arvis,   110
quem si quis videat vetus ut non fregerit aetas,
terna minus Pyliae miretur saecula famae.
namque senex longae peragit dum tempora
      vitae,   112a
centum fecundos Titan renovaverit annos,
ipse tamen velox celerem super edere corpus
audet equum validisque sedet moderator habenis.

---

    [1] aptior *Francken is probable.*

water, so that approach thereto may be easy for thy
men and uphill for the enemy. How the soldiery may
be kept robust by unceasing struggles for distinction,
to prove whose hand discharges best the slow stake
or the speedy arrow or the obstinate pilum breaking
all down before it; whose hand has skill to hold in
the swift horse with bridle tightened and let the
reins fly free for the slow, and, changing about, now
gallop on a straight course or at pleasure make him
wheel in the circle's narrow round; who excels in the
shield-guard on right or left side as he will, as on
the one or the other quarter comes the spear's heavy
rush, or in getting the swift sling home upon the
mark. Next, as soon as the struggle of venturous
battle comes, and under confronting standards the
lines prepare to close, then thou wilt not fail in
forming the order of the fight, whether it be needful
for the troops to draw into a square, so that the
dressed line runs with level front, or it be desired to
sunder the battle into two several parts, so that the
army's right may hold the left and its left the right
and the twofold hazard yield a double victory.

106 But my verses do not stray among unproved
distinctions. I sing what wars have shown. I have
a witness in the gallant soldiery of vanquished
Iapydia; a witness also in the cunning Pannonian,
scattered far and wide over the icy Alps; a witness
too in the poor son of Arupium's fields, whom whoso
sees unbroken by advanced old age will wonder less
at the three lifetimes of the Pylian legend. For
while the old man accomplishes his long life's period
Titan will have brought round a hundred fruitful
years. Yet unaided he scruples not to fling his
nimble limbs above the fleet steed's back and sit
there its master, with a strong grasp on the reins.

315

te duce non alias conversus terga Domator [1]
libera Romanae subiecit colla catenae.

nec tamen his contentus eris : maiora peractis
instant, compertum est veracibus ut mihi signis,
quis Amythaonius nequeat certare Melampus.  120
nam modo fulgentem Tyrio subtemine vestem
indueras oriente die duce fertilis anni,
splendidior liquidis cum Sol caput extulit undis
et fera discordes tenuerunt flamina venti,
curva nec adsuetos egerunt flumina cursus ;
quin rapidum placidis etiam mare constitit undis,
ulla nec aerias volucris perlabitur auras
nec quadrupes densas depascitur aspera silvas,
quin largita tuis sit multa silentia votis.
Iuppiter ipse levi vectus per inania curru  130
adfuit et caelo vicinum liquit Olympum
intentaque tuis precibus se praebuit aure
cunctaque veraci capite adnuit : additus aris
laetior eluxit structos super ignis acervos.

quin hortante deo magnis insistere rebus
incipe : non idem tibi sint aliisque triumphi.
non te vicino remorabitur obvia marte
Gallia nec latis audax Hispania terris
nec fera Theraeo tellus obsessa colono,

---

[1] *I now, with some hesitation, keep* Domator *A., following a suggestion of Professor L. Havet that it is the name of a native chief.* Salassus *Baehrens, " the Salassian."*

Thou wast commander when Domator that never
turned his back before stooped his free neck to take
the Roman chains.

[118] Nor wilt thou rest content with this. What is
coming is greater than what has come to pass, as
I have ascertained from signs that tell the truth,
which Amythaon's Melampus could not match. Thou
hadst just donned the garb of flaming Tyrian tissue,[1]
as the day dawned that ushers in the fruitful year,
when, brighter than before, the Sun lifted his head
from the clear waves and the warring winds held
their wild gusts in check, nor did the winding rivers
pursue their wonted courses. Nay, even the whirling
sea stood still, its waves at peace. And no bird is
there that glides across the airs of heaven or savage
four-footed beast that grazes in woodland thickets
but gave lavish silence to thy prayers. Jupiter
himself rode in airy chariot through the void unto
thy side, and left Olympus, neighbour of the sky
He gave himself with ear attentive to thy prayers,
and granted all, bowing the head that never lies ;
and when fire touched the altar, its glad flare rose on
high above the piled-up incense.

[135] Now at the god's call press thou on to great
achievements. Not the same triumphs should there
be for thee as others. Confronting Gaul shall not
detain thee in combat close at hand, nor the wide terri-
tory of martial Spain, nor the wild land whereon the
settlers of Thera lodged,[2] nor that where flows the

---

[1] *I.e.*, the *toga praetexta* of the consul. Messalla was consul
with Octavianus in 31.

[2] *I.e.*, Cyrene. In this reference and those that follow to
rivers in the East—Choaspes, near Susa, Gyndes (for its con-
nection with Cyrus see Herod., XI.189), in Babylonia, Oroatis, in
Susiana, &c.—the war with Antony and Cleopatra is alluded to.

# PANEGYRICVS MESSALLAE

nec qua vel Nilus[1] vel regia lympha Choaspes    **140**
profluit aut rapidus, Cyri dementia, Gyndes
aret Araccaeis aut unda Oroatia[2] campis.
nec qua regna vago Tamyris finivit Araxe,
impia nec saevis celebrans convivia mensis
ultima vicinus Phoebo tenet arva Padaeus,
quaque Hebrus Tanaisque Getas rigat atque Magynos.
  quid moror? Oceanus ponto qua continet orbem,
nulla tibi adversis regio sese offeret armis.
te manet invictus Romano marte Britannus
teque interiecto mundi pars altera sole.[3]    **150**
nam circumfuso consistit in aere tellus
et quinque in partes toto disponitur orbe.
atque duae gelido vastantur frigore semper:
illic et densa tellus absconditur umbra,
et nulla incepto perlabitur unda liquore,
sed durata riget densam in glaciemque nivemque,
quippe ubi non umquam Titan super egerit ortus.
at media est Phoebi semper subiecta calori.
seu propior terris aestivum fertur in orbem
seu celer hibernas properat decurrere luces.    **160**
non igitur presso tellus exsurgit aratro,
nec frugem segetes praebent neque pabula terrae;
non illic colit arva deus, Bacchusve Ceresve,
ulla nec exustas habitant animalia partes.
fertilis hanc inter posita est interque rigentes
nostraque et huic adversa solo pars altera nostro,
quas similis utrimque tenens vicinia caeli
temperat, alter et alterius vires necat aer:

---

[1] aut Eulaeus (*a river of Susiana*) *S. Allen.*

[2] Oroatia *editor* (*see* "*Classical Review,*" XIX. p. 214): caristia *MSS. Or perhaps* Copratia (*fr.* Coprates, *another river in S.*).

[3] *I keep the text with Mr. Housman, who explains* sole *as in* Stat. "*S.*" IV. 3, 156, *of the* "*ecliptic,*" *as interposed between the north and south temperate zones.*

Nile or the king's stream Choaspes, or where the
rushing Gyndes which maddened Cyrus lies parched,
or the waters of Oroatis in the plains of Aracca, nor
where is the wild Araxes which Tamyris made the
boundary of her kingdom, or where the Padaean, on
whose savage tables is often spread a cannibal repast,[1]
dwells in remotest lands, the neighbour of Phoebus,
and where the Hebrus and the Tanais water the
Getae and the Magyni.[1]

147 Why do I trifle thus? Wherever the Ocean's
deep encompasses the earth, no land will meet thee
with opposing force. The Briton whom Roman
prowess has not vanquished is reserved for thee,
and the other portion of the world, with the Sun's
path set between. For the Earth rests on circum-
ambient air, and into five parts is its whole sphere
distributed. And two are always ravaged by icy
cold. There the earth is buried in thick shade and
no waters slip to the end of their liquid course, but
are frozen hard to thick ice and snow, since Titan
there never shows his rising orb on high. But the
middle is always underneath the heat of Phoebus,
whether he moves nearer to the earth on his summer
orbit or whether swiftly he hastes to conclude the
winter day. So there the earth does not rise in ridges
before the deep-driven plough, nor do the cornfields
yield grain or the lands pasture. No god tends the
fields, whether Bacchus or Ceres, nor do any animals
live in those parched regions. Between it and both
the frozen zones is set a fruitful one, ours and the
region that is opposite this land of ours, attempered
to likeness by the neighbouring climes that hold them
in on either side, one air destroying all the other's

[1] The *Padaei*, a cannibal tribe in India: Herod. III., 99.
The *Magyni* (*infra*) are unknown.

hinc placidus nobis per tempora vertitur annus;
hinc et colla iugo didicit submittere taurus          170
et lenta excelsos vitis conscendere ramos,
tondeturque seges maturos annua partus,
et ferro tellus, pontus † confunditur † [1] aere,
quin etiam structis exsurgunt oppida muris.
ergo ubi praeclaros poscent tua facta triumphos,
solus utroque idem diceris magnus in orbe.

   non ego sum satis ad tantae praeconia laudis,
ipse mihi non si praescribat carmina Phoebus.
est tibi, qui possit magnis se accingere rebus,
Valgius: aeterno propior non alter Homero.          180

   languida non [2] noster peragit labor otia, quamvis
Fortuna, ut mos est illi, me adversa fatiget.
nam mihi, cum magnis opibus domus alta niteret,
cui fuerant flavi ditantes ordine sulci
horrea fecundas ad deficientia messis,
cuique pecus denso pascebant agmine colles,
et domino satis et nimium furique lupoque,
nunc desiderium superest: nam cura novatur,
cum memor ante actos semper dolor admonet annos.

   sed licet asperiora cadant spolierque relictis,     190
non te deficient nostrae memorare camenae.
nec solum tibi Pierii tribuentur honores:
pro te vel rapidas ausim maris ire per undas,
adversis hiberna licet tumeant freta ventis,
pro te vel densis solus subsistere turmis
vel parvum Aetnaeae corpus committere flammae.
sum quodcumque, tuum est.   nostri si parvula cura
sit tibi, quanta libet, si sit modo, non mihi regna
Lydia, non magni potior sit fama Gylippi,[3]

---

  [1] *For the corrupt* confunditur *Némethy reads* proscinditur,
*which* (*or* neptunus finditur *ed.*) *gives the required sense.*

  [2] non *is abrupt and* nec *has been conjectured.*

  [3] Philippi *has been conjectured.*

power. Hence comes it that our year turns kindly
through its seasons; hence that the bull has learned
to bow his neck to the yoke and the limber vine to
climb the lofty bough, and year by year the cornfield
yields its ripe fruit to its shearer, and iron ploughs
the earth and bronze the sea; yea, and towns rise
high with their pile of walls. So, then, when thy
deeds shall claim their glorious triumph, thou only
shalt have the name of great in either world.

177 I am not strong enough to advertise such glory,
no, not if Phoebus himself dictate my song. Thou
hast in Valgius one that can gird himself for these
great achievements: none other comes nearer to
immortal Homer. 'Tis not that toil with me leaves
leisure to be passed in indolence, albeit Fortune, as is
her wont, harasses me with her enmity. For though
once I had a lofty mansion glittering with wealth, and
rows of yellow furrows, pouring treasure into barns
that could not cope with the plenteous harvests, and
serried lines of cattle browsing on the hills, enough
for owner and overmuch for thief and wolf, now
naught but the sense of loss remains. For pain
springs up again as Grief remembers and reminds
me ever of the bygone years.

190 But though harder times befall and I be
stripped of what is left me, my Muse will not fail
to tell of thee. Nor shall Pierian homage only
be accorded thee. For thee I would venture
over the rushing billows of the sea, though the
stormy friths swelled with hostile winds; for thee
I would await alone the serried squadrons' charge
or commit this poor body to the flames of Aetna.
All that I am is thine. If thou have but a little
thought of me, however small it is, if thou do but
have it, neither Lydia's monarchy nor the renown of

posse Meleteas nec mallem vincere chartas.    200
quod tibi si versus noster, totusve minusve,
vel bene sit notus, summo vel inerret in ore,
nulla mihi statuent finem te fata canendi.
quin etiam mea tunc tumulus cum texerit ossa,
seu matura dies celerem properat mihi mortem,
longa manet seu vita, tamen, mutata figura
seu me finget equum rigidos percurrere campos
doctum seu tardi pecoris sim gloria taurus
sive ego per liquidum volucris vehar aera pennis,
quandocumque hominem me longa receperit
    aetas,    210
inceptis de te subtexam carmina chartis.


# DE SVLPICIA

## INCERTI AVCTORIS ELEGIAE

### [TIBVLLI LIB. III. VIII. = IV. II.]

Svlpicia est tibi culta tuis, Mars magne, kalendis;
  spectatum e caelo, si sapis, ipse veni.
hoc Venus ignoscet: at tu, violente, caveto
  ne tibi miranti turpiter arma cadant.
illius ex oculis, cum vult exurere divos,
  accendit geminas lampadas acer Amor.
illam, quidquid agit, quoquo vestigia movit,
  componit furtim subsequiturque Decor.
seu solvit crines, fusis decet esse capillis;
  seu compsit, comptis est veneranda comis.    10
urit, seu Tyria voluit procedere palla;
  urit, seu nivea candida veste venit.

great Gylippus would be more to me, nor would I
choose rather to surpass the writings of the son of
Meles. But if my verse, whether all of it or less,
shall be well known to thee or else but cross thy
lips, the Fates shall set no bounds to my singing
of thee. Nay, more even then when the grave
has covered my bones, whether the appointed day
haste betimes to bring me a speedy end or a long
life awaits me, whether a change of shape shall make
me a horse that is trained to scour the unyielding
plains or I am a bull, the pride of the slow herd, or
a bird, borne on wings through the flowing air, none
the less, when lapse of ages receives me back among
mankind, will I weave verse to append to the pages
I had begun to write on thee.


## SULPICIA'S GARLAND


## VIII

### *To Sulpicia on the First of March*

GREAT Mars, it is thy Calends, and Sulpicia is dressed
for thee. Come thyself, if thou hast wit, from heaven
to see her. Venus will pardon this; but thou, rough
god, have a care lest to thy shame thy arms drop from
thy wondering hold. From her eyes, when he would
burn the gods amain, doth fierce Love kindle his
torches twin. Whatsoever she does, whithersoever she
turns her steps, Grace follows her unseen to order
all aright. Hath she loosed her hair? Then flowing
locks become her. Hath she dressed it? With dressed
hair she is divine. She fires the heart if she chooses
to appear in gown of Tyrian hue; she fires it if she

# DE SVLPICIA

talis in aeterno felix Vertumnus Olympo
    mille habet ornatus, mille decenter habet.
sola puellarum digna est cui mollia caris
    vellera det sucis bis madefacta Tyros,
possideatque, metit quidquid bene olentibus arvis
    cultor odoratae dives Arabs segetis,
et quascumque niger rubro de litore gemmas
    proximus Eois colligit Indus aquis.         20
hanc vos, Pierides, festis cantate kalendis,
    et testudinea Phoebe superbe lyra.
hoc sollemne sacrum multos haec sumet in annos ;
    dignior est vestro nulla puella choro.


## [TIBVLLI LIB. III. IX. = IV. III.]

Parce meo iuveni, seu quis bona pascua campi
    seu colis umbrosi devia montis aper,
nec tibi sit duros acuisse in proelia dentes ;
    incolumem custos hunc mihi servet Amor.

      .      .      .      .      .

sed procul abducit venandi Delia cura.
    o pereant silvae deficiantque canes !
quis furor est, quae mens densos indagine colles
    claudentem teneras laedere velle manus ?
quidve iuvat furtim latebras intrare ferarum
    candidaque hamatis crura notare rubis ?       10
sed tamen, ut tecum liceat, Cerinthe, vagari,
    ipsa ego per montes retia torta feram,

comes in the sheen of snowy robes. Like her, on
everlasting Olympus, bounteous Vertumnus wears a
thousand garbs, and wears with grace the thousand.
Of all maids only she deserves to receive from
Tyre soft wool twice drenched in costly juice,
that hers should be all that the rich Arab, tiller of
the perfumed field, reaps from his fragrant lands;
yea, all the pearls that the swart Indian, hard by the
waters of the Dawn, picks from the red seas' shores.
Sing of her on the festal Calends, ye Pierian nymphs,
and thou too, Phoebus, proud of thy tortoise lyre.
This rite recurring shall be hers for many a year. No
maid is worthier of the favours of your quire.


# IX

### *To Cerinthus at the Chase*

Boar, spare the youth I love, whether thy haunt is
the plain's fair pastures or the deep woodland of the
hills, nor think it thy part to whet thy hard tusks for
the fray. Let Love be his guard and keep him safe
for me. . . . But the dame of Delos draws him far
away with love of venery. Oh that woods might
wither and dogs be extinct! How mad, how sense-
less is this whim to hurt soft hands, setting the
tinchel [1] round the thick-clad hills! What pleasure
is it to steal into the lairs of wild beasts and to score
thy white legs with the bramble's barbs? Yet still,
Cerinthus, so I may share thy roamings, I will my-
self carry the twisted nets across the fells, myself

---

[1] This word, used by Scott, *Waverley*, ch. xxiv., is the only
equivalent of *indago*, the circle which hunters draw round
their game.

ipsa ego velocis quaeram vestigia cervi
    et demam celeri ferrea vincla cani.
tunc mihi, tunc placeant silvae, si, lux mea, tecum
    arguar ante ipsas concubuisse plagas ;
tunc veniat licet ad casses, inlaesus abibit,
    ne veneris cupidae gaudia turbet, aper.
nunc sine me sit nulla venus, sed lege Dianae,
    caste puer, casta retia tange manu ;        20
et quaecumque meo furtim subrepit amori,
    incidat in saevas diripienda feras.
at tu venandi studium concede parenti,
    et celer in nostros ipse recurre sinus.


## [TIBVLLI LIB. III. X. = IV. IV.]


Hvc ades et tenerae morbos expelle puellae,
    huc ades, intonsa Phoebe superbe coma.
crede mihi, propera : nec te iam, Phoebe, pigebit
    formosae medicas applicuisse manus.
effice ne macies pallentes occupet artus,
    neu notet informis languida [1] membra color,
et quodcumque mali est et quidquid triste timemus,
    in pelagus rapidis evehat amnis aquis.
sancte, veni, tecumque feras, quicumque sapores,
    quicumque et cantus corpora fessa levant ;    10
neu iuvenem torque, metuit qui fata puellae
    votaque pro domina vix numeranda facit.
interdum vovet, interdum, quod langueat illa,
    dicit in aeternos aspera verba deos.
pone metum, Cerinthe ; deus non laedit amantes.
    tu modo semper ama ; salva puella tibi est.    16

---

    [1] languida *Rigler :* pallida *A. :* candida *vulg.*

follow the tracks of the fleet deer and undo the iron collar of the rushing hound. Then, then would forests please me when it can be shown I have been in thy arms, my love, beside the very toils. Then, though the wild boar come up to the nets, he shall depart unharmed lest he break the joys of eager love. But now without me let there be no loving; but, lad, be chaste, and lay chaste hands upon the nets as Diana's rule enjoins, and let any she that creeps by stealth into my place of love fall among savage wild beasts and be torn piecemeal. But do thou leave the love of hunting to thy sire and haste back quickly to my arms.

# X

*Sulpicia Sick*

COME hither and drive out the tender maid's disease, come hither, Phoebus, with thy pride of unshorn hair. Hear me and hasten; and henceforth, Phoebus, thou shalt ne'er regret to have laid thy healing hands upon the fair. See to it that no wasting blight fall on the pallid form, nor disfiguring hue mark the feeble limbs. Yea, all the mischief, all the dread things we fear, let the rushing river-waters carry out into the main. Come, holy one, and bring with thee all essences, all chants that ease the body's sickness. And torture not the youth who fears that the maid will die, and offers prayers, past counting, for his mistress. Sometimes he prays, sometimes in grief that she is sick he utters fierce words against the eternal gods. Put fear aside, Cerinthus. God harms not lovers. Do thou love ever, and thy girl is safe.

nil opus est fletu ; lacrimis erit aptius uti,     21
   si quando fuerit tristior illa tibi.     22
at nunc tota tua est, te solum candida secum     17
   cogitat, et frustra credula turba sedet.
Phoebe, fave.   laus magna tibi tribuetur in uno
   corpore servato restituisse duos.     20
iam celeber, iam laetus eris, cum debita reddet     23
   certatim sanctis gratus uterque focis.
tunc te felicem dicet pia turba deorum,
   optabunt artes et sibi quisque tuas.

## [TIBVLLI LIB. III. XI. = IV. V.]

Qvi mihi te, Cerinthe, dies dedit, hic mihi sanctus
   atque inter festos semper habendus erit.
te nascente novum Parcae cecinere puellis
   servitium et dederunt regna superba tibi.
uror ego ante alias.   iuvat hoc, Cerinthe, quod uror,
   si tibi de nobis mutuus ignis adest.
mutuus adsit amor, per te dulcissima furta
   perque tuos oculos per Geniumque rogo.
magne Geni, cape tura libens votisque faveto,
   si modo, cum de me cogitat, ille calet.     10
quod si forte alios iam nunc suspirat [1] amores,
   tum precor infidos, sancte, relinque focos.
nec tu sis iniusta, Venus ; vel serviat aeque
   vinctus uterque tibi vel mea vincla leva.
sed potius valida teneamur uterque catena,
   nulla queat posthac quam soluisse dies.

[1] suspirat *the corrected MSS.* : suspiret *A.*

No need for weeping. Then fitlier will thy tears flow
if ever she is angered with thee. But now she is
wholly thine. In the kind maid's breast are only
thoughts of thee, and a credulous company waits in
vain upon her. Phoebus, be gracious. Great praise
will be thy portion when by saving one life thou
restorest two. Then famous and jubilant wilt thou
be when in grateful rivalry both pay the debt they
owe to thy holy altar. Then the company of good
gods will call thee fortunate, and each desire thy
own craft for himself.

# XI

## *Cerinthus' Birthday*

THIS day that made thee live for me, Cerinthus, shall
be for me one to be hallowed always and set among
the festivals. When thou wast born, the voices of
the Fates proclaimed that now there was new slavery
for woman, and bestowed proud sovereignty on thee.
I burn more fiercely than them all, but joy, Cerinthus,
in the burning, if within thy breast live fires caught
from mine. May love like mine be thine, I pray
thee, by our stolen raptures, by thine eyes and thy
Birth-spirit. Great Genius, take this incense with a
will, and smile upon my prayer, if only when he
thinks on me his pulse beats high. But if perchance
even now he sighs for another love, then, holy one,
depart thou from that faithless altar. And, Venus,
be not thou unjust; either let both alike be bound
thy slaves or lift my shackles off. But rather let us
both be bound, with a strong chain that no coming

optat idem iuvenis quod nos, sed tectius optat ;
  nam pudet haec illum dicere verba palam.
at tu, Natalis, quoniam deus omnia sentis,
  adnue : quid refert, clamne palamne roget ?      20


## [TIBVLLI LIB. III. XII. = IV. VI.]

NATALIS Iuno, sanctos cape turis acervos,
  quos tibi dat tenera docta puella manu.
tota [1] tibi est hodie, tibi se laetissima compsit,
  staret ut ante tuos conspicienda focos.
illa quidem ornandi causas tibi, diva, relegat ;
  est tamen, occulte cui placuisse velit.
at tu, sancta, fave, neu quis divellat amantes,
  sed iuveni quaeso mutua vincla para.
sic bene compones : ullae non ille puellae
  servire aut cuiquam dignior illa viro.      10
nec possit cupidos vigilans deprendere custos
  fallendique vias mille ministret Amor.
adnue purpureaque veni perlucida palla :
  ter tibi fit libo, ter, dea casta, mero.
praecipit et natae mater studiosa quod optet :
  illa aliud tacita iam sua mente rogat.
uritur ut celeres urunt altaria flammae,
  nec, liceat quamvis, sana fuisse velit.
sis Iuno, grata, ut veniet cum proximus annus,
  hic idem votis iam vetus adsit amor.      20

----

[1] lota *the corrected MSS., perhaps rightly, of the ceremonial
bath.*

day can loose. The lad desires the same as 1, but
conceals his longing more; he is ashamed to say
the words aloud. But thou, Birth-spirit, a god and
knowing all things, grant the prayer. What matter
if his suit be uttered or unspoken?

# XII

### *Sulpicia's Birthday*

Juno of the birthday, receive the holy piles of incense
which the accomplished maid's soft hand now offers
thee. To-day she is thine wholly; most joyfully she
has decked herself for thee, to stand before thy
altar a sight for all to see. 'Tis in thee, goddess,
she bids us find the reason for this apparelling. Yet
there is one that in secret she desires to please.
Then, hallowed one, be kind, and let none pluck
apart the lovers : but forge, I prithee, like fetters for
the youth. Thus shalt thou match them well. To
no maid he, to no man she might fitlier be
thrall. And may no watchful guard surprise their
wooings, but Love suggest a thousand ways for his
outwitting. Bow assent and come in all the sheen
of purple palla. They are making offering to thee,
holy goddess, thrice with cake and thrice with wine,
and the mother eagerly enjoins upon her child what
she must pray for. But she, now mistress of herself,
sues for another thing in the silence of her heart.
She burns as the altar burns with the darting flames,
nor, even though she might, would she be whole.
Be grateful, Juno, so that, when the next year
comes, this love, now of long standing, may be there
unchanged to meet their prayers.

## SVLPICIAE ELEGIDIA

### [TIBVLLI LIB. III. XIII. = IV. VII.]

Tandem venit amor, qualem texisse pudori
    quam nudasse alicui sit mihi, Fama,[1] magis.
exorata meis illum Cytherea Camenis
    attulit in nostrum deposuitque sinum.
exoluit promissa Venus: mea gaudia narret,
    dicetur si quis non habuisse sua.
non ego signatis quicquam mandare tabellis,
    me legat ut nemo quam meus ante, velim,
sed peccasse iuvat, vultus componere famae
    taedet: cum digno digna fuisse ferar.        10


### [TIBVLLI LIB. III. XIV. = IV. VIII.]

Invisvs natalis adest, qui rure molesto
    et sine Cerintho tristis agendus erit.
dulcius urbe quid est? an villa sit apta puellae
    atque Arretino frigidus amnis agro?
iam, nimium Messalla mei studiose, quiescas:
    non tempestivae saepe, propinque, viae.
hic animum sensusque meos abducta relinquo,
    arbitrio quam vis non sinit esse meo.

[1] Fama *printed as a vocative with* Némethy

## SULPICIA

### XIII

#### On her Love

At last has come a love which, Rumour, it would
shame me more to hide than to disclose to any one.
Won over by my Muse's prayers, Cythera's queen
has brought and placed him in my arms. What
Venus promised she hath fulfilled. Let my joys be
told by all of whom 'tis said that they have missed
their own. Never would I choose to entrust my
messages to tablets under seal, that none might read
my thoughts before my lover. Nay, I love my fault,
and loathe to wear a mask for rumour. Let all hear
that we have met, each worthy of the other.

### XIV

#### Before her Birthday

My hated birthday is at hand, to be kept all joylessly
in the odious country and without Cerinthus. What
is more pleasant than the town? Would a grange
be fit place for a girl, or the chill river of Arretium
and its fields? Rest now, Messalla, from thy excessive
zeal for me. Journeys, my kinsman, are oft
ill-timed. They take me away, but here I leave my
soul and heart, since force forbids my living mistress
of myself.

# SVLPICIAE ELEGIDIA

## [TIBVLLI LIB. III. XV. = IV. IX.]

Scis iter ex animo sublatum triste puellae?
    natali Romae iam licet esse suo.
omnibus ille dies nobis natalis[1] agatur,
    qui nec opinanti nunc tibi forte venit.

## [TIBVLLI LIB. III. XVI. = IV. X.]

Gratvm est, securus multum quod iam tibi de me
    permittis, subito ne male inepta cadam.
sit tibi cura togae potior pressumque quasillo
    scortum quam Servi filia Sulpicia:
solliciti sunt pro nobis, quibus illa doloris
    ne cedam ignoto maxima causa toro.

## [TIBVLLI LIB. III. XVII. = IV. XI.]

Estne tibi, Cerinthe, tuae pia cura puellae,
    quod mea nunc vexat corpora fessa calor?
a ego non aliter tristes evincere morbos
    optarim, quam te si quoque velle putem.
at mihi quid prosit morbos evincere, si tu
    nostra potes lento pectore ferre mala?

---

[1] natalis *and probably other words in this couplet are corrupt.
The general sense is given in the version.*

334

## XV

### The Journey Abandoned

Dost thou know that the burden of that journey is lifted from thy girl's heart? Now she can be at Rome upon her birthday. Let us all, then, keep that day [with gladness], which comes to thee this time by unexpected chance.

## XVI

### Cerinthus Unfaithful

It is a pleasant thought that now in thy unconcern thou dost allow thyself so much at my expense,[1] that I may not trip in some unhappy fit of folly. For thee toga and strumpet loaded with wool-basket may be worthier of thy preference than Sulpicia, Servius' daughter. But they are distressed in my behalf, to whom this is the greatest cause of pain, that I may yield my place to an ignoble rival.

## XVII

### From her Sick-bed

Cerinthus, hast thou any tender thought for thine own girl, now that fever racks her feeble frame? Ah, I would not pray to triumph over the drear disease if I thought not that thou wouldst wish it too. How should it profit me to master sickness if thou canst bear my troubles with a heart unmoved?

[1] Or, possibly, "I am obliged for what thou dost allow thyself, troubling little about me."

# SVLPICIAE ELEGIDIA

## [TIBVLLI LIB. III. XVIII. = IV. XII.]

Ne tibi sim, mea lux, aeque iam fervida cura
    ac videor paucos ante fuisse dies,
si quicquam tota commisi stulta iuventa
    cuius me fatear paenituisse magis,
hesterna quam te solum quod nocte reliqui,
    ardorem cupiens dissimulare meum.

---

## INCERTI AVCTORIS

## [TIBVLLI LIB. III. XIX. = IV. XIII.]

Nvlla tuum nobis subducet femina lectum ;
    hoc primum iuncta est foedere nostra venus.
tu mihi sola places, nec iam te praeter in urbe
    formosa est oculis ulla puella meis.
atque utinam posses uni mihi bella videri !
    displiceas aliis ; sic ego tutus ero.
nil opus invidia est ; procul absit gloria vulgi :
    qui sapit, in tacito gaudeat ipse sinu.
sic ego secretis possum bene vivere silvis,
    qua nulla humano sit via trita pede.        10
tu mihi curarum requies, tu nocte vel atra
    lumen, et in solis tu mihi turba locis.
nunc licet e caelo mittatur amica Tibullo,
    mittetur frustra deficietque venus.
hoc tibi sancta tuae Iunonis numina iuro,
    quae sola ante alios est mihi magna deos.
quid facio demens ?   heu heu mea pignora cedo.
    iuravi stulte ; proderat iste timor.

## XVIII

### *An Apology*

My life, let me be no more to thee so hot a passion
as few days ago methinks I was, if in my whole
youth I have done any deed of folly of which I
would own I have repented more, than leaving thee
yesternight alone, through desire to hide the fire
within me.

## XIX

### *To his Mistress*

No woman shall filch thy place of love with me:
such our covenant when first the love-tie joined us.
Only thou dost please me; now save thee no girl in
the city is beauteous to my eyes. And, oh, might I be
the only one to think thee fair! Mayst thou be un-
pleasing to all besides. So shall I be safe. No need
for envy here; far from me be the vaunts of the
common herd; let the wise man keep his joy hushed
up within his bosom. Thus shall I live happily in
forest depths where foot of man has never worn a
path. For me thou art repose from cares, light even in
night's darkness, a throng amid the solitudes. Now,
though a mistress be sent to Tibullus from the skies,
she will be sent in vain, and desire be extinguished
This I swear to thee by thy Juno's holy power; for
to me is she great above all gods beside. What mad
thing am I doing? Alas! surrendering my hostages.
That was an oath of folly. Thy fears were my gain.

## TIBVLLVS

nunc tu fortis eris, nunc tu me audacius ures ;
   hoc peperit misero garrula lingua malum.     20
iam, facias quodcumque voles, tuus usque manebo,
   nec fugiam notae servitium dominae,
sed Veneris sanctae considam vinctus ad aras :
   haec notat iniustos supplicibusque favet.


## [TIBVLLI LIB. III. XX. = IV. XIV.]

RVMOR ait crebro nostram peccare puellam :
   nunc ego me surdis auribus esse velim.
crimina non haec sunt nostro sine facta dolore :
   quid miserum torques, rumor acerbe ?  tace.


## DOMITI MARSI

TE quoque Vergilio comitem non aequa, Tibulle,
   Mors iuvenem campos misit ad Elysios,
ne foret aut elegis molles qui fleret amores
   aut caneret forti regia bella pede.

Now wilt thou take heart, now fan my flames more boldly. This, alas! is the mischief brought me by my chattering tongue. Now, do what thou wilt, I will remain thine always, nor flee from bondage to a mistress that I know, but will sit in my chains at the altar of holy Venus. She brands law-breakers and befriends the suppliant.

## XX

### Unkind Rumour

RUMOUR says that my girl is oft unfaithful. Now could I wish my ears were deaf. These charges are not made without suffering for me. Why dost thou torture thus thy victim, bitter Rumour? Peace!

## DOMITIUS MARSUS

### On the Death of Tibullus

THEE too, Tibullus, ere thy time hath Death's un-
    feeling hand
Despatched to fare by Vergil's side to dim Elysium's
    land,
That none should be to plain of love in elegy's soft
    lay
Or in heroic numbers sweep with princes to the
    fray.

# PERVIGILIUM VENERIS
TRANSLATED BY J. W. MACKAIL
HON. LL.D. EDINBURGH AND ST.
ANDREWS; FORMERLY PROFESSOR
OF POETRY IN THE UNIVERSITY
OF OXFORD

# INTRODUCTION

THE little poem which has come down to us under the title of the *Pervigilium Veneris* is remarkable not only for its poetical merit—a delicate and bewitching beauty of phrasing and melody which survives the confusion of a corrupt and disordered text—but also as the first clear note of the new romanticism which transformed classical into mediaeval literature. It is the earliest known poem belonging in spirit to the Middle Ages.

Its date, authorship, and provenance are all unknown. It is extant in two MSS. of what is known as the *Anthologia Latina*, a collection of short Latin poems of the post-classical period. The collection may have been formed in the fourth century. Both MSS. are in the Bibliothèque Nationale at Paris. The earlier and more important, the Codex Salmasianus, or Parisiensis 10318, probably belonged to the great Cistercian library at Cluny, which was dispersed at the sack of the monastery in 1562. It was given by a friend to Salmasius early in the seventeenth century; he annotated but did not edit it. The handwriting dates it as written at the end of the seventh or beginning of the eighth century. The other MS., the Codex Pithoeanus, or Parisiensis 8071, is about 200 years later in date. It belonged to Pierre Pithou, who from it printed the poem for the first time at Paris in 1577. Modern scholars regard both MSS. as traceable to a common archetype, probably of the sixth century, in which the text had already become very corrupt.

Theories as to the date of the poem may be classed under two heads. The one attributes it to the second century, either in the principate of Hadrian (who revived the worship of Venus on a scale of great magnificence), or a generation later, in the principate of Marcus Aurelius. The other assigns it to some period between the end of the third and the middle of the fourth century, and to the African school which flourished in that period. It has a certain affinity in style and spirit with the Eclogues of Nemesianus of Carthage (*circ.* A.D. 285), and one still more striking with the few surviving fragments of Tiberianus (*circ.* A.D. 350), in language, versification, and a delicate feeling for nature. This latter date is now generally accepted. It is supported by traces in the *Pervigilium* (though these are not very certain) of the substitution of accentual for quantitative prosody, which was then beginning, and by its marked tendency towards discarding the case-inflexions of classical Latin.

As it stands in the MSS., the poem consists of ninety-two or ninety-three lines. Many of these are obviously disordered, and the refrain appears to be inserted or omitted capriciously. A note attached to the title in Codex S, "Sunt vero versus xxii," has no relevance to its length, but refers to the contents of a section of the anthology at the beginning of which it stands. Nor is it possible to rearrange with any confidence a poem which consists of loosely strung stanzas capable of being set in various patterns, and which in any case is full of studied interlacements and repetitions. The text here given is

largely conjectural, not only in its free rearrangement
and in the insertion of the refrain at regular intervals,
but also in the addition, to fill up gaps, of several lines
which have no MS. authority.

Many scholars from Pithou and Salmasius onwards
have worked at the fascinating and in great part
insoluble problems presented by the poem. In
modern times there are critical texts by Bücheler
(1858), Riese (1869), and Baehrens (1882), and more
recently by Clementi (Oxford, 1911). Many attempts
have likewise been made—none of them with much
success—to render in English verse the ringing
melody and fragile exquisiteness which make it
unique in poetry. Among these, it is only neces-
sary to mention the two most recent, those by
Mr. Clementi (*op. cit.*) and by Sir A. Quiller-Couch
(1912). Both print the Latin text used by them
opposite their English. The remarkable study and
appreciation of the poem, and the imaginative recon-
stitution of the circumstances of its origin, in Pater's
*Marius the Epicurean* are widely known.

The *trinoctium* of Venus, for which the piece was
written, or, rather, by which it was suggested, was
in its origin a popular festival, and became under the
Empire an organised observance in the established
State religion. In this poem we see it as neither
one nor the other, but as a motive of fantasy, a
summons which evokes imaginative associations, and
sets the rhythm of poetry in movement round nature
and history, love and life. Nothing could be less
like either a folk-song or an official ode. It touches
the last refinement of simplicity. In the delicately
running, softly swaying verses, that ring and glitter
and return on themselves in interlacing patterns,
there is germinally the essence and inner spirit of

345

the whole romantic movement. All the motives of
the old classical poetry survive, yet all have undergone
a new birth.

> The fairy fancies range
> And, lightly stirr'd,
> Ring little bells of change
> From word to word.

Poetry has gone back to childhood; and has re-
covered, as though for one fleeting moment and by
the spell of a capricious enchanter, the key of spring,
the freshness of morning, the innocence of youth.

# THE EVE OF ST. VENUS

# PERVIGILIVM VENERIS

## I

CRAS amet qui nunquam amavit quique amavit cras
   amet:
ver novum, ver iam canorum, ver renatus orbis est;
vere concordant amores, vere nubunt alites,
et nemus comam resolvit de maritis imbribus.

cras amet qui nunquam amavit quique amavit cras
   amet.


## II

cras amorum copulatrix inter umbras arborum
inplicat casas virentes de flagello myrteo:
cras canoris feriatos ducit in silvis choros;
cras Dione iura dicit fulta sublimi throno.

cras amet qui nunquam amavit quique amavit cras
   amet.


## III

cras erit cum primus aether copulavit nuptias:
tunc cruore de superno spumeo et ponti globo,

# THE EVE OF ST. VENUS

### I

To-morrow shall be love for the loveless, and for the lover to-morrow shall be love. Spring is young, spring now is singing, spring is the world reborn. In spring the loves make accord, in spring the birds mate, and the woodland loosens her tresses under nuptial showers.

To-morrow shall be love for the loveless, and for the lover to-morrow shall be love.

### II

To-morrow the marriage-maker of the loves amid shadows of trees weaves her verdurous bowers of myrtle-spray; to-morrow she leads her bands on festival in the singing forests: to-morrow Dione declares her laws high enthroned aloft.

To-morrow shall be love for the loveless, and for the lover to-morrow shall be love.

### III

To-morrow will be the day when the primal ether joined wedlock: then from the moisture overhead

349

caerulas inter catervas, inter et bipedes equos,
fecit undantem Dionem de maritis imbribus.

cras amet qui nunquam amavit quique amavit cras
amet.

## IV

ipsa gemmis purpurantem pingit annum floridis;
ipsa turgentes papillas de favoni spiritu
urget in nodos tepentes; ipsa roris lucidi,
noctis aura quem relinquit, spargit umentes aquas.

cras amet qui nunquam amavit quique amavit cras
amet.

## V

emicant lacrimae trementes de caduco pondere,
gutta praeceps orbe parvo sustinet casus suos:
umor ille quem serenis astra rorant noctibus
mane virgines papillas solvit umenti peplo.

cras amet qui nunquam amavit quique amavit cras
amet.

## VI

en pudorem florulentae prodiderunt purpurae
et rosarum flamma nodis emicat tepentibus.
ipsa iussit diva vestem de papillis solvere,
ut recenti mane nudae virgines nubant rosae.

cras amet qui nunquam amavit quique amavit cras
amet.

and the orbed sea-foam, amid green multitudes and finned horses, sprang Dione wave-born under nuptial showers.

To-morrow shall be love for the loveless, and for the lover to-morrow shall be love.

## IV

She herself paints the crimsoning year with flowery jewels; herself coaxes swelling buds into warm clusters under the West Wind's breath; herself sprinkles dripping wetness of the glittering dew that the night-air leaves as it passes.

To-morrow shall be love for the loveless, and for the lover to-morrow shall be love.

## V

Sparkling tears quiver in a heavy drip, the little splashing dew-bead holds together in its fall: the moisture that the stars distil on cloudless nights unfolds the maiden buds from their wet sheaths at daybreak.

To-morrow shall be love for the loveless, and for the lover to-morrow shall be love.

## VI

Lo, the petalled crimsons have unveiled their blush, and a flame of roses breaks from the warm clusters: the Goddess herself has bidden the roses loosen the raiment from their maiden buds, to be naked virgin brides in the fresh daybreak.

To-morrow shall be love for the loveless, and for the lover to-morrow shall be love.

## VII

facta Cypridis de cruore deque Amoris osculo,
deque gemmis deque flammis deque solis purpuris,
cras ruborem qui latebat veste tectus ignea
uvido marita nodo non pudebit solvere.

cras amet qui nunquam amavit quique amavit cras
amet.

## VIII

ipsa nymphas diva luco iussit ire myrteo :
it puer comes puellis ; nec tamen credi potest
esse Amorem feriatum, si sagittas vexerit :
ite nymphae, posuit arma, feriatus est Amor.

cras amet qui nunquam amavit quique amavit cras
amet.

## IX

iussus est inermis ire, nudus ire iussus est,
neu quid arcu neu sagitta neu quid igne laederet :
sed tamen cavete nymphae, quod Cupido pulcher est :
totus est inermis idem quando nudus est Amor.

cras amet qui nunquam amavit quique amavit cras
amet.

## VII

Compounded of Venus' blood and of Love's kiss and of jewels and of flames and of flushes of the sun, to-morrow the bride unashamed will unfold from the wet cluster the crimson that lurked hid in its taper sheath.

To-morrow shall be love for the loveless, and for the lover to-morrow shall be love.

## VIII

Herself the Goddess has bidden the nymphs go forth in the myrtle thicket: with the girls a boy goes in company; and yet it may not be deemed that Love is gone on festival if he carries his shafts. Go forth, nymphs; Love has laid by his weapons, he keeps festival.

To-morrow shall be love for the loveless, and for the lover to-morrow shall be love.

## IX

He has been bidden go forth unarmed, has been bidden go forth naked, that he might do no injury with bow nor shaft nor torch. But yet take heed, nymphs, because Cupid is fair; Love naked is complete, Love unarmed is the same.

To-morrow shall be love for the loveless, and for the lover to-morrow shall be love.

## X

conpari Venus pudore mittit ad te virgines :
una res est quam rogamus, cede virgo Delia,
ut nemus sit incruentum de ferinis stragibus
et recentibus virentes ducat umbras floribus.

cras amet qui nunquam amavit quique amavit cras
amet.

## XI

ipsa vellet te rogare, si pudicam flecteret ;
ipsa vellet ut venires, si deceret virginem :
iam tribus choros videres feriatos noctibus
congreges inter catervas ire per saltus tuos.

cras amet qui nunquam amavit quique amavit cras
amet.

## XII

floreas inter coronas, myrteas inter casas,
nec Ceres nec Bacchus absunt nec poetarum deus.
de tenente tota nox est perviglanda canticis :
regnet in silvis Dione, tu recede Delia.

cras amet qui nunquam amavit quique amavit cras
amet.

## X

Venus sends thee maidens as virginal as thou: "One thing it is we ask: retire, maid of Delos, that the woodland be unstained by wild creatures' slaughter, and trace her verdurous shadows over the fresh flowers."

To-morrow shall be love for the loveless, and for the lover to-morrow shall be love.

## XI

Herself she would ask thee, if she might bend thy virginity; thyself she would thou camest, if that were meet for a maiden: now for three nights wouldst thou see the bands pass along thy glades amid assembled multitudes making festival.

To-morrow shall be love for the loveless, and for the lover to-morrow shall be love.

## XII

Among flowery garlands, among myrtle bowers, Ceres and Bacchus are not absent, nor the god of the poets. All the night shall be kept awake with songs unceasingly; Dione shall be queen in the woods: do thou retire, maid of Delos.

To-morrow shall be love for the loveless, and for the lover to-morrow shall be love.

## XIII

iussit Hyblaeis tribunal stare diva floribus;
praeses ipsa iura dicet, adsidebunt Gratiae:
Hybla totos funde flores, quicquid annus adtulit;
Hybla florum sume vestem, quantus Ennae campus
 est.

cras amet qui nunquam amavit quique amavit cras
 amet.

## XIV

ruris hic erunt puellae vel puellae montium
quaeque silvas quaeque lucos quaeque fontes
 incolunt:
iussit omnes adsidere mater alitis dei,
iussit et nudo puellas nil Amori credere.

cras amet qui nunquam amavit quique amavit cras
 amet.

## XV

ut pater totum crearet veris annum nubibus
in sinum maritus imber fluxit almae coniugis,
unde fetus perque pontum perque caelum pergeret
perque terras mixtus omnes alere magno corpore.

cras amet qui nunquam amavit quique amavit cras
 amet.

# THE EVE OF ST. VENUS

## XIII

The Goddess has bidden her judgment-seat be set amid flowers of Hybla; herself will preside and declare her laws, the Graces will sit beside her. Pour forth all thy flowerage, O Hybla, the whole foison of the year; put on thy garment of flowers, O Hybla, over all the plain of Enna.

To-morrow shall be love for the loveless, and for the lover to-morrow shall be love.

## XIV

Here will be the country-maidens or the hill-maidens, and they who haunt forests and groves and springs: the mother of the winged god has bidden them all sit beside her, has bidden maids put no affiance even in naked love.

To-morrow shall be love for the loveless, and for the lover to-morrow shall be love.

## XV

To quicken the whole year from the clouds of spring, the bridegroom-shower has flowed into the lap of his fair bride, that so mingling with the vast frame he might pass through sea and through sky and through all the lands to nourish their offspring.

To-morrow shall be love for the loveless, and for the lover to-morrow shall be love.

## XVI

ipsa venas atque mentem permeanti spiritu
intus occultis gubernat procreatrix viribus.
ipsa Troianos nepotes in Latinos transtulit,
Romuleas ipsa fecit cum Sabinis nuptias.

cras amet qui nunquam amavit quique amavit cras
amet.

## XVII

pervium sui tenorem seminali tramite
perque caelum perque terras perque pontum
    subditum
ipsa duxit, ipsa venis procreantem spiritum
inbuit, iussitque mundum nosse nascendi vias.

cras amet qui nunquam amavit quique amavit cras
amet.

## XVIII

ipsa Laurentem puellam coniugem nato dedit,
moxque Marti de sacello dat pudicam virginem,
unde Ramnes et Quirites proque prole posterum
Romulum patrem crearet et nepotem Caesarem.

cras amet qui nunquam amavit quique amavit cras
amet.

# THE EVE OF ST. VENUS

## XVI

Herself the Creatress in hidden might sways flesh
and spirit from within with her enkindling life.
Herself she engrafted her Trojan offspring on the
Latins, herself made the wedding of the Sabines
with the sons of Romulus.

To-morrow shall be love for the loveless, and for
the lover to-morrow shall be love.

## XVII

Herself along the passage of the seed drew the
flooding tide of herself through sky and through the
lands and through the sea beneath, herself poured
the quickening life through their veins, and bade the
universe know the ways of birth.

To-morrow shall be love for the loveless, and for
the lover to-morrow shall be love.

## XVIII

Herself she gave her son the Laurentine maid for
bride, and gives thereafter to Mars the shy cloistered
virgin, from these to beget Ramnes and Quirites,
and for issue of posterity Romulus the sire and Caesar
the grandchild of her line.

To-morrow shall be love for the loveless, and for
the lover to-morrow shall be love.

## XIX

rura fecundat voluptas : rura Venerem sentiunt :
ipse Amor puer Dionae rure natus creditur :
hunc ager cum parturiret ipsa suscepit sinu,
ipsa florum delicatis educavit osculis.

cras amet qui nunquam amavit quique amavit cras
amet.

## XX

ecce iam super genestas explicant tauri latus,
quisque coetus continetur coniugali foedere :
subter umbras cum maritis ecce balantum gregem,
et canoras non tacere diva iussit alites.

cras amet qui nunquam amavit quique amavit cras
amet.

## XXI

iam loquaces ore rauco stagna cycni perstrepunt :
adsonat Terei puella subter umbram populi,
ut putes motus amoris ore dici musicos,
et neges queri sororem de marito barbaro.

cras amet qui nunquam amavit quique amavit cras
amet.

# THE EVE OF ST. VENUS

## XIX

The country quickens with love's delight, the country feels Venus' touch: Love himself, the child of Dione, is deemed country-born. Him, while the field broke to birth, herself she took up into her bosom, herself nursed with the dainty kisses of flowers.

To-morrow shall be love for the loveless, and for the lover to-morrow shall be love.

## XX

Lo, now the bulls lay a broad flank upon the broom; each community is held together in wedlock-band. Lo, beneath the shade the bleating flock with their lords, and tuneful birds that the Goddess has bidden not be mute.

To-morrow shall be love for the loveless, and for the lover to-morrow shall be love.

## XXI

Now hoarse-mouthed swans crash trumpeting over the pools; the maid of Tereus makes descant under the poplar shade, that you would think tunes of love issued trilling from her mouth, and not a sister's complaint of a barbarous lord.

To-morrow shall be love for the loveless, and for the lover to-morrow shall be love.

## XXII

illa cantat, nos tacemus : quando ver venit meum ?
quando fiam uti chelidon ut tacere desinam ?
perdidi musam tacendo, nec me Apollo respicit :
sic Amyclas, cum tacerent, perdidit silentium.

cras amet qui nunquam amavit quique amavit cras
    amet.

## XXII

  She sings, we are mute : when is my spring coming ?
when shall I be as the swallow, that I may cease to
be voiceless ?  I have lost the Muse in silence, nor
does Apollo regard me :  so Amyclae, being mute,
perished by silence.

  To-morrow shall be love for the loveless, and for
the lover to-morrow shall be love.

# APPENDIX

## PERVIGILIVM VENERIS

*This text is printed as close to the MSS. as possible. Conjectural changes have been noted, but not corrections of spelling, or where the text depends on one MS. only.*

CRAS amet qui numquam amavit quique amavit cras
           amet!
ver novum : ver iam canorum : ver renactus orbis est !
vere concordant amores, vere nubunt alites
et nemus comam resolvit de maritis imbribus :
cras amorum copulatrix inter umbras arborum     5
inplicat casas virentis de flagello myrteo,
cras Dione iura dicit fulta sublimi throno.
Cras amet qui numquam amavit quique amavit cras
           amet !

tunc cruore de superbo spumeo pontus globo
caerulas inter catervas, inter et bipedes equos    10
fecit undantem Dionen de marinis imbribus.
Cras amet qui numquam amavit quique amavit cras
           amet !

ipsa gemmis purpurantem pingit annum floridis,
ipsa surgentes papillas de Favoni spiritu
urget in nodos feraces, ipsa roris lucidi,    15

---

2 ver renactus orbis est *Bährens :* ver natus orbis est *T :* vere natus iovis est *S.*
  6 casas *Pithoeus :* gazas *T :* gaza *S.*
  11 marinis *Rivinus :* maritis *codd.*
  13 floridis *Rigler :* floribus *codd.*
  15 nodos *amicus Scriverii :* notos *S :* totos *T :* toros *Pithoeus.* feraces *Bährens :* penates *S :* pentes *T.*

noctis aura quem relinquit, spargit umentis aquas.
et micant lacrimae tumentes de caduco pondere :
gutta praeceps orbe parvo sustinet casus suos.
iam pudorem florulentae prodiderunt purpurae:
umor ille, quem serenis astra rorant noctibus,      20
mane virgineas papillas solvit umenti peplo.
ipsa iussit mane totae virgines nubant rosae :
facta Cypridis de cruore deque Amoris osculis
deque gemmis deque flammis deque solis purpuris
cras ruborem, qui latebat veste tectus ignea      25
unico marita nodo non rubebit solvere.
Cras amet qui numquam amavit quique amavit cras
amet!

ipsa Nymphas diva luco iussit ire myrteo :
it puer comes puellis ; nec tamen credi potest,
esse Amorem feriatum, si sagittas vexerit ;      30
"ite, Nymphae, posuit arma, feriatus est Amor :
iussus est inermis ire, nudus ire iussus est,
neu quid arcu neu sagitta neu quid igne laederet."
sed tamen, Nymphae, cavete, quod Cupido pulcher
est :
totus est inermis idem quando nudus est Amor.      35
Cras amet qui numquam amavit quique amavit cras
amet!

conparis Venus pudore mittit ante virgines :
"una res est quam rogamus : cede, virgo Delia,
ut nemus sit incruentum de ferinis stragibus.
ipsa vellet te rogare, si pudicam flecteret,      40
ipsa vellet ut venires, si deceret virginem.
iam tribus choros videres feriatis noctibus

---

[17] micanat *S:* mecanat *T, corr. Lipsius.*
[19] iam *Bergk:* in *codd.*      [21] tumenti *codd.*, umenti *vulgo.*
[22] totae *Orelli:* tute *S:* tue *T.*
[23] Cypridis *O. Mueller:* prius *codd.*
[26] unico *Pithoeus:* unica *codd.*      [29] it *Pithoeus:* et *codd.*

congreges inter catervas ire per saltus tuos
floreas inter coronas, myrteas inter casas.
nec Ceres nec Bacchus absunt nec poetarum deus. 45
detinenter tota nox est perviclanda canticis:
regnet in silvis Dione : tu recede, Delia."
Cras amet qui numquam amavit quique amavit cras
              amet!

iussit Hyblaeis tribunal stare diva floribus :
Praeses ipsa iura dicet, adsidebunt Gratiae.   50
Hybla, totos funde flores, quidquid annus adtulit ;
Hybla, florum subde vestem, quantus Ennae campus
ruris hic erunt puellae vel puellae montium   [est!
quaeque silvas quaeque lucos quaeque montes in-
iussit omnes adsidere pueri mater alitis,   [colunt.
iussit et nudo puellas nil Amori credere.   55
Cras amet qui numquam amavit quique amavit cras
              amet!

et recentibus virentes ducat umbras floribus . . .
Cras erit quom primus aether copulavit nuptias,
ut pater totum creavit vernis annum nubibus :   60
in sinum maritus imber fluxit almae coniugis,
unde fetus mixtus omnis aleret magno corpore.
ipsa venas atque mentem permeanti spiritu
intus occultis gubernat procreatrix viribus,   64
perque caelum perque terras perque pontum sub-
pervium sui tenorem seminali tramite   [ditum

 [46] detinenter *Schenkel :* detinente *S :* detinent et *T.*
 [50] praesens *codd.,* corr. *Dousa.* dicit adsederunt *codd., corr.
Dousa.*
 [52] subde *Scriverius,* vestem *Salm. :* superestem *S :* rumper-
este *T.* Ennae *Lipsius :* ethne *T :* et nec *S :* Aetnae *Pithoeus.*
 [54] locos *T,* corr. *Pithoeus.*
 [58] rigentibus *codd.,* corr. *Pithoeus.*
 [59] quom *Buecheler :* quo *S :* qui *T.*
 [60] totum *Salm. :* totis *codd.*

inbuit iussitque mundum nosse nascendi vias.
Cras amet qui numquam amavit quique amavit cras
amet!

ipsa Troianos nepotes in Latinos transtulit,
ipsa Laurentem puellam coniugem nato dedit,    70
moxque Marti de sacello dat pudicam virginem,
Romuleas ipsa fecit cum Sabinis nuptias,
unde Ramnes et Quirites proque prole posterum
Romuli matrem crearet et nepotem Caesarem;   74
Cras amet qui numquam amavit quique amavit cras
amet!

rura fecundat voluptas, rura Venerem sentiunt;
ipse Amor puer Dionae rure natus dicitur.
hunc ager cum parturiret, ipsa suscepit sinu,
ipsa florum delicatis educavit osculis.   79
Cras amet qui numquam amavit quique amavit cras
amet!

ecce iam super genestas explicant apri latus,
quisque laetus quo tenetur coniugali foedere.
subter umbras cum maritis ecce balantum greges;
et canoras non tacere diva iussit alites:
iam loquaces ore rauco stagna cygni perstrepunt.  85
adsonat Terei puella subter umbram populi,
ut putes motus amoris ore dici musico
et neges queri sororem de marito barbaro.
illa cantat: nos tacemus? quando ver venit meum?
quando faciam uti chelidon vel tacere desinam?  90
perdidi Musam tacendo nec me Phoebus respicit.
sic Amyclas cum tacerent perdidit silentium.
Cras amet qui numquam amavit quique amavit cras
amet!

[81] aonii *codd.* : apri *Bährens suggests.*
[82] laetus *Bährens :* tutus *S :* tuus *T.*

# INDEX TO CATULLUS

# INDEX TO CATULLUS

# INDEX TO CATULLUS

# INDEX TO TIBULLUS

*The references are according to the division into three books.*
*D.M. = the "Epitaph" by Domitius Marsus.*

373

# INDEX TO TIBULLUS

Printed in Great Britain by Richard Clay & Sons, Limited,
BUNGAY, SUFFOLK.

# THE LOEB CLASSICAL LIBRARY

## VOLUMES ALREADY PUBLISHED

### Latin Authors

APULEIUS. THE GOLDEN ASS (METAMORPHOSES). W. Adlington (1566). Revised by S. Gaselee. (*4th Imp.*)

AULUS GELLIUS. J. C. Rolfe. 3 Vols.

AUSONIUS. H. G. Evelyn White. 2 Vols.

BOETHIUS: TRACTS AND DE CONSOLATIONE PHILOSOPHIAE. Rev. H. F. Stewart and E. K. Rand. (*2nd Imp.*)

CAESAR: CIVIL WARS. A. G. Peskett. (*2nd Imp.*)

CAESAR: GALLIC WAR. H. J. Edwards. (*4th Imp.*)

CATULLUS. F. W. Cornish; TIBULLUS. J. B. Postgate; AND PERVIGILIUM VENERIS. J. W. Mackail. (*8th Imp.*)

CICERO: DE FINIBUS. H. Rackham. (*2nd Imp.*)

CICERO: DE OFFICIIS. Walter Miller. (*2nd Imp.*)

CICERO: DE SENECTUTE, DE AMICITIA, DE DIVINATIONE. W. A. Falconer. (*2nd Imp.*)

CICERO: DE REPUBLICA AND DE LEGIBUS. Clinton Keyes.

CICERO: LETTERS TO ATTICUS. E. O. Winstedt. 3 Vols. (Vol. I. *4th Imp.*, Vols. II. and III. *2nd Imp.*)

CICERO: LETTERS TO HIS FRIENDS. W. Glynn Williams. 3 Vols. Vol. I.

CICERO: PHILIPPICS. W. C. A. Ker.

1

CICERO: PRO ARCHIA, POST REDITUM, DE DOMO, ETC. N. H. Watts.

CICERO: TUSCULAN DISPUTATIONS. J. E. King.

CICERO: PRO CAECINA, PRO LEGE MANILIA, PRO CLUENTIO, PRO RABIRIO. H. Grose Hodge.

CLAUDIAN. M. Platnauer. 2 Vols.

CONFESSIONS OF ST. AUGUSTINE. W. Watts (1631). 2 Vols. (*3rd Imp.*)

FRONTINUS: STRATAGEMS AND AQUEDUCTS. C. E. Bennett.

FRONTO: CORRESPONDENCE. C. R. Haines. 2 Vols.

HORACE: ODES AND EPODES. C. E. Bennett. (*7th Imp.*)

HORACE: SATIRES, EPISTLES, ARS POETICA. H. R. Fairclough.

JUVENAL AND PERSIUS. G. G. Ramsay. (*4th Imp.*)

LIVY. B. O. Foster. 13 Vols. Vols. I.–IV. (Vol. I. *2nd Imp.*)

LUCRETIUS. W. H. D. Rouse. (*2nd Imp.*)

MARTIAL. W. C. A. Ker. 2 Vols. (*2nd Imp.*)

OVID: HEROIDES AND AMORES. Grant Showerman. (*2nd Imp.*)

OVID: METAMORPHOSES. F. J. Miller. 2 Vols. (Vol. I. *4th Imp.*, Vol. II. *3rd Imp.*)

OVID: TRISTIA AND EX PONTO. A. L. Wheeler.

PETRONIUS. M. Heseltine; SENECA: APOCOLO-CYNTOSIS. W. H. D. Rouse. (*5th Imp.*)

PLAUTUS. Paul Nixon. 5 Vols. Vols. I.-III. (Vol. I. *3rd Imp.*)

PLINY: LETTERS. Melmoth's Translation revised by W. M. L. Hutchinson. 2 Vols. (*3rd Imp.*)

PROPERTIUS. H. E. Butler. (*3rd Imp.*)

QUINTILIAN. H. E. Butler. 4 Vols.

SALLUST. J. C. Rolfe.

SCRIPTORES HISTORIAE AUGUSTAE. D. Magie. 3 Vols. Vols. I. and II.

SENECA: EPISTULAE MORALES. R. M. Gummere. 3 Vols. (Vol. I. 2nd Imp.)

SENECA: MORAL ESSAYS. J. W. Basore. 3 Vols. Vol. I.

SENECA: TRAGEDIES. F. J. Miller. 2 Vols. (2nd Imp.)

STATIUS. J. H. Mozley. 2 Vols.

SUETONIUS. J. C. Rolfe. 2 Vols. (3rd Imp.)

TACITUS: DIALOGUS. Sir Wm. Peterson and AGRICOLA AND GERMANIA. Maurice Hutton. (3rd Imp.)

TACITUS: HISTORIES. C. H. Moore. 2 Vols. Vol. I.

TERENCE. John Sargeaunt. 2 Vols. (5th Imp.)

VELLEIUS PATERCULUS AND RES GESTAE. F. W. Shipley.

VIRGIL. H. R. Fairclough. 2 Vols. (Vol. I. 6th Imp., Vol. II. 3rd Imp.)

# Greek Authors

ACHILLES TATIUS. S. Gaselee.

AENEAS TACTICUS: ASCLEPIODOTUS AND ONA-
SANDER. The Illinois Greek Club.

AESCHINES. C. D. Adams.

AESCHYLUS. H. Weir Smyth. 2 Vols. (Vol. I. 2nd Imp.)

APOLLODORUS. Sir James G. Frazer. 2 Vols.

APOLLONIUS RHODIUS. R. C. Seaton. (3rd Imp.)

THE APOSTOLIC FATHERS. Kirsopp Lake. 2 Vols.
(Vol. I. 4th Imp., Vol. II. 3rd Imp.)

APPIAN'S ROMAN HISTORY. Horace White. 4 Vols.
(Vol. IV. 2nd Imp.)

ARISTOPHANES. Benjamin Bickley Rogers. 3 Vols.
(2nd Imp.) Verse trans.

ARISTOTLE: THE "ART" OF RHETORIC. J. H.
Freese.

ARISTOTLE: THE NICOMACHEAN ETHICS. H.
Rackham.

ARISTOTLE: POETICS AND LONGINUS. W. Hamilton
Fyfe; DEMETRIUS ON STYLE. W. Rhys Roberts.

ATHENAEUS: DEIPNOSOPHISTAE. C. B. Gulick. 7
Vols. Vols. I and II.

CALLIMACHUS AND LYCOPHRON. A. W. Mair;
ARATUS. G. R. Mair.

CLEMENT OF ALEXANDRIA. Rev. G. W. Butterworth.

DAPHNIS AND CHLOE. Thornley's Translation revised by
J. M. Edmonds; AND PARTHENIUS. S. Gaselee. (2nd
Imp.)

DEMOSTHENES, DE CORONA AND DE FALSA
LEGATIONE. C. A. Vince and J. H. Vince.

DIO CASSIUS: ROMAN HISTORY. E. Cary. 9 Vols.

DIOGENES LAERTIUS. R. D. Hicks. 2 Vols.

EPICTETUS. W. A. Oldfather. 2 Vols. Vol. I.

EURIPIDES. A. S. Way. 4 Vols. (Vol. I. 3rd Imp.,
Vols. II. and IV. 4th Imp., Vol. III. 2nd Imp.) Verse trans.

EUSEBIUS: ECCLESIASTICAL HISTORY. Kirsopp
Lake. 2 Vols. Vol. I.

GALEN: ON THE NATURAL FACULTIES. A. J. Brock. (*2nd Imp.*)

THE GREEK ANTHOLOGY. W. R. Paton. 5 Vols. (Vol. I. *3rd Imp.*, Vol. II. *2nd Imp.*)

THE GREEK BUCOLIC POETS (THEOCRITUS, BION, MOSCHUS). J. M. Edmonds. (*5th Imp.*)

HERODOTUS. A. D. Godley. 4 Vols. (Vols. I.-III. *2nd Imp.*)

HESIOD AND THE HOMERIC HYMNS. H. G. Evelyn White. (*3rd Imp.*)

HIPPOCRATES. W. H. S. Jones and E. T. Withington. 4 Vols. Vols. I.-III.

HOMER: ILIAD. A. T. Murray. 2 Vols. (Vol. I. *2nd Imp.*)

HOMER: ODYSSEY. A. T. Murray. 2 Vols. (Vol. I. *4th Imp.*, Vol. II. *2nd Imp.*)

ISAEUS. E. W. Forster.

ISOCRATES. G. B. Norlin. 3 Vols. Vol. I.

JOSEPHUS: H. St. J. Thackeray. 8 Vols. Vols. I.-III.

JULIAN. Wilmer Cave Wright. 3 Vols.

LUCIAN. A. M. Harmon. 8 Vols. Vols. I.-IV. (Vol. I. *3rd Imp.*, Vol. II. *2nd Imp.*)

LYRA GRAECA. J. M. Edmonds. 3 Vols. (Vol. I. *2nd Ed.*)

MARCUS AURELIUS. C. R. Haines. (*2nd Imp.*)

MENANDER. F. G. Allinson.

OPPIAN, COLLUTHUS, TRYPHIODORUS, A. W. Mair.

PAUSANIAS: DESCRIPTION OF GREECE. W. H. S. Jones. 5 Vols. and Companion Vol. Vols. I. and II.

PHILOSTRATUS · THE LIFE OF APOLLONIUS OF TYANA. F. C. Conybeare. 2 Vols. (Vol. I. *3rd Imp.*, Vol. II. *2nd Imp.*)

PHILOSTRATUS AND EUNAPIUS: LIVES OF THE SOPHISTS. Wilmer Cave Wright.

PINDAR. Sir J. E. Sandys. (*4th Imp.*)

PLATO: CHARMIDES, ALCIBIADES, HIPPARCHUS, THE LOVERS, THEAGES, MINOS AND EPINOMIS. W. R. M. Lamb.

PLATO: CRATYLUS, PARMENIDES, GREATER HIPPIAS, LESSER HIPPIAS. H. N. Fowler.

PLATO: EUTHYPHRO, APOLOGY, CRITO, PHAEDO, PHAEDRUS. H. N. Fowler. (5th Imp.)

PLATO: LACHES, PROTAGORAS, MENO, EUTHYDEMUS. W. R. M. Lamb.

PLATO: LAWS. Rev. R. G. Bury. 2 Vols.

PLATO: LYSIS, SYMPOSIUM, GORGIAS. W. R. M. Lamb.

PLATO: STATESMAN, PHILEBUS. H. N. Fowler; ION. W. R. M. Lamb.

PLATO: THEAETETUS AND SOPHIST. H. N. Fowler.

PLUTARCH: MORALIA. F. C. Babbitt. 14 Vols. Vol. I.

PLUTARCH: THE PARALLEL LIVES. B. Perrin. 11 Vols. (Vols. I., II. and VII. 2nd Imp.)

POLYBIUS. W. R. Paton. 6 Vols.

PROCOPIUS: HISTORY OF THE WARS. H. B. Dewing. 7 Vols. I.–IV.

QUINTUS SMYRNAEUS. A. S. Way. Verse trans.

SOPHOCLES. F. Storr. 2 Vols. (Vol. I. 5th Imp., Vol. II. 3rd Imp.) Verse trans.

ST. BASIL: LETTERS. R. J. Deferrari. 4 Vols. Vols. I. and II.

ST. JOHN DAMASCENE: BARLAAM AND IOASAPH. Rev. G. R. Woodward and Harold Mattingly.

STRABO: GEOGRAPHY. Horace L. Jones. 8 Vols. Vols. I.–V.

THEOPHRASTUS: ENQUIRY INTO PLANTS. Sir Arthur Hort, Bart. 2 Vols.

THUCYDIDES. C. F. Smith. 4 Vols. (Vol. I. 2nd Imp.)

XENOPHON: CYROPAEDIA. Walter Miller. 2 Vols. (Vol. I. 2nd Imp.)

XENOPHON: HELLENICA, ANABASIS, APOLOGY AND SYMPOSIUM. C. L. Brownson and O. J. Todd. 3 Vols.

XENOPHON: MEMORABILIA AND OECONOMICUS. E. C. Marchant.

XENOPHON: SCRIPTA MINORA. E. C. Marchant.